TREES OF THE SOUTHEASTERN STATES

TREES OF THE SOUTHEASTERN STATES

Including Virginia, North Carolina, South Carolina,
Tennessee, Georgia, and northern Florida

BY

WILLIAM CHAMBERS COKER, Ph. D., LL. D.

Kenan Research Professor of Botany and Director of the Arboretum
in the University of North Carolina

AND

HENRY ROLAND TOTTEN, Ph. D.

Professor of Botany in the University of North Carolina

CHAPEL HILL
THE UNIVERSITY OF NORTH CAROLINA PRESS

Copyright © *1934, 1937, and 1945,* by
The University of North Carolina Press
All rights reserved

Manufactured in the United States of America
ISBN 0–8078–0160–7
Library of Congress Catalog Card Number 37–10946
Revised edition

First printing, December 1945
Second printing, March 1954
Third printing, January 1967
Fourth printing, January 1973

PREFACE TO THIRD EDITION

MOST OF THE CHANGES or additions in this third edition
relate to the extension of the range of many of the species.
From Professor S. A. Cain's work in the Great Smoky
Mountains, we have also noted dimensions of a number of
trees which are larger than heretofore known for our area.
Only two species have been added, *Quercus oglethorpensis*,
and *Fraxinus nigra*. The name *Aesculus neglecta* var.
georgiana has been changed to *A. sylvatica*, with the former name as a synonym. *Magnolia cordata* has been reduced to a variety of *M. acuminata*, and its range has been
greatly extended.

In all cases in which the figure illustrating a species is
not included within the description, the name has been
inserted to avoid any confusion.

Chapel Hill, N. C.,
November, 1944.

PREFACE TO SECOND EDITION

In this second edition of the *Trees of the Southeastern States,* we are including the state of Tennessee in the area covered. This has required the addition of 11 species, and one (Munson plum) as native rather than introduced. The distribution of the trees of Tennessee has not so far been worked out as it should be by us or apparently by anyone else, at least so far as published. Any information that our readers can send us on this subject will be gratefully received. For most of the information we have secured on such distribution, we gladly acknowledge our debt to Professor C. E. Moore of State Teachers College, Memphis, Tenn., Professor H. M. Jennison of the University of Tennessee, and Mr. A. F. Sanford, Knoxville, Tennessee. We have of course made full use of the work of Dr. Gattinger (see bibliography). Other changes from the first edition consist of further notes on distribution and size, the addition of one exotic escape in Florida, and the treatment of *Viburnum lentago* as a tree. We have made only two changes in nomenclature.

Since the publication of our first edition we have to announce the heavy loss of Dr. T. G. Harbison, curator of the herbarium at the University of North Carolina. His generous and continued coöperation with us in all our work has been of the greatest importance and in his death we suffer a loss that cannot be replaced. We have secured his herbarium from the family. This herbarium consists mainly of southern woody plants but is also exceptionally rich in certain groups of herbaceous plants. These additions, together with the Ashe herbarium and our own extensive collections, have placed us in a very favorable position for the study of our southern trees and shrubs.

Chapel Hill, N. C.,
October 30, 1936.

PREFACE TO FIRST EDITION

SINCE the publication in 1916 of our little book on the *Trees of North Carolina* we have continued our study on the trees of the Southeastern States. We have personally visited many sections of these states, and have been greatly assisted by the generous collections of correspondents. Among these we must first mention Mr. T. G. Harbison of Highlands, N. C., who has not only contributed largely to our herbarium but who has recently been working with us in Chapel Hill for several months. His knowledge of the type localities and individual trees, gained through many years of travel through the Southern States, has been of very great assistance throughout. He has accompanied us on two of our extensive collecting trips into Georgia and Florida and on a number of excursions in North and South Carolina. Mr. W. W. Ashe, of Washington, D. C., whose death in 1932 was a personal loss to us, had been most generous in furnishing us materials and information, and his large and valuable herbarium, since acquired by the University of North Carolina, has helped us greatly. Among other correspondents to whom we are most indebted for information and materials are Mr. J. S. Holmes, State Forester of North Carolina, of Raleigh, Prof. H. L. Blomquist of Duke University, Durham, N. C., Prof. Herman Kurz of Florida State College for Women, Tallahassee, Mr. H. A. Rankin of Fayetteville, N. C., Prof. R. S. Freer of Lynchburg College, Lynchburg, Va., Prof. Julian Miller of the University of Georgia, Athens, Mr. James Henry Rice, Jr., of Wiggins, S. C., Mr. E. J. Alexander of the New York Botanical Garden, Mr. W. W. Eggleston of the Bureau of Plant Industry, Washington, D. C., Rev. Charles Raynal of Statesville, N. C., Prof. Earl H. Hall of the Woman's College of the University of North Carolina, Greensboro, Dr. Hal M. Stuart of Beaufort, S. C., Prof. E. C. Coker and Mr. F. H. Haskell of Columbia, S. C., and Mrs. R. L. Creal of Bryson City, North Carolina. Professor J. N. Couch of our department brought back much valuable material to us from an extensive trip in Florida. For loans of material and information we wish to thank the New York Botanical Garden, the United States National Herbarium, the Charleston Museum, and the Missouri Botanical Garden. The drawings have been made by Miss Nell Henry, Mrs. Alleda Burlage, Mrs. S. H. Hobbs, Mrs. Mary deB. Graves, Mrs. Cecil Johnson, Miss Velma Matthews, and Miss Alma Holland. We are also indebted to the last two for much valuable work in the preparation of the manuscript and in the reading of the proof.

Chapel Hill, N. C.
April 12, 1934

TREES OF THE SOUTHEASTERN STATES

INTRODUCTION

THE TREES of the Southeastern States in their variety, beauty, and landscape effect are probably not equaled by any other similar area in the world. There are many more kinds of trees in North Carolina alone than in the whole of Europe. We are describing in this book 241 native trees, not counting varieties and also omitting a large number of so-called species of hawthorn that are mentioned more or less casually. We are also including 22 foreign trees that have now escaped from cultivation and become established as wild. It is not possible to say just how many trees occur in our territory. The number would vary with the personal opinion of each student and the constantly changing attitude toward what really constitutes a species. Any such effort is further complicated by the impossibility of drawing any sharp distinction between trees and shrubs (see below).

Under the genus *Crataegus* we call attention to the very large number of so-called new species of hawthorns that have been described. Many of these are of doubtful validity as real species and it is out of the question to go into a full discussion of them in a book of this type.

To help the beginner we are including two plates, one of leaf characters and one of flowers. In our descriptions we have used as few technical terms as we could with clearness and in the glossary at the back we define these terms.

The common names of oaks and pines, as well as other trees, are so varied and confused in different parts of the country that any determination of the species by this means is impossible. We cannot put down all the common names of trees and to do so would be no help. Therefore the student should be careful, when he sees a common name in this book, not to jump to the conclusion that a tree called by that name in his community is the one given in the book. In any serious attempt to become acquainted with the trees,

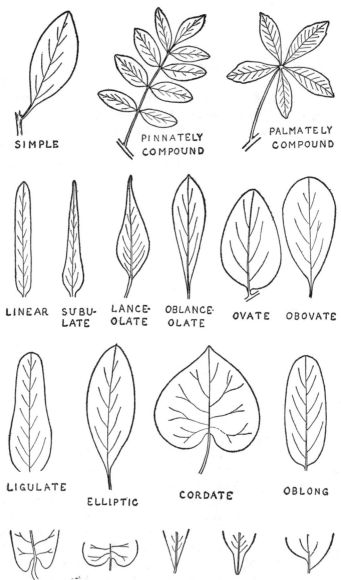

SIMPLE

PINNATELY COMPOUND

PALMATELY COMPOUND

LINEAR   SUBU-LATE   LANCE-OLATE   OBLANCE-OLATE   OVATE   OBOVATE

LIGULATE

ELLIPTIC   CORDATE   OBLONG

AURICULATE   CORDATE   CUNEATE   DECURRENT   OBLIQUE

Typical Leaves

scientific names should be used and the descriptions carefully followed.

We have not tried to make this book a text in systematic botany. In many cases we give the floral structure but in some others where the flowers are small and optically insignificant we omit such details. Botanically such flowers are of course as significant as any others but to the majority using this book their descriptions would not be interesting and would be read only casually if at all. Any student with a real botanical interest should turn to the systematic manuals such as those of Small, Gray, or Britton and find these details for himself. Flowering dates given without other reference indicate the beginning dates of flowering as recorded of plants growing at Chapel Hill, if Chapel Hill is in the region inhabited by the plant; flowering dates for plants not growing at Chapel Hill indicate dates of collections in flower, rather than the beginning of flowering. The beginning date varies considerably with the earliness or lateness of the season for the spring flowering plants though there is little variation in the summer and fall flowering ones. The length of the daylight period is the controlling factor rather than temperature in these latter groups, as has been shown by the work of Garner and Allard of the United States Department of Agriculture.

The bibliography that we give on page 401 includes only the most important books together with a few of the more easily accessible and comprehensive articles. In addition to these many other references are given in the text. In our citations the first number indicates the volume, the second the page, and the third the year. Though they will not be available to many, we include the classical works of Catesby, Walter, and Elliott. Students should at least know that these works exist and if they are in the neighborhood of an important library they may be able to find these books and get acquainted with them. Bartram's *Travels* is a fascinating record of his experiences while botanizing in the South. It is full of the most interesting observations on the vegetation, Indians, and animals, as

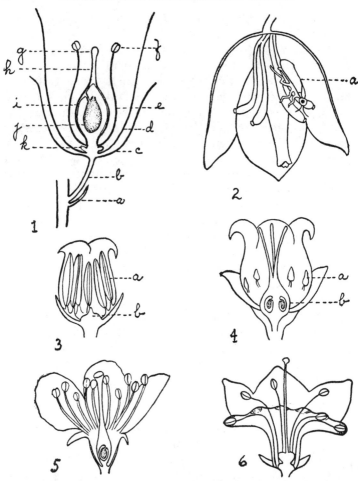

1. Section of typical flower. *a*, bract; *b*, pedicel; *c.* sepal; *d*, petal; *e*, filament; *f*, anther; *g*, stigma; *h*, style; *i*, ovary; *j*, ovule; *k*, nectar gland. *e* and *f* together form the stamen; *g*, *h*, and *i* make up the pistil.

2. Yucca, monocot type. Perianth of similar parts; calyx and corolla not distinctly different. *a*, Pronuba moth on stamen.

3, 4. Persimmon. Male and female flowers different; petals fused into a bell; male flowers smaller with functional stamens (*a*) and aborted pistil (*b*); female flowers with functional pistil (*b*) and aborted stamens (*a*).

5. Plum. Flower with a calyx cup, the stamens and petals borne on its margin.

6. Kalmia. For description see Kalmia, p. 359.

well as the early settlers. It is one of the best travel books
ever written and should be read as a splendid example of
early American writing. A reprinting in 1928 is now
available.

A number of shrubs occurring in our range may reach
the size of little trees in the most favorable spots, and a
good many of them are included in one or more of our
manuals of American trees. As is to be expected, there is
no sharp distinction either in size or habit between a shrub
and a tree. A tree is supposed to have a single trunk and
to be at least ten or fifteen feet high. If we included here
all of our shrubs that sometimes have single trunks and
reach such a height, we would add considerably to this
book. As they are rarely found with such dimensions, we
think it best to exclude them. In comparing the number
of trees in any one state or section with those in another,
one must consider the different attitudes of authors in regard to the inclusion of such plants.

We are giving below a list of these larger shrubs.

Alnus rugosa (Du Roi) Spreng. Smooth Alder.

Aronia arbutifolia (L. f.) Ell. Chokeberry.

Azalea arborescens Pursh. Azalea.

Azalea nudiflora L. Pink Azalea or Wild Honeysuckle.

Baccharis halimifolia L. Pencil Bush, Salt Myrtle, Jocko
   Bush.
   A tree at Myrtle Beach, S. C., is 14 feet high and 4
   inches in diameter, and there is another of about the
   same size at Rockingham, N. C.

Cephalanthus occidentalis L. Buttonbush, Button Willow.
   A specimen in Bartow County, Ga., is 15 feet high and
   5 inches thick, according to Harper (*Southern Wood-
   lands* 1, No. 4: 2. 1907).

Clethra acuminata Michx. Mountain Sweet Pepperbush.
   One specimen in a swamp near Highlands, N. C., is 18
   feet high and 4¼ inches thick one foot from the ground.

Cornus Amomum Miller. Silky Cornel, Swamp Dogwood.

Cornus asperifolia Michx. Rough-leaved Dogwood.

Cornus stricta Lam. Stiff Cornel.

Corylus americana Walt. Hazelnut.

Crataegus. Many species.

Euonymus atropurpureus Jacq. Burning Bush.

Ilex laevigata (Pursh) A. Gray. Smooth Winterberry.

Ilex longipes Chapman.

Ilex verticillata (L.) A. Gray. Winterberry.

Lyonia ferruginea (Walt.) Nuttall [*Xolisma ferruginea* (Walt.) Heller]. Titi.

    Harper says that it reaches a height of 20 feet and diameter of 4 inches in Coffee County, Georgia.

Ptelea trifoliata L. Hop Tree.

Rhus copallina L. Winged Sumach.

    At Gatlinburg, Tenn., there are two trees of this species which measure over 4 inches in diameter four and a half feet from the ground.

Rhus glabra L. Smooth Sumach.

    A specimen at Cullasaja Falls, Macon County, N. C., is 7 inches in diameter one and a half feet from the ground.

Robinia Boyntonii Ashe.

Robinia hispida L. Rose Acacia.

Sambucus canadensis L. Elder.

Staphylea trifolia L. Bladdernut.

    One specimen seen by Harper in Georgia was 5 or 6 inches in diameter, and he reports one from Floyd County, Ga., which was 25 feet high.

Styrax americana Lam. Storax.

    A tree with a single trunk near Hartsville, S. C., measured in April 1933 was about 18 feet high and 2 inches in diameter two feet from the ground.

Styrax grandifolia Ait. Storax.

    Reaches a height of 20 feet and a diameter of $3\frac{1}{2}$ inches near Chapel Hill, N. C. One in the Coker Arboretum at Chapel Hill is $3\frac{7}{8}$ inches in diameter.

Viburnum cassinoides L. Withe-rod, Possum Haw.

Viburnum nudum L. Smooth Withe-rod.

KEY TO THE GENERA

Trees with linear or scale-like leaves (all evergreen
except *Taxodium*); seeds not borne in a closed
ovary
GYMNOSPERMS   p.   7

Trees broad-leaved (except in *Tamarix*), not cone
bearing (Magnolias, Sweet Gum, Alders, and
Birches have fruits superficially cone-like, but
seeds are borne in closed ovaries, not on top of
a flat cone scale as in true cones)
ANGIOSPERMS   p.   8

GYMNOSPERMS

Trees with fleshy fruits about the size of a wild
plum or cherry
Taxaceae   I

Trees with true cones (berry-like in *Juniperus*)
Pinaceae   II

I. Taxaceae

Fruit oval with a pulpy flesh, resembling a small
plum. It is really an exposed seed
Tumion taxifolium, Stinking Cedar   p.   52

Fruit consisting of a small dark seed nearly surrounded by a pulpy red coat
Taxus floridana, Florida Yew   p.   54

II. Pinaceae

1. Leaves needle-like, united into bundles
Pinus, Pines   p.   15

   Leaves small, scale-like or linear, not united into
bundles 2

2. Fruit resembling a small berry, but really a little
fleshy cone about the size of a pea or smaller;
leaves not over ⅜ inch long
Juniperus, Cedars   p.   47

   Fruit a dry cone when mature, showing separate
scales 3

3. Leaves very small and scale-like; fruit a small
round cone about the size of a pea; a tree of
coastal swamps
Chamaecyparis thyoides, Juniper   p.   47

   Leaves very small and scale-like, the leafy twig as
if pressed; cones small, elongated (¼-½ inch
long); a small rare tree of the mountains, not
rare in cultivation
Thuja occidentalis, American Arborvitae   p.   45

   Leaves linear, angular-roundish or flattened; cones
larger than the above 4

4. Trees not evergreen; cones spherical
Taxodium, Cypresses　　p. 42
Trees evergreen; cones elongated, not spherical....　5
5. Leaves without a distinct stalk; cones erect
Abies, Firs　　p. 40
Leaves with an abrupt little stalk that remains on the twigs when the leaves fall; cones hanging down ....　6
6. Leaves flat
Tsuga, Hemlocks　　p. 36
Leaves 4-sided
Picea, Spruces　　p. 33

ANGIOSPERMS

Leaves parallel-veined; evergreen
Monocotyledons
Leaves net-veined; majority not evergreen
Dicotyledons

Monocotyledons

Leaves several feet wide, fan-shaped
Sabal Palmetto, Palmetto　　p. 55
Leaves narrower, less than 3 inches wide, lance-shaped
Yucca, Spanish Bayonet　　p. 57

Dicotyledons

Leaves compound ....　I
Leaves simple ....　II　p. 10

I. Leaves compound

Leaves alternate on the twig....................　A
Leaves opposite on the twig....................　B　p. 9

A. Leaves compound, alternate on the twig

1. Leaves twice compound* ....　2
Leaves once compound ....　7
2. Trunk and branches thorny or prickly ....　3
Trunk and branches not thorny ....　5
3. Leaves more than two feet long
Aralia spinosa, Hercules Club　　p. 344
Leaves less than one foot long.................　4
4. Fruit 12-18 inches long, many-seeded
Gleditsia triacanthos, Honey Locust　　p. 257
Fruit 1-3 inches long with 1-3 seeds; trees of the deep coastal swamps
Gleditsia aquatica, Water Locust　　p. 258

* *Gleditsia* may also bear once compound leaves.

5. Leaflets with teeth
   Melia Azedarach, China-berry — p. 268
   Leaflets without teeth 6
6. Leaflets one-sided
   Albizzia Julibrissin, "Mimosa" — p. 265
   Leaflets symmetrical
   Gymnocladus dioica, Kentucky Coffee Tree — p. 265
7. Odor of leaves offensive when crushed
   Ailanthus altissima, Tree of Heaven — p. 267
   Odor of leaves not offensive when crushed........ 8
8. Fruit a flat pod................................ 9
   Fruit not a flat pod........................... 10
9. Branches with short thorns; twigs and leaf stalks not sticky
   Robinia Pseudoacacia, Black Locust — p. 261
   Branches with or without short thorns; twigs and leaf stalks very sticky
   Robinia viscosa, Clammy Locust — p. 263
   Branches without thorns; twigs and leaf stalks not sticky
   Cladrastis lutea, Yellow Wood — p. 260
10. Fruit a small one-seeded capsule; branches and leaves spiny; leaves fragrant when bruised
    Xanthoxylum Clava-Herculis, Prickly Ash — p. 270
    Fruit a nut with the hull dividing into four parts when ripe (scarcely dividing in Pig-nut Hickory)
    Hicoria, Hickories — p. 80
    Fruit a light brown or yellowish, coriaceous, translucent berry; a rare tree found near the coast
    Sapindus marginatus, Soapberry — p. 308
    Fruit a nut with a fibrous hull which does not split away 11
    Fruit small, red or white 12
11. Hull and nut oblong, pointed
    Juglans cinerea, Butternut — ⱴ. 79
    Hull and nut nearly spherical
    Juglans nigra, Black Walnut — p. 77
12. Twigs smooth; fruits orange-red
    Sorbus americana, Mountain Ash — p. 200
    Twigs smooth; fruits whitish
    Rhus vernix, Poison Sumach — p. 273
    Twigs densely fuzzy; fruits red
    Rhus typhina, Staghorn Sumach — p. 272

B. Leaves compound, opposite on the twig

1. Leaflets clustered at the end of the leaf stalk (palmately compound)
   Aesculus, Buckeyes — p. 300
   Leaflets not clustered at the end of the leaf stalk (pinnately compound) 2

2. Leaflets at least in some cases lobed; fruit double
   with two wings

    Acer Negundo, Ash-leaved Maple   p. 299

 Leaflets not lobed; fruit simple with an apical wing

      Fraxinus, Ashes   p. 374

II. Leaves simple

Leaves simple, alternate on the twig.............. A

Leaves simple, opposite on the twig.............. B p. 14

A. Leaves simple, alternate on the twig

1. Fruit an acorn

      Quercus, Oaks   p. 110

 Fruit not an acorn............................ 2

2. Branches thorny 3

 Branches not thorny 6

3. Edges of leaves not toothed or lobed............. 4

 Edges of leaves with teeth or lobes.............. 5

4. Fruit large, heavy, greenish

    Maclura pomifera, Osage Orange   p. 172

 Fruit a black berry

    Bumelia, Buckthorn   p. 363

5. Fruit an apple (botanically a pome) ¾ inch or
   more thick; flowers very fragrant

    Malus, Crabapples   p. 201

 Fruit a ''haw'' looking like a little apple (botanically a pome-like drupe), less than ¾ inch thick

    Crataegus, Hawthorne   p. 210

6. Edges of leaves not toothed or lobed............. 7

 Edges of leaves with teeth or lobes.............. 27

7. Leaves evergreen 8

 Leaves not evergreen 19

8. Leaves more than 2½ inches broad

    Magnolia grandiflora, Magnolia   p. 176

 Leaves averaging less than 2½ inches broad....... 9

9. Leaves aromatic when bruised 10

 Leaves not aromatic when bruised............... 12

10. Twigs smooth; leaves white underneath

    Magnolia virginiana, Sweet Bay   p. 178

 Twigs tomentose, puberulous, or rarely nearly
   glabrous; leaves not white beneath 11

11. Twigs slightly hairy or nearly glabrous; peduncles
    ½-1 inch long

    Persea Borbonia, Smooth Red Bay   p. 192

 Twigs tomentose; peduncles usually 2-3 inches long

    Persea palustris, Red Bay   p. 191

12. Twigs hairy at least when young............... 13

 Twigs smooth 16

13. Leaf blades more than 3½ inches long; petals
    united into a tube 14

 Leaf blades less than 3½ inches long; petals
   fused at least at base 15

 Leaf blades 2½-6 inches long; petals free

    Elliottia racemosa   p. 354

14. Leaf blades about 3½ times as long as broad; calyx lobes broad and blunt
    Rhododendron maximum, Great Laurel   p. 356
    Leaf blades about twice as long as broad; calyx lobes very short and pointed
    Rhododendron catawbiense, Rose Bay   p. 358
15. Twigs sticky when young, becoming smooth at latter part of season; fruit a pod
    Kalmia latifolia, Mountain Laurel   p. 359
    Twigs not sticky; leaves often with prickly edges; fruit a red "berry"
    Ilex Cassine, Dahoon Holly   p. 281
16. Fruit a "berry" (botanically a drupe)..........   17
    Fruit not a "berry" (drupe)   18
17. Leaves very narrow, not rarely with very short teeth near the end; berry red
    Ilex myrtifolia, Myrtle-leaved Holly   p. 282
    Leaves oblong-lanceolate, berry black
    Laurocerasus caroliniana, Laurel Cherry   p. 254
18. Fruit not winged; flower clusters axillary
    Cyrilla racemiflora, He Huckleberry   p. 276
    Fruit winged; flower clusters terminal
    Cliftonia monophylla, Titi   p. 277
19. Leaves very small and scale-like
    Tamarix gallica, Tamarisk   p. 343
    Leaves not scale-like   20
20. Leaves large, averaging over 6 inches long........   21
    Leaves less than 6 inches long..................   22
21. Leaves without a disagreeable odor when crushed
    Magnolia   p. 173
    Leaves with a disagreeable odor when crushed
    Asimina triloba, Pawpaw   p. 190
22. Blade of leaf as broad or nearly as broad as long..   23
    Blade of leaf much longer than broad...........   24
23. Leaves often heart-shaped at base; fruit a flat pod
    Cercis canadensis, Redbud   p. 255
    Leaves not heart-shaped at base; fruit a 3-lobed capsule
    Sapium sebiferum, Chinese Tallow Tree   p. 269
    Leaves oval or obovate, not heart-shaped at base; fruit small one-seeded pods scattered in a large feathery inflorescence
    Cotinus americanus, Smoke Tree   p. 274
24. Fruit a persimmon (botanically a berry)
    Diospyros virginiana, Persimmon   p. 367
    Fruit not a persimmon, over 2 inches thick
    Maclura pomifera, Osage Orange   p. 172
    Fruit not a persimmon, less than 2 inches thick...   25
25. Fruit a dry, oblong, shiny brown, wrinkled "berry" (drupe) about ¾ inch long; a small tree of far southern swamps
    Leitneria floridana, Corkwood   p. 76
    Fruit a dry, sweet, globose, orange colored or reddish "berry" (drupe) about ¼ inch thick
    Celtis laevigata, Hackberry   p. 166

Fruit a red "berry" (drupe) about 1 inch or more
 long, very acid
     Nyssa ogeche, Ogeechee Lime   p. 347
 Fruit a blue, purple, or black "berry" (drupe)... 26
26. Veins from midrib strongly curving toward tip
     Cornus alternifolia, Blue Dogwood   p. 353
 Not as above
       Nyssa, Gums   p. 345
27. Blade of leaf as broad as long or less than twice
  as long as broad 28
 Blade of leaf much longer than broad 37
28. Blade of leaf broad and notched at the end
    Liriodendron tulipifera, Tulip Poplar   p. 188
 Blade of leaf pointed at the end................ 29
29. Leaves evergreen, thick and leathery
       Ilex opaca, Holly   p. 279
 Leaves not evergreen 30
30. Fruit stalks attached to a leaf-like bract
       Tilia, Lindens   p. 310
 Not as above 31
31. Leaves palmately 3-5-lobed, large 32
 Leaves not as above 33
32. Leaves glabrous, toothed
    Liquidambar Styrariflua, Sweet Gum   p. 197
 Leaves hairy on lower side, not toothed
  Sterculia platanifolia, Japanese Varnish Tree   p. 338
33. Leaves large with many irregular lobes and teeth;
  bark white and flaky
    Platanus occidentalis, Sycamore   p. 198
 Leaves not lobed; fruit an apple
      Malus, Apple   p. 201
 Leaves not lobed, shining; fruit a pear
     Pyrus communis, Pear   p. 207
 Not as above 34
34. Leaf blade 6 inches or more long, not lobed
    Populus heterophylla, Cotton-wood   p. 59
 Leaf blades small or deeply lobed................ 35
35. Leaf stalks flattened
     Populus, Poplars   p. 59
 Leaf stalks not flattened...................... 36
36. Leaves smooth, none lobed, fruit a woody, 2-seeded
  pod
    Hamamelis virginiana, Witch Hazel   p. 195
 Leaves smooth or only slightly tomentose below,
  smooth or harsh above, some lobed; not increasing
  by suckers; fruit a multiple berry
     Morus, Mulberries   p. 170
 Leaves densely soft tomentose below, harsh above;
  plant increasing by suckers
  Broussonetia papyrifera, Paper Mulberry   p. 172
37. Leaves evergreen 38
 Leaves not evergreen 39

38. Fruit a red berry   *Ilex*, Hollies   p. 278

    Fruit a silky pod
      Gordonia Lasianthus, Loblolly Bay   p. 341

    Fruit a small drupe covered with a gray wax
      Myrica cerifera, Wax Myrtle   p. 75

39. Teeth of leaves with bristly tips
      Castanea, Chestnut and Chinquapins   pp. 105, 107

    Teeth of leaves not bristle-tipped................ 40

40. Leaves over 4 times as long as broad
      Salix, Willows   p. 64

    Leaves less than 4 times as long as broad......... 41

41. Leaves with conspicuous parallel veins from the midrib to the edge (In the two Amelanchiers the veins extend nearly to the edge before branching) 42

    Leaves without conspicuous parallel veins from the midrib 49

42. Bark smooth or with only slight furrows and cracks 43
    Bark quite rough or papery.................... 45

43. Leaf margins undulate
      Hamamelis virginiana, Witch Hazel   p. 195

    Leaf margin smooth or minutely toothed
      Rhamnus caroliniana, Buckthorn   p. 309

    Leaf margin distinctly toothed 44

44. Bark whitish; trunk without ridges, leaves coarsely toothed
      Fagus grandifolia, Beech   p. 104

    Bark dark brown, young bark with odor of wintergreen; trunk without ridges; leaves finely toothed
      Betula lenta, Cherry Birch   p. 100

    Bark very dark; trunk with ridges; leaves finely toothed
      Carpinus caroliniana, Hornbeam   p. 96

45. Bark and twigs with odor of wintergreen
      Betula lutea and *B. lenta*, Yellow and Cherry Birches   pp. 99, 100

    Bark and twigs not aromatic.................... 46

46. Bark falling away in papery layers
      Betula papyrifera var. *cordifolia* and *B. nigra*
      Paper and Black Birches   pp. 102, 103

    Bark not falling away in papery layers........... 47

47. Bark rough; fruit small with two flat wings
      Ulmus, Elms   p. 159

    Bark rough-scurfy; fruit not as above........... 48

48. Fruit a cluster of hop-like bracts
      Ostrya virginiana, Hop Hornbeam   p. 97

    Fruit a tuberculate drupe
      Planera aquatica, Water Elm   p. 164

49. Leaves without teeth, usually but not always lobed, aromatic
      Sassafras variifolium, Sassafras   p. 193

    Leaves not as above (some nearly without teeth in *Symplocos*) 50

50. Leaves distinctly sour to taste
          Oxydendrum arboreum, Sourwood   p. 361
   Leaves sweet to taste
          Symplocos tinctoria, Horse Sugar   p. 368
   Leaves not distinctly sour or sweet.............. 51
51. Fruit winged
          Halesia, Silverbells   p. 370
   Fruit not winged 52
52. Fruit a small drupe varying from orange-red to dark purple; leaves toothed or entire; bark often with corky warts
          Celtis, Hackberries   p. 165
   Fruit a small or large pome or drupe, often a bright red; leaves always toothed 53
   Fruit a small dry pod borne in catkins
          Salix, Willows   p. 64
   Fruit a larger dry pod borne singly
          Stewartia   p. 338
53. Flowers borne in elongated racemes.............. 54
   Flowers not borne in racemes 55
54. Flowers less than ½ inch wide
          Padus, Choke Cherries   p. 252
   Flowers over ½ inch wide
          Amelanchier, Shad-bushes   p. 207
55. Flowers not over ¼ inch wide, of two sexes on different trees
          Ilex, Hollies   p. 278
   Flowers larger, perfect 56
56. Flowers in axillary clusters (umbels) of several; fruit a plum, cherry, or peach
          Prunus, Plums, Cherries, and Peaches   p. 243
   Flowers single in the axils of the leaves; fruit a sweet little black berry
          Vaccinium arboreum, Sparkleberry   p. 362

B. Leaves simple, opposite on the twig

1. Edges of leaf not toothed or lobed............... 2
   Edges of leaf with teeth or lobes................ 8
2. Leaves heart-shaped, large...................... 3
   Leaves not heart-shaped........................ 4
3. Fruit a short, ovate pod
          Paulownia tomentosa, Poulownia   p. 389
   Fruit a long, slender pod
          Catalpa, Catalpa   p. 387
4. Leaves evergreen; flowers in axillary clusters, fragrant
          Osmanthus americanus, Devil-wood   p. 386
   Not as above 5
5. Leaves less than 2 inches long, some may be obscurely toothed near the apex
          Viburnum obovatum, Small-leaved Viburnum   p. 393
   Leaves over 2 inches long...................... 6

6. Primary veins arising from the lower two-thirds of the midrib only, strongly curving toward the tip; flower head surrounded by 4 white or pink, petal-like leaves; fruit red *Cornus florida*, Dogwood   p. 351
   Not as above   7
7. Leaves hairy; stipules between leaf stalks in spring; part of calyx lobes pink and greatly enlarged; fruit a dry pod
   Pinckneya pubens, Georgia Bark   p. 390
   Leaves hairy or glabrous at maturity; no stipules; flowers in loose drooping clusters, fragrant, petals long and narrow; fruit a dark blue, fleshy drupe
   Chionanthus virginica, Fringe Tree   p. 384
8. Leaves distinctly toothed but not lobed
   Viburnum, Haws   p. 393
   Leaves toothed and lobed
   Acer, Maples   p. 288
   Leaves obscurely toothed above the middle, but not lobed   9
9. Leaves less than 2 inches long
   Viburnum obovatum, Small-leaved Viburnum   p. 393
   Leaves over 2 inches long
   Forestiera acuminata, Swamp Privet   p. 383

PINACEAE (PINE FAMILY)

PINUS (Tourn.) L.

1. Leaves 5 or more in a bundle
   Pinus Strobus, White Pine   No. 1
   Leaves less than 5 in a bundle.................   2
2. Leaves over 10 inches long; cones usually 6-9 inches long
   Pinus palustris, Long-leaf Pine   No. 2
   Leaves not over 10 inches long; cones smaller.....   3
3. Cones 3-5½ inches long.....................   4
   Cones not over 3 inches long...................   5
4. Leaves 2 or 3 in a bundle; cones with a distinct, strongly curved stalk
   Pinus Elliottii, Slash Pine   No. 3
   Leaves usually 3 in a bundle; cones almost sessile
   Pinus taeda, Loblolly Pine   No. 4
5. Leaves usually 3 in a bundle...................   6
   Leaves usually 2 in a bundle, rarely 3...........   7
6. Leaves 6-8 inches long
   Pinus serotina, Pond Pine   No. 5
   Leaves 3-4 inches long
   Pinus rigida, Black Pine   No. 6
7. Cones about 3 inches long, prickles stout
   Pinus pungens, Table Mountain Pine   No. 11
   Cones about 2-2½ inches long, prickles weak.....   8

1. Pinus Strobus L. White Pine.

THIS is a large and beautiful pine which reaches its southern limit in the high mountains of northeastern Georgia.

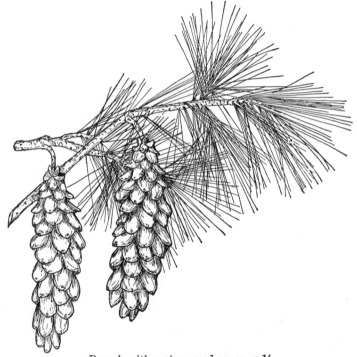

Branch with mature seed cones, x ¼.

In that state and in South Carolina it is scarce and of little importance. In North Carolina and Virginia it is common in the mountains and is a valuable timber tree. In North

Carolina it extends as far east as the junction of Deep and Rocky rivers in Chatham and Lee counties. This remarkable outpost, which is about seventy-five miles farther east than the nearest grove to the west (see below), was first reported by J. A. Holmes (*Journ. Eli. Mitch. Sci. Soc.* **1**: 87. 1884). We visited this locality first in 1921 and found several large trees there. People living near said that 35,000 feet of white pine lumber were sawed from this hill and the hill across the river in Lee County about 1911. On a visit to the Lee County side in 1933 we found White Pines scattered along the bluffs and hills for over a mile. The largest tree measured 3 feet in diameter three feet from the ground. Over a hundred trees would be over 10 inches in diameter and saplings and seedlings were abundant. In Davie County there is a flourishing grove near the northwest corner of the county on the old Jacob Holman farm (now the Jim Cleary farm), one tree being about 100 feet high and 4 feet 3⅗ inches in diameter at the top of a mulch heap 18 inches deep; ten trees were counted about six miles southeast of this grove and about one mile south of Cana, and one tree near Bear Creek about three miles west of Mocksville. Unfortunately this last was felléd in 1933.

Bark dark gray and smooth; needles a delicate bluish green, slender, borne in groups of five or rarely more, 3-5 inches long; cones long and slender, with thin scales, maturing the second year.* This is apparently the largest pine of the eastern United States; in the north it is said to reach a diameter of seven feet (possibly more). It is much used as an ornamental, but in cultivation it frequently has a white, waxy, bark aphis (*Chermes pinicorticis* Fitch), which greatly disfigures the trees and often seriously injures them. The best remedy is abundant nourishment. An entirely prostrate form of this species, spreading in mats, is known from the mountains of Newfoundland. A similar form is known to horticulture (*Rhodora* **34**: 168. 1932).

*In all pines the cones require two seasons' growth to mature.

2. Pinus palustris Mill. **Long-leaf Pine, Southern Pine.**
THIS is a large tree found in the coastal plain and sandhill regions with some extension into adjacent areas from southeastern Virginia to Florida. In North Carolina it grows as far west as Cary in Wake County and near the Badin dam in Stanly County and as far inland as Kirksey in Greenwood County, South Carolina. In Georgia it extends in the mountains to altitudes of 1,500 feet.

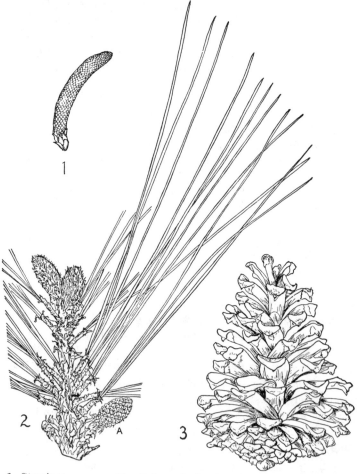

1, Staminate cone, x ½. 2, branch showing year old cone (A), two stout apical buds, and leaves, x ¼. 3, mature seed cone, x ⅓.

Leaves in threes, 10-15 inches long; cones very large, 6-8 (rarely 9) inches long, appearing in abundance only at intervals of several years. Though ruthlessly destroyed by turpentine and sawmill operations for many years, this well known and highly valuable timber and turpentine tree is still vigorously fighting to propagate itself, and in many areas, especially in the sandhills, it is doing so successfully. The young trees stand fire to a remarkable degree and when mixed with other pines are often the only ones left alive after being burned over. Prof. R. W. Graeber of North Carolina State College reports a tree of this species in Duplin County, eight miles southeast of Delway, that is $3\frac{7}{10}$ feet in diameter four and a half feet from the ground, and 110 feet tall. There is in certain sections of North Carolina, especially around Rockingham, a remarkable weeping variety in which the needles reach a length of twenty-four inches. Flowering in Johnson County, N. C., March 13, 1931.

A hybrid between *P. palustris* and *P. taeda,* which has been named *P. sondereggeri* by H. H. Chapman, has been reported as not uncommon in a number of places in Louisiana (Chapman, *Journ. Forestry* 20: 729. 1922). He thinks that the seed parent is the Long-leaf Pine. Prof. Korstian of Duke University writes that he has clearly recognized such a hybrid tree in Pender County, North Carolina. He has planted in the Duke Forest about 500 seedlings that he thinks are this hybrid. These seeds came from Pender County.

3. Pinus Elliottii Engelm. Slash Pine.

THIS is a tall tree about the same size as the Long-leaf Pine. It occupies an area just south of Charleston, S. C., on the sea islands and inland to near Branchville, then above Fairfax towards points south of Augusta and other parts of Georgia to northern Florida and south to the Everglade region. Small's *Manual of the Southeastern Flora* (1933) recognizes three species in the Slash Pine group, all three occurring in Georgia. We cannot agree with this interpretation.

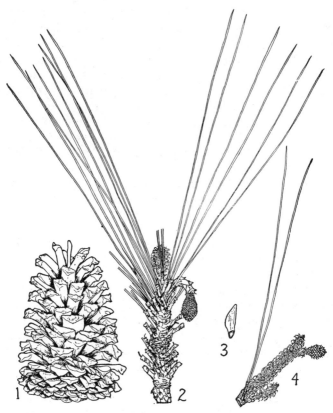

1, Mature open cone. 2, twig with leaves, bud, and one year old cone. 3, seed. 4, twig with two weeks old cone. All x ⅓.

Bark purplish brown, peeling off in thin, almost papery layers, very characteristic; leaves shorter and more polished than those of the Long-leaf Pine, borne mostly in twos, sometimes in threes, about 6-9 (4-10) inches long; male cones cylindrical, ¾-1½ inches long, scales purplish brown; young female cones at time of flowering ovate; year old cones ovate, ⅞ inch long by ⅝ inch thick, scales and prickles still pointing forward; mature cones a handsome reddish brown color, more or less shining as if varnished, on stalks about ¾-1 inch long, quite variable in size even on trees in the same grove or at times on the same tree, when open 2½-5½ inches long and 2-3½ inches thick, shaped like those of the Long-leaf Pine, prickles very small and sharp; wings of seeds unusually thin and transparent compared with other pines. The young cones are pointed

Twigs showing year old cones from the same tree. All x ⅖.

forward but during the first month or two of growth the stalks as a rule curve sharply backward and remain in this position until maturity. The Slash Pine yields a much larger percentage of turpentine than the Long-leaf Pine, some say as much as 50 per cent, but it is not so resistant to fire as that species. It is now being planted by the Department of Conservation and Development in a number of localities in North Carolina to determine its suitability in that state (*Conservation and Industry* 8, No. 12, p. 14.

1931). The Carolina Fiber Company of Hartsville, S. C., is planting large tracts of Slash Pine in lower South Carolina in a reforestation program. They are much pleased with it and report a very rapid growth in youth. Year old seedlings set out in 1930 in old fields were, in 1933, 8 to 10 feet high. Mr. P. H. Rogers, president of the company, says that these trees have received some attention as follows: "the first year corn was planted between the rows and the two following years peas were harrowed in, and this will be done again this year." He also says that it is very important that the trees be set the first year that the fields are abandoned and that Slash Pine should be planted only in fairly well drained fields, using *P. echinata* and *P. taeda* in the wet lands.

There has been a difference of opinion as to whether there is only one Slash Pine in our territory or more than one. After repeated examination of the pines from Miami northward we are convinced that there is only one Slash Pine in this territory. The Cuban Pine *(P. caribaea, P. cubensis)*, the common and only pine of the Caribbean Islands, may get into the Florida Keys. We cannot say as to this. We have numerous collections of good material of *P. Elliottii* from Allendale County in South Carolina, from Waycross and Quitman in Georgia, and from near Tallahassee, Palm Beach, Miami, and Kelsey City in Florida. Flowering at Kelsey City on January 10, 1933, and about 15 miles below Miami on January 24, 1933.

4. **Pinus taeda** L. **Loblolly Pine, Old Field Pine, North Carolina Pine, Forest Pine.**

THIS is a large tree which is abundant in the coastal plain and eastern piedmont of Virginia and North Carolina and throughout most of South Carolina, Georgia, southeastern Tennessee, and in northern and central Florida. In the coastal plain it is the pine that covers old fields; in the eastern piedmont old fields are covered by *P. echinata;* and farther west by *P. virginiana*. Westward from the coastal plain the Loblolly Pine rapidly becomes less abundant and in North Carolina disappears in Alamance and Randolph counties in the central part of the state, but farther south

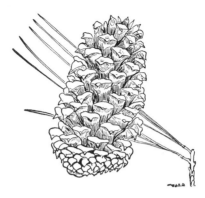

Open seed cone and bundles of
leaves, x ⅓.

Peattie reports a splendid specimen on a hill that is practically an extension of Melrose Mountain in Polk County,
"perhaps the Loblolly Pine that is closer to the mountains
than any other in the state." We have a sheet from Peattie
(No. 1600) from this tree. The open cone is only 1¾ inches
long, but otherwise it is typical *P. taeda*, as are also the
leaves. Mr. J. S. Holmes, State Forester of North Carolina,
estimates (Geol. and Econ. Survey, *Press Bull.* **116.** 1914)
that the Loblolly comprises about 20 per cent of our pines
in the neighborhood of Chapel Hill but that even at Hillsboro, in a distance of only fourteen miles, it drops to 15 per
cent.

Leaves about 6 inches long, three in a bundle; cones 3-5
inches long, sessile or with a very short stalk. The largest
pine we have seen or heard of in the southeastern states
belongs to this species. It is growing on the edge of a swamp
in Wilson County, N. C., near Stantonsburg on the farm of
Mr. C. P. Farmer. We visited it recently and found it to
be 5 feet 8⅕ inches in diameter four feet from the ground,
and 5 feet 6⅖ inches in diameter six feet above ground.
Some one had cut into the trunk about two feet from the
ground so that we could pull off a chip showing the four
outermost rings. These rings averaged ⅑ inch in width.
At this rate the tree would show about 312 rings four feet
from the ground. This rate of growth is very much greater
than that usually indicated by old pines near the surface,

showing that it must have been very favorably situated. A small pine only about three feet from it, which had recently been cut down, had a wood diameter of 20½ inches and showed 172 rings, the rings averaging only about ⅟₁₈ inch in width. In the northern states the White Pine is said to reach even larger dimensions than this, but we have not seen any so large in the south. Large old trees of *P. taeda* and *P. echinata,* scattered among hardwood trees, show a large amount of heart-wood and are called "forest pines." Nearly everyone thinks these are of different kind from the old field pines but they are not. For a comprehensive study of the Loblolly Pine from a commercial point of view see Ashe, *Bull.* 24, N. C. Geol. and Econ. Surv., 1915. Flowering March 31 to April 23.

5. **Pinus serotina** Michx. **Pond Pine, Marsh Pine, Pocoson Pine.**

THIS is a good sized tree common in swamps and wet flats of the coastal plain throughout most of our area but rare north of southeastern Virginia. Back of the dunes at Myrtle Beach we have seen this pine with *P. palustris* and *P. taeda* growing within a few feet of each other. In the pine flats it is often mixed with *P. palustris.* In North Carolina it is found as far west as the eastern edge of the piedmont and has been reported even from the eastern part of Alamance County. It is common in the eastern part of northern Florida but rare in the western part (Harper).

Leaves usually in threes, rarely in fours, 6-8 inches long; cones broadly top-shaped, solid, with small weak prickles, about 2-2¾ inches long and of the same width when open. They remain closed usually for several years, sometimes for as much as 12 years, and in these closed cones the seeds remain capable of germination (Coker, *Journ. Eli. Mitch. Sci. Soc.* 26: 43. 1910). This tree has much the appearance of *P. taeda,* except for the cones, and in the market the lumber of the two is not distinguished. In the second edition of Sargent's *Manual of Trees* this pine is considered a variety of *P. rigida.* This disposition we are quite unable to accept. They differ not only in

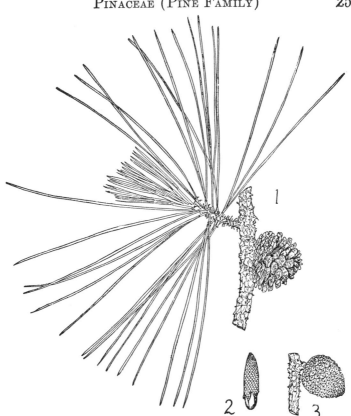

1, Branch with leaves and mature open seed cone, x ¼.
2, staminate cone, x ⅚. 3, mature unopened seed cone, x ¼.

leaves, cones, and stature but in soil requirements and regional distribution.

6. Pinus rigida Mill.   Black Pine, Pitch Pine, Mountain Pine.

THIS is a small tree which is common at moderate altitudes and extends in stunted form up to 4,500 feet in the mountains in our area from Virginia to Georgia. In the adjacent piedmont it is found as far east as Lincoln and Yadkin counties, with one apparently outlying station reported from Warren County, in North Carolina and Greenville in South Carolina.

Branch with mature seed cone; twig showing leaves. All x ½.

Leaves usually in threes, rarely in twos or fours, 3-4½ (5½) inches long; cones resembling those of the Short-leaf Pine but larger, about 2-3 inches long. Sargent says that this tree may reach a diameter of 3 feet, but in our area it is usually not more than 2 feet. The timber is usually knotty and of little commercial importance.

7. Pinus echinata Mill. Rosemary Pine, Short-leaf Pine, Yellow Pine, Old Field Pine, Forest Pine.

THIS is a large and important timber tree, which is found throughout our region southward to northern Florida. It is more abundant in the middle district, much rarer in the coastal plain where it descends to the neighborhood of streams or damp flats, and in the mountains is found only at low elevations (up to 3,300 ft.) In Florida it occurs chiefly in the western and middle sections of the northern part.

Leaves short, 3-5 inches long, not twisted, usually two in a bundle, sometimes three; cones very small, about 2

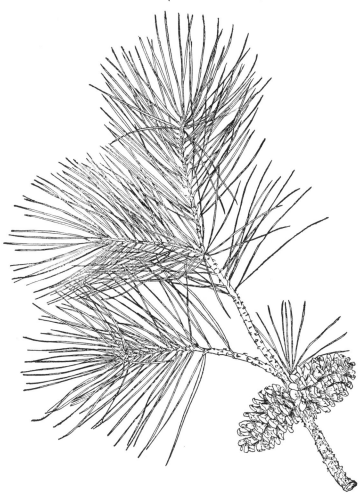

Branch with leaves and mature seed cones, x ⅛.

inches long or less. Old trees grown in thick woods are free of limbs and knots to near the top, and such are commonly called Forest Pines. A fine specimen of this species growing on a rich hillside near Chapel Hill (destroyed by lightning in 1908) was probably the largest pine tree in Orange County. From the rings it was about 203 years old. Flowering April 4 to April 22.

8. **Pinus glabra** Walter.   **Walter's Pine, Spruce Pine.**

THIS is a beautiful tree of damp coastal woods in our area
from the lower Santee River in South Carolina southward
to central and western Florida.   It is plentiful along much

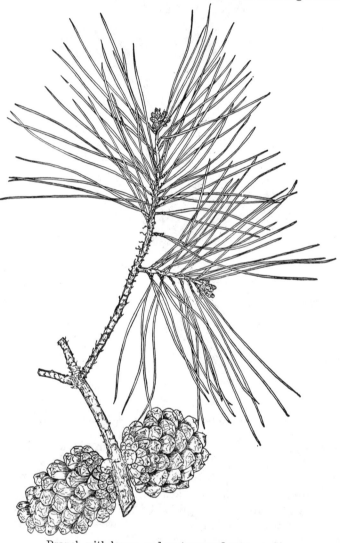

Branch with leaves and mature seed cones, **x ⅗**

of the highway between Charleston and Beaufort, South Carolina. Very rarely does it occur in pure stands.

Bark much smoother than in most pines; branches drooping; leaves pale, slender, two in a bundle, 2-4 inches long (reaching 5 inches in cultivation at Chapel Hill); male cones very small and densely clustered; mature seed cones small, 1½-2 inches long and up to 2 inches broad when open, the prickles small and delicate. This tree reaches about the same size as the Long-leaf Pine. In general effect Walter's Pine resembles the White Pine but is closely related to the Scrub Pine in the Black Pine group.

In John Bartram's *Diary of a Journey through the Carolinas, Georgia, and Florida*, annotated by Dr. Francis Harper and published by the American Philosophical Society in 1942, we find that on September 25, 1765, Bartram meets with a pine near Savannah, Georgia, which he describes clearly enough to leave no doubt that he refers to the pine that Walter first named *Pinus glabra* about twenty-three years later. Bartram gave no scientific name but called it ''spruice pine,'' his spelling for spruce pine, a name used for it to this day.

9. Pinus virginiana Mill. Scrub Pine, Jersey Pine, Spruce Pine, Possum Pine.

THIS is a small tree which is abundant on dry hills, bluffs, and old fields in the piedmont and lower mountains (3,800 feet) and rare in the coastal plain from Virginia to Georgia. Near Chapel Hill it is found only on very poor or hilly places. In North Carolina it is found sparingly as far east as Wilmington. In South Carolina and Georgia it is known from a few places in the sandhills, such as Chesterfield County, South Carolina, and from near Augusta, Georgia. Through northern Virginia it is the most abundant tree and many of the forests are of practically pure stands of Scrub Pine.

Bark almost smooth; branches drooping; leaves short, twisted, about 1¾-2½ inches long, generally two in a bundle; cones very small and abundant, 1½-2 inches long. The old open cones remain on the tree for years so that the tree appears full of them. Flowering from March 30 to April 22.

Pinus virginiana. Branch with leaves, year old cones, and mature seed cone, x ½.

10. Pinus clausa Chapman. Sand Pine.

This is a small spreading tree which inhabits in our area poor soil from southern Georgia to Peace River on the west coast and also along almost the entire east coast of Florida. In the upper peninsular region it is said to extend through from coast to coast. In many places on the east coast it is the only pine that can stand conditions on the poorer sandy

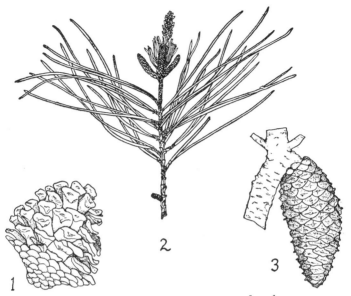

1, Open seed cone. 2, twig with leaves and male cones.
3, unopened seed cone. All x ½.

dunes and flats. Not rarely it is found growing with a peculiar cedar-like shrub, *Ceratiola*.

Bark on twigs and small branches very smooth, grayish brown, then gray, becoming fissured and plated only on the older branches; twigs very slender and pliable; bud scales deep red-brown, nearly smooth; leaves slender, short, about 2-3¼ inches long, two in a bundle; male cones purplish brown, slender, about ¾ inch long or shorter, maturing about the third week in March in 1932 near Palm Beach, Florida; collected in flower December 31, 1933, near Daytona, Florida; young female cones during the first spring a peculiar creamy yellow color, ovate, about ¾ inch long with rather stout prickles nearly at right angles; year old cones no longer, slightly thicker, red-brown, the scales slightly more ascending; mature cones polished red-brown, soon losing this polish and becoming dull grayish brown, ovoid-pyramidal, 1⅞-2½ inches long by 1 inch thick below when closed, about 1¾-2 inches thick when open; prickles when mature no longer than when young, easily breaking away, seated on small gray protuberances. Near Apopka, Florida, it reaches a height of 75 feet and a diameter of 15 inches. This pine seems to be easily killed by fire and along the highway on the east coast of Florida many thousands of dead trees present a sad picture.

11. Pinus pungens Lamb. Table Mountain Pine, Burr Pine, Hickory Pine.

THIS is a small or medium sized tree of irregular growth found in our area on rather poor soil in the mountains and on ridges east of them from Virginia to Georgia, as on Table Mountain and Pilot Mountain, North Carolina, top of Barney's Wall, Giles County, Virginia, and reported on Piny Mountain about 10 miles south of Table Rock, South Carolina (S. A. Ives). The easternmost records we now have in North Carolina are just northeast of High Point and in southwest Mecklenburg County on the Catawba River.

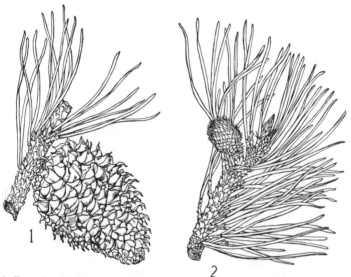

1, Branch with leaves and mature seed cone.   2, branch showing year old cone. All x ⅓.

Leaves two in a bundle, strong, about 1½-3½ inches long; cones heavy, often in clusters of three, about 3-3½ inches long, remarkable for the very broad and strong spines with bent tips; seeds glaucous, blue-black, triangular, about $\frac{3}{16}$ inch long, wing long, triangular, about $\frac{3}{4}$ inch long by $\frac{1}{4}$-$\frac{5}{16}$ inch wide. While some of the cones open the first year, others remain closed for a number of years. Thomas Meehan reports that seeds from old cones are quite as good as those from freshly matured ones, and that even clean seeds survive for as much as six years (*Bot. Gaz.* 5: 75. 1880). Compare with *Pinus serotina*. Seeds of most pines are, on the contrary, short-lived. The largest standing tree of this species we have seen is on the Harbison farm about two miles from Highlands, N. C. It was (1941) 2 feet $10\frac{1}{3}$ inches thick four and a half feet from the ground and 61 feet high, measured by Mr. Tom Harbison who carried a tape to the topmost twig. That this could be done is evidence of the rigidity and toughness of the branches. Another large tree is near the eastern limit of the species, a single specimen about $1\frac{1}{2}$ miles south of Cana in Davie County, North Carolina. This tree is in good soil and is 1 foot 7 inches in diameter three feet above the ground and about 70 feet high, as high as the Short-leaf Pines around it, but standing out conspicuously from the other trees on account of its large cones and the stubs of dead branches that reach nearly to the ground. The cones are very persistent, being found on the main body of the tree within ten feet of the ground. A section in the museum in Raleigh from Henderson County, N. C., has a diameter of 2 feet 4 inches. Sargent says that the wood is brittle, but we have found it very tough. Branches even near the top are so tough that they can be tied into knots and are practically unbreakable. The common name, Hickory Pine, is evidently based on its toughness.

PICEA Link.

Leaves dark green; cones usually over 1 inch long, most
  of them falling soon after maturity
              Picea rubens, Red Spruce   No. 1
Leaves bluish green (glaucous); cones usually not over
  1 inch long, hanging on for years after maturity
            Picea mariana, Black Spruce   No. 2

1. Picea rubens Sargent (P. rubra Link). Red Spruce.

THIS is a fine large tree of the far north extending through western North Carolina. It makes up a large part of the Balsam groves of Grandfather, Mitchell, the Black Mountains, Clingman's Dome and the Smokies in general in North Carolina, and there it is often called "He Balsam." In Virginia it occurs on Pine Mountain, Grayson County (Small), on Stonyman Mountain near Luray, Page County (Tidestrom), along the headwaters of Little Stony Creek, Giles County (Massey), and in Highland County (Freer). It appears not to occur in South Carolina. In the higher altitudes it is often mixed with the true Balsam or Fraser's Fir.

1-3, Cones of various sizes, x ¾.

Twigs stout on exposed or fruiting branches, slender on shaded branches and on young trees, bright brown, then blackish, set with short stiff hairs; outer bud scales with long hair-like points, even extending into cilia beyond the bud on delicate branches; leaves ⅜-¼ inch long, more or less four-cornered, curved upward, borne on stout little stalks called sterigmata that are left on the twig when the leaves fall off, extending in all directions around the twigs; cones more or less polished, red-brown, pendent, about 7/8-1¾ inches long, undernourished or imperfect ones smaller, maturing in one year and mostly falling off soon after maturity but smaller ones often hanging on until late in the following summer, margins of cone scales slightly eroded; seed very small with a short broad wing.

Small has described a spruce on slopes, summits, and cliffs at Blue Ridge, N. C., and in Virginia, which he has named *P. australis*. We have studied our southern spruces from a number of places in western North Carolina and we cannot find any consistent differences between them and the northern *P. rubens*. The cones vary greatly in size in the same localities. Some of them smaller and some of them larger than the cones of the northern spruce as given in all the manuals. The smaller cones are not associated with more delicate or glabrous twigs. In our illustration we show three figures of cones, the central one larger (2½ inches) than any record of the northern *P. rubens*. It is true that the tree from which this cone was taken had been planted at Highlands, brought down from the Balsam Mountains of North Carolina, and this may have had something to do with the unusual size.

There are two foreign spruces that are much more commonly planted in the southern states than the native ones. They are the Norway Spruce, *Picea Abies* Karst., and the Oriental Spruce, *P. orientalis* Carr. Both of these can be distinguished from our southern spruce by the fact that the outer scales of the buds are not prolonged into a hair-like tip. A hand lens will show this character clearly. This difference makes it easy to distinguish these at all times of the year. The Norway Spruce can be distinguished from the Oriental Spruce by the much longer cones, up to 5 inches, and by the reflexed scales of the buds making them look like little flowers. The Oriental Spruce has compact little buds and cones about 1¾-2¾ inches long.

2. Picea mariana B. S. & P. Black Spruce, Lash-horn.

THE Black Spruce which is a common tree in the north in cold sphagnum bogs, has been reported as far south as the mountains of North Carolina. However, its presence in North Carolina has been and still is uncertain. In Virginia it seems to be authentically reported from White Top Mountain, near the North Carolina line (Harbison and Small), and from Pine Mountain and Mt. Rogers (Small

Twig with mature cone, x ⅘.

and Vail). Eggleston writes (letter of June 20, 1932) that he thinks he saw this tree on the southern edge of Linville, North Carolina, on Route 691 to Pineola in a sphagnum swamp. He did not examine it, however. It is said that this spruce can be distinguished at a distance by its bluish color, the leaves being glaucous. We have recently visited the Cranberry bog at Pineola and found a number of spruce trees there, but all were Red Spruce, though locally the spruce growing in the bog is called ''White Spruce.'' The cones of the Black Spruce are decidedly smaller than those of the Red Spruce and they hang on for many years after maturity.

Twigs stout, brown soon becoming blackish, more or less thickly set with short hairs (rarely nearly glabrous); leaves bluish green (glaucous), about ¼-½ inch long; cones about ¾-1¼ inches long, the scales slightly eroded on the margins.

TSUGA (Endl.) Carr.

Leaves extending in one plane, cones ½-¾ inch long
        Tsuga canadensis, Hemlock   No. 1
Leaves spreading in all directions; cones 1-1½ inches long
        Tsuga caroliniana, Carolina Hemlock   No. 2

1. Tsuga canadensis (L.) Carr. Hemlock.

THIS fine Hemlock is plentiful in good moist soil in the mountains from North Carolina northward and occurs sparingly in South Carolina and Georgia and in Jackson (Harbison) and Winston, Franklin, and Jefferson counties, Alabama (Harper, *Castanea* 8: 115. 1943). The most southern station known in South Carolina is at Carson's Shoals not far from Marietta (S. A. Ives). It is supposed to be confined to the mountains, but was reported nearly fifty years ago by J. A. Holmes from one place in Wake County, N. C., on a northward-facing bluff of Swift Creek at an elevation of not more than 350 feet (*Journ. Eli. Mitch. Sci. Soc.* 1: 86. 1884). We visited this mountain-like bluff, known as "Spruce Pine Hill," about ten miles southwest of Raleigh first in 1916. On a recent visit (1933) we counted eleven trees in the group, but the trees were not in a vigorous condition and there were few saplings and seedlings, not so many as in 1916. Evidently most of the young plants have been carried away. However, J. A. Holmes in the reference cited above stated that "the larger trees do not present a healthy, vigorous appearance; and are quite certain to be short-lived." At that time four or five trees measured 12 to 15 inches in diameter. In 1933 the largest one measured 22 inches in diameter. May they be spared another fifty years!

Leaves short, flat, about ½ inch long, with two white

Twig with mature seed cones, x ⅖.

streaks beneath; cones small, about ⅝-1 inch long, pendulous, maturing the first year. A tree near Highland
Falls, Highlands, N. C., measured in August, 1932, was 4
feet ⅓ inch in diameter five feet from the ground. The
"Priestley Hemlock" in Richardson Woods, Highlands,
was 5 feet 10 inches in diameter five feet above the ground
in the summer of 1932. Prof. Cain of the University of
Tennessee reports one in the Great Smoky Mountains that
is 5 feet 8 inches in diameter at breast height. The Hemlock is very highly valued as an ornamental tree and is
important for its timber and tanbark. Several horticultural forms are known, among them a spreading semi-
prostrate bush (var. *pendula*).

2. Tsuga caroliniana Engelm. Carolina Hemlock.

THIS is a smaller tree than the Canada Hemlock, is less
abundant, and has a different habitat. It is found only on
dry slopes and rocky ridges at moderate elevations from
Virginia to northern Georgia. In Virginia it grows on the
east slope of Flat Top Mountain, Peaks of Otter, Bedford
and Botetourt counties at elevations from 2,100 to 4,000
feet, on the west end of Petite's Gap on western slopes of
High Cock Knob of Blue Ridge, and on the west slope of
Thunderhill Mountain, Rockbridge County (in our herbarium, R. S. Freer), also in Craig County, and Small and
Vail mention it from Little Brushy Mountain and on slopes

Twig with mature seed cones, x ⅖.

of Farmer Mountain on New River. A number of other localities are added in a list by Professor Freer in *Claytonia* for July, 1936. In North Carolina it is found on places such as Pinnacle Mountain (near Kanuga), Banner's Elk, Linville Gorge, and Blowing Rock. Its farthest eastern station known to us is on bluffs at the Cascades at foot of Moore's Knob (Sauratown Mountains) in Stokes County, North Carolina. At this station the species mingles with Canadian Hemlock on the side of the gorge. On ridges around Highlands, North Carolina, it is common and reaches its greatest size. One of the largest on Wild Cat Cliff is about 65 feet high and measures 2 feet 2¾ inches in diameter three feet from the ground. In South Carolina the only records we have are at Caesar's Head just outside the North Carolina line (Coker), Table Mountain (Gibbes, see below), on Little Pinnacle Mountain near Caesar's Head, and on Little Rich Mountain two miles south of the North Carolina state line (S. A. Ives). In Georgia it occurs at Tallulah Falls. It is also reported on the Tennessee side of the Smoky Mountains.

Leaves flat, up to ¾ inch long, pointing in all directions around the twig; cones oblong, about 1-1½ inches long, the scales longer than broad; seed and wing straw-yellow, about ⅝ inch long and ³⁄₁₆ inch wide, shiny, the seed about ⅕ inch long, pointed at both ends; cones fully ripe and shedding seeds at Tallulah Falls on August 29, 1932. In 1933 all the seeds had fallen at Wild Cat Cliff near Highlands. N. C., by September 9, while on September 14 seeds were just beginning to fall in Linville Gorge. This tree was first discovered on Table Mountain, Pickens County, S. C., in 1837 by Dr. L. R. Gibbes, who recognized it as distinct in 1856. He gave it the manuscript name of *Pinus laxa,* but Gray discouraged him and he never published it. It was not until twenty-five years later that Engelmann named the tree (see note in *Journ. Eli. Mitch. Sci. Soc.* **44**: 124. 1928). The Carolina Hemlock differs from *T. canadensis* in having the leaves pointing in all directions around the twig, in the larger cones with longer scales, and in the less spreading growth. The Carolina Hemlock is a very beautiful tree in cultivation, perhaps the handsomest of any eastern American conifer, combining in a remarkable way delicacy, symmetry, and strength.

ABIES (Tourn.) Hill.

Bracts of cones projecting beyond the scales and turning
  downward; cones 1¾-2½ inches long
                    Abies Fraseri, Fraser's Fir   No. 1
Bracts of cones not projecting beyond the cone scales
  or scarcely so; cones 2-4 inches long
                    Abies balsamea, Balsam Fir   No. 2

1. Abies Fraseri (Pursh) Poir. She Balsam, Balsam, Fraser's Fir.

THIS is the true Balsam of the highest mountains in northern and southern Virginia, North Carolina, and eastern Tennessee. Kellerman collected it on Cheat Mountain, Randolph County, West Virginia, at an elevation of 3,700 feet. It occurs mixed with spruce or in nearly pure stands mostly at elevations of 5,000 feet or more as on Mt. Mitchell, Cold Mountain (Haywood County), Roan Mountain, Grandfather Mountain, and Clingman's Dome in North Carolina.

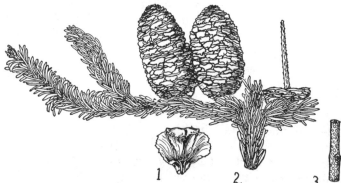

1, Cone-scale with its bract, x 1. 2, branch showing leaves, mature seed cones, and the axis of a cone after the falling of most of the seeds, cone-scales, and bracts, x ½. 3, twig showing circular scars left when the leaves fall, x ½.

Leaves fragrant, narrow, flattish, white below, at least when young, a scar instead of a stalk being left on the branch when the leaf falls; cones standing upright on the branches near the top of the tree, 1¾-2½ inches long, the scales usually broader than long, bracts long, projecting well beyond the scales and strongly reflexed downward, maturing the first year. The cones do not fall at maturity but the cone scales fall off, leaving the axis standing as in all the firs. This is also the habit of the true cedars (Deodara, Mt. Atlas, and Lebanon). Here and there in the bark are large blisters filled with clear liquid resin, which may be used as a healing lotion for cuts and for other uses to which Canada Balsam (obtained from *A. balsamea*) is put. The presence of this liquid resin (fancifully compared to milk) gives the common name She Balsam to the tree, while the spruces lacking it are often called He Balsams. A section of Fraser's Fir in the museum in Raleigh from Mitchell County, N. C., has a diameter of 2 feet ¼ inch. This species does better in cultivation in the southern states than *A. balsamea* and retains its beauty longer, but it cannot be grown successfully outside of the lower mountains.

2. **Abies balsamea** (L.) Miller. **Balsam Fir, Balsam, Canada Balsam.**

THIS tree is very rare in our area, reaching its southern limit in the high mountains of Virginia, such as on Crescent Rock in the Blue Ridge (Page and Madison counties), and on the summit of Mt. Rogers, Grayson County. It is the common Balsam of the far north and Canada and furnishes the balsam of commerce. Regarding the identity of the Virginia and West Virginia form, Dr. R. S. Freer writes (*Claytonia* 2, No. 1, 1935):

"In a previous paper (*Bartonia* No. 15, 1933) the occurrence of this tree at Crescent Rock in Page County was discussed, and mention made of the fact that specimens collected here by Steele had been incorrectly identified as *A. Fraseri*. Collections of *Abies* material were made on Cheat Mountain, Randolph County, West Virginia, on the trip to the shale slopes mentioned above, and Dr. Wherry later made collections five miles southeast of Davis, Tucker County, West Virginia. At both these latter places, the *Abies* seemed to be identical with that from Crescent Rock. There is a growing feeling that all of this *Abies* material

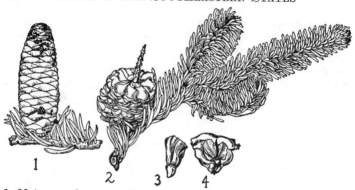

1, Mature seed cone, x ½.   2, branch with leaves and a cone from which part of the seeds and cone-scales have fallen, x ½.   3, seed, x 1.   4, cone-scale with its bract, x 1.

is not *balsamea*, but the intermediate form designated by Fernald *Abies balsamea* var. *phanerolepis*. The botanists of the University of West Virginia are inclined so to distribute an *Abies* growing around the Cranberry Glades of Pocahontas County, and this appears to be identical with the Cheat Mountain *Abies*.''

Leaves fragrant, narrow, flattish, white below, at least when young, a scar instead of a stalk being left on the branch when the leaf falls; cones standing upright on the branches near the top of the tree, about 2-4 inches long, scales broader than long, falling off the axis at the maturity of the seed; bracts small, usually shorter than the scales; seeds with a thin brown wing. *Abies balsamea* may easily be distinguished from *A. Fraseri* by the shorter cone bracts, which are nearly or quite concealed by the scales. The leaves are very similar but may be slightly longer and are said to be frequently pointed in *A. balsamea*, while in *A. Fraseri* they are often slightly emarginate.

TAXODIUM Richard.

Leaves extending in one plane
    Taxodium distichum, Swamp Cypress   No. 1
Leaves pressed against the twig and all around it
    Taxodium ascendens, Pond Cypress   No. 2

1. Taxodium distichum (L.) Richard. Swamp Cypress, Bald Cypress.

This is a large and important timber tree of the coastal

plain swamps throughout our area, and it is common in bottom lands of western Tennessee. It is conspicuous in all the deeper swamps and follows the rivers as far as the sandhills or rarely beyond. On the Neuse River it comes within a few miles of Raleigh, North Carolina, and on Haw River extends into Alamance County.

Bark thin, about ⅛-⅜ inch thick (tree 14 inches in diameter; specimen from H. A. Rankin of Fayetteville, N. C.), with low narrow ridges; leaves flat, narrow, and spreading in one plane on slender short branches that fall with the leaves in autumn; male cones very small, spher-

Branch with leaves, x ⅖.

ical, produced in slender, compound, drooping panicles appearing nearly fully grown the summer preceding their opening, very conspicuous on the trees in winter; seed cones spherical, about ¾ inch in diameter, with thick scales which bear two seeds each, maturing the first year. When young the cypress has a symmetrical conic shape as in most conifers but later under forest conditions the shape is entirely reversed, the top expanding almost horizontally, crowning a long bare trunk. This is also the habit of the true cedars (Deodara, Lebanon, Mt. Atlas). The wood is very durable and is highly valued for shingles and other exposed construction. Though confined to the swamps, this cypress and the next will do well in any good upland soil and are very ornamental. In 1913 a large cypress tree was cut in Lenoir County, N. C., that had a diameter of 11 feet 1 inch four feet from the ground, and showed 818 rings (figures by H. H. Brimley). Probably the largest cypress tree now standing in North Carolina is on the bank of Turnbull Creek near the mouth of Little Turnbull Creek in Bladen County. Lionel Melvin has reported this tree to us with the following measurements: 10 feet 6 inches in diameter two feet above the ground, 8 feet 4½ inches five and a half feet above the ground, and 6 feet 4 inches seven and one-half feet above ground. A fine specimen is the "Sovereign Cypress" of Seminole County, Florida, which with a diameter of 13 feet 6 inches eighteen inches above ground is the largest conifer we know of east of the Mississippi River. In *American Forests* **48:** 4, 1942, there is a fine photograph of this tree. We think that the age there mentioned is greatly overestimated. We have a section of a Bald Cypress from Levy County, Florida, kindly donated by the Cummer Cypress Company of Jacksonville, that is 6½ feet in diameter, taken not nearer than six feet from the ground. It shows about 950 rings (a region a few inches wide in the center has decayed). For other accounts of large cypress trees, see *Journ. Eli. Mitch. Sci. Soc.* **46:** 86, 1930.

Two insect galls appear on *Taxodium distichum*. One is a conspicuous turbinate whitish gall, considered by Schweinitz to be a fungus and named *Merulius Cupressi* (later *Cantharellus*), but Berkeley showed it to be an insect gall. Our trees are not true cypresses. The true cypresses (genus *Cupressus*) are evergreen and are found in our country only in the western states.

2. Taxodium ascendens Brongniart. Pond Cypress.

THIS is a tree which inhabits savannas and poorly drained bogs in the coastal region from the Dismal Swamp to Florida. It is usually smaller than the Swamp Cypress.

Bark coarsely ridged, soft, red-brown, much thicker than in Swamp Cypress, up to ¾-1 inch (trees about 2 feet in diameter; specimens from H. A. Rankin of Fayetteville, N. C.), with heavier, thicker slabs; leaves needle-like, short and slender, pressed against the twig except in the case of

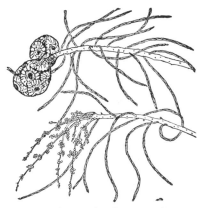

Upper twig showing leaves and mature seed cones; lower twig showing clusters of staminate cones. All x ⅔.

seedlings and strong shoots where the leaves may be spreading; male and seed cones as in *T. distichum*. Like the Swamp Cypress, this tree may be grown successfully in upland soils. Both species of cypress, when growing in water or in very wet soil, form an enlarged base (most abrupt in *T. ascendens*) and send up from the roots "cypress knees" to aerate the roots. Flowering in cultivation at Chapel Hill on April 12, 1929.

THUJA L.

1. Thuja occidentalis L. American Arborvitae.

THIS is one of the rarer and more local trees of our section. It is found only in the mountains and comes no farther south than North Carolina, where it occurs only on limestone soil along Cripple Creek and Linville River, on the headwaters of the New River in Alleghany and Ashe counties, and near Jefferson and Sparta. In Virginia it is more frequent, occurring sometimes in quantity. In that state it has been found at the following points, always on limestone: in the valley of the Middle Fork of the Holston River, along Hungry's Mother Creek, alt. 2,075-2,300 ft., and along Reed Creek near Wytheville (Small and Vail, *Mem. Torr. Bot. Club* 4: 167. 1893), and in Alleghany

Thuja occidentalis. 1, Branch with leaves and one open cone. 2, branch with mature cones. *T. orientalis.* 3, Branch with mature cones. All x ½.

County (Steele); and we have found it at Natural Bridge, Rockbridge County, on Walker Creek in Giles County, and on Dismal Creek in Bland County. It is reported on the Holston River in the mountains of Tennessee by Gattinger.

Leaves minute and scale-like; cones small and elongated, about ¼-½ inch long, maturing the first year. The finest specimens of this tree we have seen wild were at Natural Bridge, Va., in Cedar Creek ravine. The largest of these measured 5 feet 1½ inches four and a half feet from the ground. Dr. Chester A. Reed has estimated that these trees are growing at the rate of one inch in diameter in thirty years, and that the largest one there is over 1,600 years old. As this is one of the most popular conifers in cultivation, with many horticultural forms now offered by the trade, and as the Oriental Arborvitae is also very popular in cultivation, we thought it of interest to add to the cut a drawing of the cone of the Oriental Arborvitae, *T. orientalis.* The difference may be seen at a glance. Flowering in cultivation at Chapel Hill on February 27, 1731.

CHAMAECYPARIS Spach.

1. Chamaecyparis thyoides (L.) BSP. Juniper, White Cedar.

THIS is the ''Juniper'' of the coastal plain swamps from Maine to Florida. It is found inland to Moore County, North Carolina, to central South Carolina, and to Talbot County, Georgia.

Leaves scale-like, in general appearance much resembling the Red Cedar; fruit a small dry cone about the size of a pea, maturing the first year; seeds very small, 1-3 to a scale, flat with thin lateral wings. The wood is light brown, very durable, and valuable for telephone poles and other exposed construction. This tree often reaches a height of 40 feet and a diameter of 2 feet. A section in the museum in Raleigh from Craven County, N. C., has a diameter of 2 feet 9¼ inches. Korstian and Brush have recently published an important bulletin on the White Cedar (*Technical Bull.* **251,** U. S. Dept. Agric. 1931). See also Buell and Cain, *Ecology* **24:** 85, 1943.

JUNIPERUS (Tourn.) L.

Leaves very small and scale-like; a common tree
Juniperus virginiana, Cedar   No. 1
Leaves about ⅜ inch long, linear, flat, and sharp; a rare shrub or small tree of the mountains
Juniperus communis var. *montana,* Mountain Juniper   No. 2

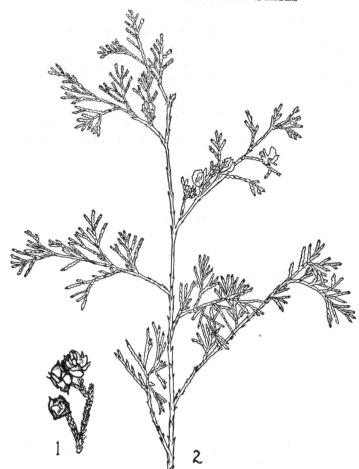

Chamaecyparis thyoides. 1, Twig with open cones, x 1¼.
2, branch with leaves and cones, x ½.

1. Juniperus virginiana L.   Cedar, Red Cedar.

THIS is a tree which is found in our range as far south as
northern Florida. It is common in the piedmont but rare
in the coastal plain except near the sea, and is absent in the
mountains except at low elevations (extends up to 4,000
ft. in N. C.). It forms extensive forests of almost pure
stands on limestone hills of the middle Tennessee River
basin.

Leaves small, pointed, scale-like (in very young plants lance-like), four-ranked in alternate pairs; male cones very small, borne on the tips of small twigs, abundant; female flowers (young cones) inconspicuous, also on the tips of short twigs; fruit subglobose, berry-like, blue, covered with a glaucous bloom. The color of the leaves is quite variable, some trees being decidedly bluish. The shape of the tree is usually narrowly pyramidal but in some localities, as in Chapel Hill, it is often open and spreading. It may reach

1, Twig with male cones, x 3. 2, twig with female flowers, x 3.
3, branch with leaves, fruit (A), cedar-apple (B) and bag-worm case (C), x ½.

a height of 40 feet and a diameter of 2-3 feet or more. The largest Cedar in Chapel Hill is 3 feet 4⅓ inches in diameter three feet from the ground.

The date of flowering of the male trees varies widely, in our notes from January 25 to March 15. The male flowers begin opening earlier than the female, e.g., male trees began flowering in 1914 on February 2, while the female trees did not begin until March 16; in 1915 the male trees began flowering February 12, while the female trees were delayed until March 25. In 1915 practically all of the pollen was shed before the female trees bloomed, and although they formed a few normal-looking berries with seeds of usual size the seeds were empty. The young berries developed normally until about the middle of June and then began dropping rapidly. The Red Cedar matures its fruit the first season and fertilization takes place about June 8 if the trees have been pollinated. Sprays from an old tree on a plantation near Hartsville, S. C., sent to us in December, 1931, were very heavily fruited but the berries were of a peculiar shape, mostly turbinate with flattish tops. In the place of seeds every one of many opened contained a white grub. This tree and another near it have very open heads with decidedly pendent branches, but the branchlets and twigs are far less delicate than in the Barbados Cedar, *J. Barbadensis*. This last is reported in the manuals from Georgia and Florida, but there is a specimen from Summerville, S. C., in the New York Botanical Garden Herbarium which is determined as *J. Barbadensis*. It is very much like the Red Cedar, the principal difference being the more delicate, pendent branchlets and twigs. Our Red Cedar is a very variable tree and many forms have been propagated. These vary in density and shape of tree (columnar, prostrate, dwarf, etc.) and color and disposition of leaves. A number of these variations have been described under horticultural names (see Rehder, *Manual of Cultivated Trees and Shrubs*, 1940). A cedar from the northern Bahama Islands and possibly eastern Cuba has been described by Britton as *Juniperus lucayana*. Some authors now refer our coastal cedar of the lower south to this species rather than to *J. Barbadensis*.

The Red Cedar is very susceptible to a rust which causes large gall-like tumors, called cedar apples (fig. B), on the twigs. These are often taken for fruits by the ignorant. In the spring these tumors send off long yellow, gelatinous processes which make a very conspicuous mass. Spores from these processes infect the leaves of apple trees, causing yellowish splotches. When spores from these infections are blown to cedars again they cause the formation of tumors to repeat the rotation. This with the scab and fire blight are the most serious diseases of apples in this country. A peculiar caterpillar called a bagworm (a moth, female wingless) which makes for itself a protective bag upon which it sticks twigs and fruits of the cedar, is often a troublesome pest (fig. C). This same bagworm will sometimes almost defoliate Arborvitae, White Cedar, and Cypress *(Taxodium)* trees.

Our native trees that we call cedars are not true cedars. The true cedars belong to the genus *Cedrus* and are confined to Northern Africa, Asia Minor (also Island of Cyprus), and the Himalayan region. They are the Mt. Atlas Cedar, the Cedar of Lebanon, and the Deodara Cedar, all well known in cultivation in this country. They have large cones standing upright on the branches and are not closely related to our junipers.

2. **Juniperus communis** var. **montana** Ait. **Mountain Juniper.**

THIS is typically a prostrate shrub, forming dense mats up to 10 feet or more in diameter. It is found from Greenland southward to South Carolina. In the south it is rare and mostly confined to rocky slopes in the mountains or foothills. The only exception we know of is its occurrence at Aiken, South Carolina, as recorded by Ravenel (*Bull. Torr. Bot. Club* 6: 93. 1876). In one place on Mt. Satulah in North Carolina it has taken the form of a small dwarf tree with a crooked trunk about 3 inches thick and 2 or 3 feet long, with a flat spreading top about 3 feet wide. In South Carolina it grows on a rocky slope near the top of Paris Mountain near Greenville (Coker) and on a sandy hill near Aiken; in North Carolina on the summit and sides of Mt. Satulah in Macon County and on Crowder's Mountain in Gaston County (Hunter, Gray Herb.). Harbison said that the fine mat in the lawn of the Sloan Gardens in the town of Highlands at the foot of Mt. Satulah is original there. So far our only Virginia record is from Seward Forest near Triplett (U. N. C. Herb.).

Young bark yellowish to dark purple; leaves whorled in threes, long lance-shaped and pointed at the tip, flattened with the margin curved upward, rather spreading, about $\frac{3}{8}$-$\frac{5}{8}$ (rarely $1\frac{1}{16}$) inch long, the upper side with 2 broad glaucous stripes which practically meet in the center, nearly covering the midrib or sometimes forming only one stripe; fruit a blue or black berry with a gray bloom, about $\frac{5}{16}$ inch thick, maturing in the third year.

In the prostrate clumps noted on Mt. Satulah and Paris Mountain the branches send out adventitious roots at intervals. According to Dr. Alfred Rehder of the Arnold Arboretum (letter of Dec. 18, 1931) adventitious roots from the branches have been reported for the following conifers: *Juniperus horizontalis, Juniperus conferta, Picea Abies, Picea mariana,* and *Taxus canadensis.*

The typical *Juniperus communis* L. is supposed to have the tree form, but rarely reaches a height of 12 feet. We have never seen it in the south, but T. G. Harbison (letter of Jan. 28, 1932) says: "At one time there were a few small trees of this species growing with *Juniperus virginiana* at a little lower altitude on a bench below where the var. *montana* grows on Satulah Mountain. About thirty years ago a fire killed all of the *J. communis* and nearly all of the *J. virginiana.* This tree form can scarcely be distinguished from the prostrate variety except by its habit."

TAXACEAE (YEW FAMILY)

TUMION Raf.

1. Tumion taxifolium (Arn.) Greene (**Torreya taxifolia** Arnott). **Stinking Cedar.**

THIS small, handsome evergreen tree and the next represent a family of gymnosperms which is found in the southern

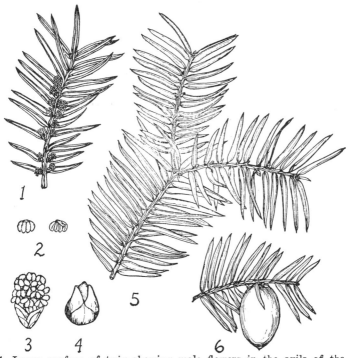

1, Lower surface of twig showing male flowers in the axils of the leaves, x ½. 2, stamens, x 2. 3, male flower, x 2. 4, female flower, x 2. 5, upper surface of twig with leaves, x ½. 6, twig with mature fruit, x ½.

states only in a very limited area. *Tumion* is found on bluffs along the Apalachicola River in Gadsden and Liberty counties, and also near the southwest end of Lake Ocheesee, Jackson County, Florida, and extends a mile or two into Georgia. They are among the rarest trees in the United States. (For literature on the distribution of *Tumion*, see Harper, *Torreya* **19**: 119, 1919; and Kurz, *Torreya* **27**: 90, 1927). *Tumion* is interesting to North Carolinians as having been first discovered by our excellent botanist, H. B. Croom.

Bark brown with scaly ridges; leaves bright green, shining, spreading right and left in a single plane, linear, sharp-pointed, about 1-1¾ inches long, almost sessile, pale beneath; male and female flowers on separate trees, male in dense spherical clusters; female flowers in twos (only one of which develops), inconspicuous, forming a purple, plum-like fruit with the pulpy flesh over a large hard seed. The fleshy part is an excess growth, called an aril, from around the base of the seed, which at maturity has completely covered the seed and seems to be a part of it. The crushed leaves and fruit have a rather offensive, resinous odor, hence the name Stinking Cedar. There stands in the yard of Poplar Mount farm, Warren County, N. C., a fine specimen of this tree, which in 1939 was 6½ feet in circumference four and one half feet from the ground.

TAXUS (Tourn.) L.

1. Taxus floridana Nuttall. Florida Yew.

THIS is a small rare tree found only in a few places on the bluffs of the Apalachicola River in Liberty and Gadsden counties, Florida, from Aspalaga south to near Bristol, e.g., Alum Bluff (U. N. C. Herb., H. Kurz) and in an acid swamp about ten miles south of the bluffs (Kurz, *Torreya* **27: 90. 1927.** This was first found and recorded by H. B. Croom (*Amer. Journ. Sci. and Arts* **26: 314. 1834**). He gave it no specific name, thinking that it might be the same as the European one.

Branches spreading; twigs slender; leaves spreading right and left in one plane, linear, sharply pointed, about ½-¾ inch long, bent at the base, on very short stalks; male flowers in the form of a small globular head borne in the axils of the leaves; female flowers single, very small, developing into a little hard dark pointed nut surrounded to near the top by a pulpy bright red coat or aril. This is eaten by birds. Male flowers open at Alum Bluff, Fla., on January 10, 1933.

The Florida Yew is the only southern tree representative of the genus to which belongs the well known Yew Tree *(T. baccata)* of Europe. The only other eastern American yew is the low spreading plant, *Taxus canadensis*, of the more northern states and Canada. South of Pennsylvania the only stations known for *T. canadensis* are in Virginia, as near the mouth of Hungry's Mother Creek, altitude 2,075

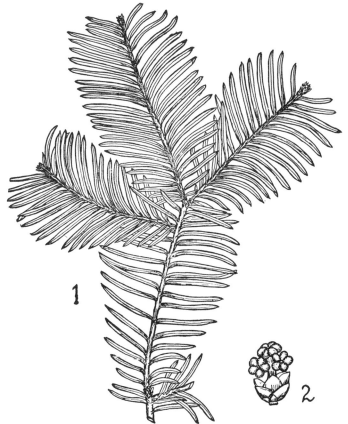

1, Branch with leaves, x ⅘. 2, male flower, x 5.

feet; banks of the Middle Fork of Holston River below the Falls, altitude 2,050 feet (Small and Vail, *Mem. Torr. Bot. Club* **4:** 167. 1893), and near Bell Grove, Maryland.

ARECACEAE (PALM FAMILY)

SABAL Adans.

1. **Sabal Palmetto** (Walt.) R. & S. **Palmetto, Cabbage Palmetto.**

THE semi-tropical Palmetto, with large fan-like leaves at the top of the thick stems, is found abundantly on Smith's

Island at the mouth of the Cape Fear River in North Carolina, where it reaches a height of thirty feet. So far as we can find this is now its northern limit. The only other North Carolina station we know of is Gause's Landing, Brunswick County (7 miles from the S. C. line), where H. A. Rankin reports to us probably a dozen trees about 15 feet high in sandy fields. Michaux *(Silva)* says that it occurs about Cape Hatteras and this statement is repeated even by Sargent in the new edition of his *Manual*. There seems to be no confirmation of any such record since Michaux's day. Croom *(Amer. Journ. Sci. and Arts* **26**: 315. 1834) says that Michaux extended it too far north but does assert: "It grows on the coast of North Carolina some ten or twenty miles north of Cape Fear inlet, but I have never met with it in the neighborhood of Cape Lookout or Topsail Inlet." We also have no confirmation of this record. In South Carolina and Georgia this tree grows on the sea islands or in the immediate neighborhood of salt water. It is plentiful on South Island near Georgetown *(Rhodora* **36**: 30. 1934). In Florida it is more widely distributed but is not known west of St. Andrews Bay (Harper).

Flowers numerous in open clusters, hanging from among the leaves; fruit subspherical, about ⅓ inch thick, black and shining, composed of some pulp and one large "seed" (drupe). Curtis *(Woody Plants of North Carolina.* 1860) says: "The trunk of this tree is of great value in the construction of wharves, as they are not subject to injury from sea-worms. . . . The inner portion of the young plant is very tender and palatable, somewhat resembling the Artichoke and Cabbage in taste, (hence its name of *Cabbage Tree,)* and is often taken for pickling, and the stock is ruined by the process. Thus for a pound or two of pickles, no better either than many other kinds, the growth of half a century is destroyed in a moment, and posterity left to the wretched inheritance of vain mourning for the loss of the greatest beauty of our maritime forest."

The Blue Stem or Dwarf Palmetto, *S. minor* (Jacq.) Pers. [*S. glabra* (Mill.) Sarg.], is found in low grounds along streams in the coastal section from North Carolina to Florida, but it is a shrub and never reaches tree size. In

North Carolina it occurs as far inland as Whiteville in Columbus County and in low grounds at the junction of Cove Creek with the Neuse River, five miles east of Fort Barnwell in Craven County, and north to Perquimans County. The Saw Palmetto, *Serenoa serrulata* (Michx.) Hooker, with the leaf stalk armed with saw-like teeth is found in sandy soil from lower South Carolina to Florida. We have no authentic record of its occurrence in North Carolina, but strange to say it is reported on islands in Back Bay, Virginia, by Weatherby and Griscom (*Rhodora* **36:** 31. 1934). In southern Florida it reaches tree size but is only a shrub in our territory. A fourth palmetto, the Needle Palm, *Rhapidophyllum Hystrix* (Fraser) H. Wendl., another armed shrub, has been reported from the shaded pine lands in the extreme southeastern part of South Carolina and southward to Florida.

LILIACEAE (LILY FAMILY)

YUCCA (Rupp.) L.

Leaves narrow, smooth, margin toothed the whole length; summer-flowering
    Yucca aloifolia, Spanish Bayonet   No. 1
Leaves narrow, rough on lower surface, margins not toothed the whole length; late-flowering
    Yucca gloriosa, Spanish Dagger

1. Yucca aloifolia L. Spanish Bayonet.

ASIDE from the Palmetto, the yuccas are the only monocot trees in our range. The Spanish Bayonet is inherently a coastal plant and is a familiar object in cultivation along all our inhabited beaches from North Carolina southward. It is hardy and considerably used as an ornamental as far inland as the piedmont of North Carolina. Dr. C. E. Moore reports that it is found occasionally as an escape from cultivation in Shelby County, Tennessee.

Trunk either single or with one or two upright branches, and usually with a clump of suckers growing up around the base; rarely over 12 feet high; leaves long, narrow, sharp-pointed, clustered at the top, the margins with sharp little teeth; individual flowers white and drooping, borne

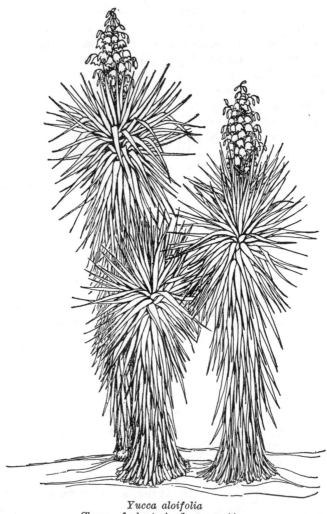

Yucca aloifolia
Clump of plants in flower, x ⅟₂₅.

in large showy upright terminal panicles, appearing in the
summer; fruits dark purple, elongated and usually knotty
and ridged, looking somewhat like short bananas, with a
purplish, bitter-sweet pulp. The pollination in *Yucca* is
very remarkable. A little white moth (called *Pronuba*)
lays its eggs in the ovary and then stuffs pollen into the

three-lobed stigma. The little grubs eat some of the seeds, leaving others that propagate the plant. (See figure on p. 4).

Another coastal yucca, *Y. gloriosa* L., occurring from North Carolina to Florida, is treated as a tree in the manuals but is very rarely over two or three feet high except near its southern limit. It is a very decorative species, even more attractive than the above, from which it differs in the larger head of flowers, appearing in late summer or fall, and paler green leaves without sharp teeth on the margins.

Two other small yuccas without obvious trunks, both of which are known as Bear Grass (*Y. flaccida* Haworth and *Y. filamentosa* L.), are native in our range. Both are cultivated for ornament.

SALICACEAE (WILLOW FAMILY)

POPULUS (Tourn.) L.

1. Leaf blade often 6 inches or more long, petioles round
       Populus heterophylla, Cottonwood   No. 1
   Leaf blade smaller, petioles flattened   2
2. Teeth on margins of leaves large, less than 14 on each side   3
   Teeth on margins of leaves small, more than 14 on each side   4
3. Petioles averaging over 2 inches in length
       Populus grandidentata, Large-toothed Poplar   No. 3
   Petioles averaging less than 2 inches in length, some leaves on tree usually white-tomentose beneath
       Populus alba, White Poplar   No. 5
4. Petioles smooth (young petioles with scattered, very short hairs), flatter than in the next below
       Populus deltoides, Carolina Poplar   No. 2
   Petioles hairy
       Populus candicans, Balm of Gilead   No. 4

1. Populus heterophylla L. Cottonwood.

THIS is a fine tall tree of the deep swamps in the coastal region in our area from Virginia southward to the Apalachicola River, Florida, and Dr. C. E. Moore says it is common in bottom lands in western Tennessee. In North Carolina it is known definitely from the lower Cape Fear and from Pasquotank, Northampton, Pender, Lenoir, Robeson,

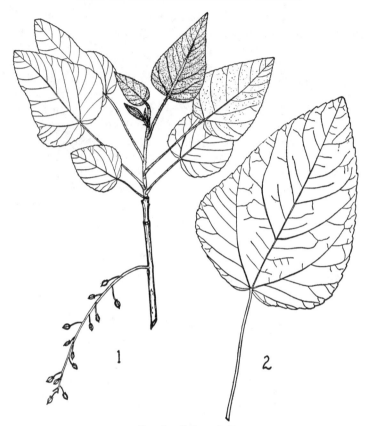

Populus heterophylla
1, Branch with young fruits and young leaves.   2, leaf.   All x ⅓.

and Chatham counties, but it is probably present in similar swamps in many other places in the eastern half of the state. We have a specimen from Florence County, South Carolina.

Leaves ovate with long points, 4-8 inches long, and about 3-5 inches wide, heart-shaped at the base, regularly toothed, densely coated below with long tawny down when young, becoming less downy to glabrous at maturity, petioles about 2-4 inches long, usually glabrous at maturity; fruit a small brown pod about ½ inch long on a short pedicel in racemes about five inches long, maturing before the leaves are grown; seeds minute, hairy, and carried about by the wind as in all poplars.

2. Populus deltoides Marsh. Carolina Poplar, Cottonwood.

THIS is a large tree found especially along streams throughout our area. It is given by Pinchot and Ashe as appearing in the piedmont plateau and they do not refer it to any other section of North Carolina, but Curtis says it is abundant in the lower sections of the southern states. According to our observations, it is most common in the coastal plain and enters sparingly into the piedmont. It is wild in swamps near Charlotte (Brier Creek), along the Cape Fear River in Harnett County, and has been found on Morgan's Creek in Orange County, North Carolina. House also reports this tree from the North Carolina mountains. In Florida we collected it along the Apalachicola River near River Junction.

Twig with leaves and catkin, x ⅖.

Bark rather smooth, gray; leaves heart-shaped, large, 4-5 (rarely 7) inches long and nearly or quite as broad, smooth and shining on both sides, with many rounded teeth, drooping and trembling on long petioles; male and female flowers on separate trees, male flowers crowded in large catkins, female flowers short-stalked on a long catkin; fruit a small, pointed pod with silky-hairy seeds as in all poplars. This is the poplar that is so much planted for quick effect in streets and lawns. It is short-lived and easily broken and should give place to better kinds. Some consider the tree found in the southern states as *P. deltoides virginiana* (Castiglioni) Sudworth, while others consider it *P. balsamifera virginiana* (Castiglioni) Sargent. A tree five miles from Macon, Georgia, is 2 feet 8 inches in diameter five feet from the ground.

3. Populus grandidentata Michx. Large-toothed Poplar.

THIS is a medium sized tree of cool rich soil, essentially of more northern range. It is certainly a rare tree in our South Atlantic states, and there is confusion as to its natural distribution in our territory. Most of the manuals and reference books confine its range to the mountains and its southern limit to North Carolina (Sargent, Britton, Sudworth). Pinchot and Ashe (1897) concur in these

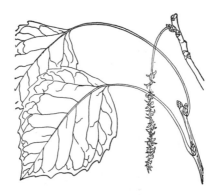

Twig with leaves; pistillate
catkin. All x ⅖.

statements. Earlier Ashe (*Journ. Eli. Mitch. Sci. Soc.* **10:** 17. 1893) had confined it to the upper part of the piedmont, as did Curtis in his *Woody Plants of North Carolina*. Mr. J. S. Holmes writes us that E. H. Frothingham has seen it on Looking Glass Rock, Pisgah National Forest, Transylvania County, North Carolina, and House reports it from the same location. In this state we have specimens from the base of a craggy ridge, Mt. Pisgah, Haywood County side (Blomquist). Harbison writes that he has collected it near Goldsboro and has seen it at Wilmington, North Carolina. It may be an escape at these places. In Virginia we have collected it in several places in Giles County, and Prof. R. S. Freer reports it from Green Pond, Kennedy Mountain near Stuart's Draft, Augusta County. Elliott includes it in his *Key to Georgia Trees.*

Leaves broadly ovate, pointed at the tip, blade about 3-4 inches long and 2-3 inches wide, with distant blunt teeth, very deep green above, light green below, when unfolding white-tomentose below, after maturity smooth and not shining; petioles flattened, 2-3½ inches long; male and female flowers borne in long catkins on separate trees; fruit an ovoid capsule bearing many seeds with a tuft of white hairs. In the Coker Arboretum at Chapel Hill it makes a strong healthy tree with a narrow crown and deep green foliage. It is a valuable tree for giving variety and tone to decorative plantings. Suckers from the roots appear here and there near the parent, but not nearly so abundantly as in the European White Poplar.

The variety *P. grandidentata meridionalis* Tidestrom, with broadly ovate-acuminate leaves and numerous teeth has been reported from Virginia and North Carolina.

4. **Populus candicans** Aiton. [**P. balsamifera** var. candicans (Aiton) Gray]. **Balm of Gilead.**

THE Balm of Gilead, in which only the female trees are known and of unknown origin, is commonly planted in the north and not rarely escaped as far south as North Carolina. We have North Carolina specimens from along the Cullasaja River in Macon County, from Polk County, and from Orange County. It is common along Pigeon River in Haywood County, west of Canton, North Carolina (Blomquist). Leaves heart-shaped, with long points, blade 2-7 inches long and 1½-6 inches broad, closely and shallowly serrate, with or without glands on the teeth, base cordate to truncate, the veins beneath, the petiole, and the blade margin usually more or less hairy; petioles 1-3 inches long, slightly flattened. The very large red buds of this plant are varnished with an abundance of a sticky, fragrant resin and furnish the drug known as the Balm of Gilead.

5. Populus alba L. European White Poplar, Aspen.

THE European White Poplar, a native of Europe and Central Asia, is easily recognized by its whitish bark and the dense white tomentum on the lower surface of the leaves. This tomentum may disappear

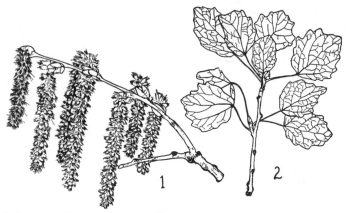

1, Branch with staminate catkins. 2, twig with leaves. All x ⅓.

on the mature leaves. The staminate catkins are about 2½-3 inches long and ½ inch thick, the brown scales densely covered with long, gray hairs. We do not recall having seen a female tree in our section. This may account for the fact that we have never found a seedling in the woods. The form most commonly planted has the habit of forming root suckers freely, and when once planted is hard to eradicate and may quickly become a nuisance in lawns. Old deserted homesteads may become converted into dense thickets of this tree, although the house has disappeared for generations.

SALIX (Tourn.) L.

1. Branchlets strongly drooping
                Salix babylonica, Weeping Willow   No. 6
   Branchlets not drooping or only slightly drooping   2
2. Leaves green beneath..........................   3
   Leaves whitish beneath.......................   4
3. Leaves closely toothed, petioles distinct
                Salix nigra, Black Willow   No. 1
   Leaves distantly toothed, nearly sessile
                Salix interior, Sand Bar Willow   No. 5
4. Branchlets brittle-jointed.....................   5
   Branchlets not brittle-jointed.................   7
5. Petioles practically glabrous at maturity
                Salix Harbisonii, Harbison Willow   No. 2
   Petioles pubescent to tomentose at maturity.......   6

6. Branchlets green, leaves with white silky hairs on
   both surfaces
                 Salix alba, White Willow   No. 7
   Branchlets yellow or reddish; leaves glabrous above
   at maturity
                 Salix alba var. *vitellina*, Yellow Willow   No. 7a
7. Leaves broad, blade less than 4 times as long as
   broad, short-pointed
                 Salix discolor, Glaucous Willow   No. 4
   Leaves narrow, blade more than 4 times as long as
   broad, long-pointed.............................. 8
8. Fresh leaves dark green above, turning black or
   dark brown on drying; flowers appearing before
   the leaves; seed pod covered with silky hairs
                 Salix sericea, Silky Willow
   Fresh leaves light green above, not noticeably dark-
   ening on drying; flowers appearing with the
   leaves; seed pods not covered with silky hairs   9
9. Stipules if present acute...................... 10
   Stipules obtuse
                 Salix longipes var. *Wardii*, Ward's Willow
10. Petioles averaging over ¼ inch long
                 Salix longipes, Black Willow   No. 3
    Petioles averaging less than ¼ inch long
                 Salix longipes var. *venulosa*, Black Willow   No. 3

1. Salix nigra Marsh. Black Willow.

THIS is a common small tree along streams throughout our
area from the coast to an altitude of about 3,000 feet. Sargent and Sudworth do not extend the range of the Black
Willow to the coastal plain of either North or South Carolina. We do not understand this, as what we call *S.
nigra* is the abundant willow fringing all the big rivers of
the coastal plain. Approaching the more coastal region,
the Black Willow becomes scarcer and *S. longipes* and *S.
Harbisonii* more abundant, but all three are found on the
damper places of the sand dunes of the shore. We distinguish *S. nigra* from *S. longipes* and *S. Harbisonii* by the
bright green, shining under side of the leaf, and from *S.
longipes* by the more brittle-jointed twigs. We have abundant collections of *S. nigra* in our herbarium from many
points in the coastal plain of North and South Carolina.

Bark dark; leaves light green, lanceolate, 3-6 inches
long, ¼-¾ inches wide, somewhat curved, finely glandular-

toothed on the margin, smooth and shining on both sides, paler green below but not whitish; petioles short and slender, 1/16-1/4 inch long, pubescent when quite young, with the pubescence on the upper side in a small furrow persisting, with minute glands at the base of the blade; male and female flowers on different trees, both borne in many-flowered catkins appearing with the leaves, calyx and corolla none, stamens 3-5, the yellow anthers making the male catkins conspicuous, pistil one, maturing into a short, light brown, sharply pointed pod which at maturity splits into two halves; seeds green and very minute, covered with long delicate hairs which float them lightly through the air. Unless the seed sprouts almost at once it

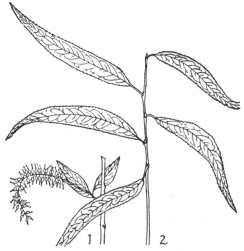

1, Twig with fruits. 2, twig with leaves.
All x 1/2.

will die. The delicate light green foliage of this willow can be used to fine effect in landscape work. A tree 5 miles northeast of Macon, Georgia, along Rock Creek is 2 feet 11 inches in diameter three feet above the ground and has a spread of 60 feet. Flowering from April 3 to April 22.

Small includes *Salix marginata* Wimmer next to *S. nigra* as a distinct species found on river banks and in

ьwamps from North Carolina to Louisiana. Schneider
thinks that the plant described by Small belongs partly to
S. Harbisonii. The principal differences given by Small
are: leaves of *S. marginata* ¾-2 inches long; bracts of
male catkins acute, while they are blunt in *S. nigra*. Sargent does not mention this species in the second edition of
his *Manual,* and Britton gives it as a synonym of *S. nigra.*

2. Salix Harbisonii Schneider. Harbison's Willow.

THIS is a small tree up to 50 feet high, sometimes only a
shrub, named by Camillo Schneider for T. G. Harbison,
who first discovered the tree near Savannah, Georgia. It is
found along rivers and in swamps from the Dismal Swamp
in Norfolk County, Virginia, to Duval County, Florida, and
as far west as Goldsboro in North Carolina, Aiken County
in South Carolina, Augusta and the Flint River in Georgia,
and to near the Apalachicola River in Florida. We have
collections from Cuyler's Swamp, near Savannah, Georgia,
from the highway causeway near the Savannah River, Jas-
per County, South Carolina, and from the Isle of Palms,
South Carolina. In our propagating grounds we have a
young tree now about 20 feet high that was brought up in
1926 from Goshen Creek in the northwestern part of
Duplin County, North Carolina.

Bark dark, ridged; branchlets reddish brown and very
brittle-jointed; leaves green above, whitish below, 2-5
inches long, from slightly less than ¼-¾ inch wide, linear
lanceolate to narrowly elliptic, often curved, finely glandular toothed, glabrous at maturity, a few stomata on the
upper surface; petioles about ¼ inch long, minutely
glandular at the blade, glabrous at maturity; stipules absent or quite small or up to ¼ inch long on vigorous twigs;
flowers appearing with the leaves, 3-9 stamens in the male
flowers; seed pods on long stalks, glabrous.

This plant is closely related to the Black Willows, and
Schneider has suggested the possibility of its being a hybrid
between *S. nigra* and *S. longipes.* From *S. nigra* it differs

1, Twig with female flowers, x ½.   2, female flower, x 2½.
3, twig with mature leaves, x ½.

in the very pale under surface of the leaf and in the more
glabrous petiole at maturity; from *S. longipes* it differs in
the brittle-jointed twigs, in the usual presence of minute
glands at the junction of the petiole and blade, in that the
petiole is glabrous at maturity, and in the presence of
stomata on the upper surface of the leaves. Dr. Carlton R.
Ball of the United States Department of Agriculture, who
has been studying our southern willows for some time, is

convinced that this is not sufficiently distinct from *S. longipes* (letter of Jan. 28, 1939).

3. Salix longipes Shuttl. Black Willow.

THIS is a small tree up to 30 feet high, but often only a shrub, that is found along streams and swamps. Three forms or varieties have been described from our area. The first or typical species was first described from Cuba and was later found through most of Florida as far west as the Saint Marks River in Wakulla County, and northward along the coast to North Carolina. The variety *vénulosa* has a wider range than the typical species, as it has been reported from Craven County, North Carolina, near the coast to northern and western Florida, up the Savannah River to near Augusta, Georgia, in Louisiana, southwestern Oklahoma, and western Texas. The variety *Wardii* has been described as found from the banks of the Potomac River, District of Columbia, and Alleghany County, Maryland, through most of Virginia and westward through the central states. We have collections of this variety, however, from the banks of Goshen Creek in Duplin County, North Carolina, which extends the range of this variety considerably farther south.

The trunk of typical *S. longipes* has dark, ridged bark, the branchlets gray-brown to red-brown, pubescent to nearly glabrous, not brittle-jointed; leaves green above, whitish below, 2-6½ inches long, ⅓-1⅛ inches wide, lanceolate, mostly acuminate, some curved, usually finely glandular-toothed, though in some instances the teeth are so small and so distant that were it not for the minute glandular points the margins could be considered hardly more than wavy, tomentose early in the season, becoming glabrous above and pubescent to glabrous below, no stomata on the upper surface; petioles mostly about ½ inch long; tomentose, very rarely glandular at the junction with the blades; stipules minute or up to ¾ inch in diameter on fast growing shoots, ovate to reniform, acute, toothed above the middle, falling early; flowers in catkins on short leafy branchlets, each flower of the male catkin with 3-7 stamens; fruit a small pod ⅛-¼ inch long, broad below and nar-

S. longipes var. *Wardii*. Branch with leaves and
open pods, x ½.

rowed, usually abruptly, upward from about the middle,
glabrous; pedicels distinct but short; seeds with an abundance of silky hairs.

Salix longipes var. *venulosa* differs from the typical
species in the narrower leaves and in the shorter petioles.

Salix longipes var. *Wardii* (Ward's Willow) differs
from the typical species in that the stipules are rounded or
at least obtuse, the branchlets tend to be more glabrous,
and the leaves are not so long-pointed.

Salix longipes and its varieties have long been confused with *S. nigra* and with *S. Harbisonii* (see their history in Schneider's Notes on American Willows in the *Journal Arnold Arboretum* 1: 24. 1919). They differ from *S. nigra* in that their leaves have a whitish, practically glaucous under surface, in the rarity of glands at the junction of blade and petiole, and in that the twigs are not brittle-jointed; from *S. Harbisonii* they differ in the tomentose petioles, in the rarity of glands at the junction of blade and petiole, in the absence of stomata in the upper epidermis, and in that the twigs are not brittle-jointed. They differ from *S. discolor,* another native willow with a whitish under surface of the leaf, in that their leaves are of a narrower type, are thinner, the veins are less prominent beneath, and the teeth are less coarse.

4. Salix discolor Muhl. Glaucous Willow, Pussy Willow.

THIS is a shrub or small tree of northern range reported by Ashe as occurring along mountain streams in North Carolina (*Journ. Eli. Mitch. Sci. Soc.* 34: 130. 1918). Small also includes it from North Carolina. We have a collection from Macon County, North Carolina, that seems to be this.

Twigs practically glabrous or with a few hairs; leaves elliptic to lanceolate, green above, at maturity pale and glabrous below, with a prominent yellow midrib, blade 1½-6 inches long and ½-1½ inches wide, margins serrate to crenulate or nearly entire; petioles ¼-1 inch long; stipules pubescent, broadly cordate, and shallowly toothed; flowers appearing before the leaves and often brought in for their ornamental value and called Pussy Willow. For the more common Pussy Willow see page 74.

5. Salix interior Rowlee (S. longifolia Muhl.) Sand-bar Willow.

THIS is a small tree or spreading shrub occurring in our area only along river banks in southern and western Tennessee and northeastern Virginia and Cape Henry.

Twig with fruits, x ¾.

Twigs slender, reddish, smooth or sometimes pubescent; bark of trunk dark, furrowed. Leaves linear-lanceolate, sharply pointed, usually curved, up to 4 inches long and ⁵⁄₁₆ inch broad, generally smaller, blade silky when young but soon glabrous on both surfaces; margin with small, slender, projecting, distant teeth. Catkin axes and bracts pubescent; female catkin usually 1½-2 inches long, male about 1¼ inches long, male flowers with only two stamens. Fruit about ¼ inch long, brown, usually glabrous.

6. Salix babylonica L. Weeping Willow.

THE well known Weeping Willow, a native of China, is occasionally spontaneous near settlements, probably from branches that have been thrown out in trash. Flowering March 26, 1920.

Twig with leaves; twig with catkins. All x ⅖.

7. Salix alba L. White Willow.

THE White Willow, a native of Europe, Africa, and Asia, is rarely spontaneous as far south as Virginia.

7a. Salix alba var. vitellina Stokes. Yellow Willow.

Twig with fruit; twig with leaves. All x ⅖.

THE YELLOW WILLOW, a native of the same region as the species, has been extensively planted and has escaped widely in western Virginia, and is rarely found as an escape in other parts of our area. Both the species and the variety are large trees with whitish, silky or glaucous leaves. The Yellow Willow has yellowish twigs. South of Virginia we have collected it from near Chapel Hill and along the roadside near Waynesville, North Carolina.

There are four other native willows in our territory that have a whitish under surface to the leaves, but we cannot consider them as trees. The largest of these is the Silky Willow (*S. sericea* Marsh). This willow, which reaches a height of 15 feet or more, might by some be considered a tree, but since it always forms a clump of many stems it is only a large shrub. The leaves of this plant are dark green above, whitish below, and through most of the season the white lower surface is covered with silky hairs. The winter buds are about the size and general shape of a grain of wheat, and are a great aid in identifying the plant late in the season when most of the silky hairs have disappeared from the leaves or the leaves have fallen. It is the willow that along many of our small streams forms the dense, dark green willow thickets, the tops of the thickets seemingly planed down to one level. Above these usually tower scattered trees of the Black Willow *(S. nigra)*, belying its name, as the general effect of its foliage is so much lighter than that of the Silky Willow. The Prairie Willow (*S. humiiis* Marsh), a much smaller shrub, is not rare in both wet places and rather dry hill and mountain sides through Virginia and North Carolina, and has been reported from Georgia and Florida. We expect to find it in South Carolina, but as yet we have no specimens from that state. The plant is related to the Glaucous Willow *(S. discolor)* and like it has thick leaves, prominently veined below, and its branches from male plants are ornamental and commonly brought in as ''Wild Pussy Willows,'' when in flower. The leaves vary much, narrowly elliptic to oblanceolate, 1½-4 inches long, ⅓-1 inch wide, always whitish below, but varying from a tomentose to glabrous under surface. The glabrous form has been called *S. humilis rigidiuscula* And. The Dwarf Gray Willow (*S. tristis* Ait.) is even smaller than *S. humilis*, rarely more than 2 feet high, and is found on rather poor wet or dry soil throughout our area. The leaves of this plant are typically about 1½ inches long and ⅛ inch wide, though longer and broader in the mountains where they seem to intergrade into *S. humilis*, and for this reason the plant is by some considered only a variety of *S. humilis*. The most commonly cultivated Pussy Willow, also called Goat Willow (*Salix caprea* L.), is a small tree with broad, tomentose leaves (in shape and size resembling apple leaves), a native of Europe and Asia. It is not found escaped in our area. The Heart-leaved Willow (*Salix cordata* Muhl.), with leaves usually rounded or heart-shaped at the base and either green or pale beneath, is found in wet places along streams as far south as North Carolina, but this willow, too, is only a shrub. Two other shrubby willows of northern range have been reported (Massey and Ball) from Virginia, *S. lucida* from Roanoke County and *S. petiolaris* from Wythe County.

MYRICACEAE (SWEET GALE FAMILY)

MYRICA L.

1. Myrica cerifera L. Wax Myrtle, Bayberry.

THIS is an attractive dioecious evergreen tree or shrub of the coastal plain throughout our area, growing in damp woods or flats and forming handsome clumps among the dunes. Myrtle Beach gets its name from this plant.

Branch with leaves and fruits, x ½.

Leaves narrow, elongated, up to 4 inches long, margins serrate or entire, dotted with orange glands below, fragrant; flowers simple, without a perianth, borne in short, bracted catkins in the leaf axils; fruit a small drupe, in clusters of several, covered with granules of gray wax. When this wax is melted from the berries it is used to make fragrant, greenish wax candles. Some of the largest specimens we have seen are near Georgetown, S. C., in low sandy woods near Black River (Springwood Lodge). One tree was 10⅕ inches thick one foot from the ground and about 20 feet high with a rounded spreading top. We have found one other larger tree near Brookgreen Gardens, S. C., that is 15 inches thick three feet from the ground and with a spread of 40 feet. In full flower on April 19, 1936, at Hartsville, South Carolina.

LEITNERIACEAE (CORKWOOD FAMILY)

LEITNERIA Chapm.

1. **Leitneria floridana** Chapm. **Corkwood.**

THIS is a small tree or shrub confined in our territory to the lower Altamaha River in Georgia and to salty swamps near Apalachicola, Florida.

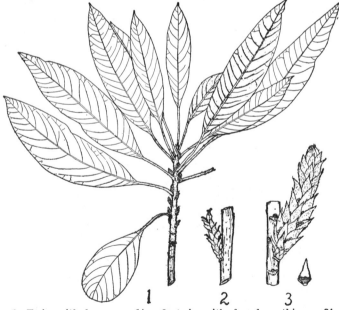

1, Twig with leaves, x ⅓. 2, twig with female catkin, x ⅔. 3, twig with male catkin and a male flower, x ⅔.

Leaves alternate, oblong to elliptic, about 4-7 inches long, margins even, pubescent below; flowers dioecious, both male and female in small catkins, calyx and corolla missing in male, nearly so in female; fruit a dry flattened drupe, single or a few together, about ¾ inch long and ¼ inch wide, surface rugose, containing a single nutlet. The wood is very light, more so than that of any other North American tree. It is used for corks and floats.

JUGLANDACEAE (WALNUT FAMILY)

JUGLANS L.

Hull and nut nearly spherical
    Juglans nigra, Black Walnut   No. 1
Hull and nut oblong, pointed
    Juglans cinerea, Butternut   No. 2

1. Juglans nigra L. Black Walnut.

THIS is a large, well known, and very valuable timber tree, which is sparsely scattered in rich woods throughout our states as far south as western Florida. It is found principally in the piedmont and mountain region, and probably was never a native inhabitant of the sandhill region. However, in many sections of the coastal region they are said by the late James Henry Rice to be plentiful, as on Chee-Ha and Waccamaw necks, South Carolina.

Leaves large, compound, the leaflets 13-27, serrate, glabrous or with a few hairs above, pubescent along the veins below; petioles pubescent; male flowers crowded in long slender catkins; female flowers borne several together on a short stalk, small, greenish, without petals and with two long, plumose stigmas, the calyx adherent to the ovary except for four short lobes above; fruit usually globose with a thick rough unopening hull, which is derived from the torus, involucre, and calyx; nut dark brown, ridged, the meats highly prized for candies, cakes, etc. They are very variable both in size and quality. In some the kernels come out easily in large pieces; in others they can be taken out only with difficulty and in broken pieces. The United States foresters are asking for information as to the location of trees producing the best nuts. The Black Walnut is handsome in cultivation, but the leaves appear late and drop early. Flowering from May 3 to May 14.

Juglans nigra.
1, Male catkin. 2, twig with a leaf. 3, fruit.
4, nut. All x ¼.

On the James River in Virginia, on the "Rowe Farm" opposite "Lower Brandon," there stands a remarkable hybrid walnut that is 25 feet in circumference six feet from the ground and has a spread of 123 feet. It is supposed to be a hybrid between the English Walnut *(J.*

regia) and either our Black Walnut or Butternut (for a photograph see *Journ. Hered.* **5**: March, 1914).

2. Juglans cinerea L. White Walnut, Butternut.

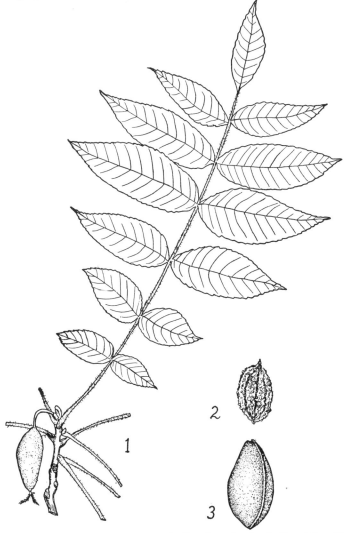

1, Twig with a leaf and young fruit. 2, nut. 3, fruit. All x ¼.

THIS is usually a small tree (rarely of good size) which is scattered in damp bottoms and along streams in the mountains at lower elevations, in the upper piedmont of Virginia and the Carolinas, and along the mountains to Georgia. In Virginia, we have collected it in Giles County at 4,100 feet elevation, and Erlanson reports it in woods west of Williamsburg, and R. S. Freer says that it is "abundant along slopes of Blackwater Creek, West Lynchburg," and it is reported from Amelia County (*Claytonia* 1: 34. 1934). Curtis, writing of its distribution in North Carolina, says that he has not met with it east of Wilkes but was informed that it was occasionally found as far down as Orange and Randolph counties. We have not seen or heard of it in Orange but J. V. Hoffman reports it growing in the State College Forest near Flat River in the northern part of Durham County, North Carolina. Faulty fruits washed down the Roanoke River are common along the shores of Albemarle Sound. Dr. Julian Miller says that Mountain City, Ga., is about the southern limit for this tree.

Leaves large, the leaflets 11-17, oblong-lanceolate, serrate, at maturity slightly hairy above, pubescent below, the leaf stalks and twigs pubescent and very sticky; fruit ovoid-oblong, covered with sticky hairs, hull thick, the edible nut being about twice as long as wide, covered with thin sharp plates. A section of a Butternut tree from Buncombe County, N. C., now in the museum in Raleigh has a diameter of 2 feet 1½ inches.

HICORIA Raf.

1. Bark of trunk flaky or scaly (in *H. ovalis* sometimes
   only the upper part of tree with flaky bark).... 2
   Bark not flaky.................................... 7
2. Leaves scurfy-hairy or pubescent................. 3
   Leaves smooth.................................... 5
3. Hull of fruit thin with prominent ridges
   Hicoria myristicaeformis, Nutmeg Hickory   No. 1
   Hull of fruit very thick......................... 4
4. Nut small, shell thin
   Hicoria ovata, Scaly-bark Hickory   No. 8
   Nut large, shell thick
   Hicoria laciniosa, Big Shell-bark Hickory   No. 7

5. Hull usually contracted into a neck at the base
   Hicoria glabra, Pig-nut Hickory   No. 11
   Hull not contracted into a neck at the base.........   6
6. Hull of fruit thick, shell thin
   Hicoria carolinae-septentrionalis,
   North Carolina Scaly-bark Hickory   No. 9
   Hull of fruit thin, shell thin
   Hicoria ovalis, Small-fruited Hickory   No. 10
7. Leaflets broad.................................   8
   Leaflets narrow...............................   9
8. Leaflets smooth, serrate to the base; fruit with a
   persistent hull and usually with a neck at the base
   Hicoria glabra, Pig-nut Hickory   No. 11
   Leaflets hairy, base not serrate; nut with a thick
   shell
   Hicoria alba, White-heart Hickory   No. 6
9. Leaflets 5-9, very pale below due to minute silvery or
   brownish scales; hull of fruit yellow with minute
   particles; meat sweet
   Hicoria pallida, Pale Hickory   No. 5
   Leaflets 7-9; apical bud yellow, long, narrow and
   irregular; hull of fruit prominently ridged in
   the upper half, shell smooth and thin; meat very
   bitter
   Hicoria cordiformis, Bitternut   No. 4
   Leaflets 7-13; hull sharply winged; nut flattened,
   shell rough; meat bitter
   Hicoria aquatica, Water Hickory   No. 2
   Leaflets 9-17; nut shell smooth; meat sweet
   Hicoria pecan, Pecan   No. 3

1. Hicoria myristicaeformis Britt. Nutmeg Hickory.

THIS is a large tree found in our range, according to Sargent and others, only along river banks and swamps in the eastern section of South Carolina. Michaux reported it from Goose Creek; Ravenel found several trees at the headwaters of Cooper River not far from Black Oak, and (in a letter to Gibbes) said that it occurs in swamps near Pooshee in St. John's, Berkeley; J. H. Rice wrote that it is found at Wiggins; and F. H. Haskell of Columbia reports it in the Wateree Swamp near Haygood, Kershaw County.

Leaves 7-12 inches long, leaflets 5-9, oblong, lanceolate to ovate-lanceolate, serrate, sessile or with very short stalks, dark green above, white below early in the season but changing to brown later, nearly glabrous above with a slightly pubescent midrib, terminal one and upper pair about the same size, $3\frac{1}{2}$-6 inches long and $1\frac{1}{2}$-$3\frac{1}{4}$ inches

Twig with leaves; fruit.   All x ⅓.

broad; nut ellipsoidal, rounded at the ends, smooth, shell thick; husk thin, distinctly ridged at the sutures, splitting nearly to the base and drawn out below to a long angular base.

2. **Hicoria aquatica** (Michx. f.) Britton.   **Water Hickory.** THIS is usually a rather small tree and little known to the public. Its distribution is not carefully worked out in our states, but it occurs in the deeper swamps of the coastal plain from southeastern Virginia to Florida, and Dr. C. E. Moore reports it from bottoms of Wolf River in Shelby County, Tennessee. In North Carolina it is known from the Cape Fear and Pamlico Sound regions. A plant has been reported on the lower Neuse River as a Pecan (Seeman,

Down Goose Creek, p. 40) that we think is this species. Harper reports it from "along the Meherrin River on the line between Southampton County, Virginia, and Northampton County, North Carolina." In South Carolina it is common in the Santee Swamp, and we have it from the flats of Black River near Kingstree and from James Island. It is probably common in all the deeper swamps of lower South Carolina and Georgia.

Twig with leaves; nut. All x ⅓.

Leaves large, compound, the leaflets about 7-13, rather small, lanceolate, pointed at both ends, serrate, glabrous above and glabrous or tomentose below, especially on the slender midrib; hull thin and with four distinct wings; nut very flat, reddish and strongly roughened by irregular ridges; meat very bitter and inedible except for squirrels. We have a tree of this interesting hickory growing in the Coker Arboretum at Chapel Hill. It was sent to us from the eastern part of North Carolina about twenty years ago. On the St. John's River near Palatka and other places farther south in Florida is found a variety of this hickory in which the nuts are smaller and without the longitudinal

wrinkles.   This has been named the variety *australis* by
Sargent.

3. **Hicoria pecan** Engl. and Graebn. **Pecan.**

Branch with fruits and separate nuts, one in section, x ⅓.

THIS highly important and now extensively cultivated nut tree is native in low grounds of the Mississippi valley and southwestward, coming eastward only to Alabama. In our territory it is native only in western Tennessee. It is too well known to need a lengthy description. Of the trees in our area it most resembles the Water Hickory, *H. aquatica,* in the leaves and is sometimes confused with it when the fruits are not seen. These two trees have more leaflets than any other hickory and are much alike in shape. Both are swamp trees and hybrids between the two are known. The Pecan nut is extremely variable in many characters, such as size, shape, thickness of shell, and quality of meat. The tree grows to be very large. One on Cane River in Natchitoches Parish, Louisiana, has a circumference of 19 feet 6 inches and a height of 150 feet (*Journ. Hered.* 6: 418. 1915). A tree on Green Street in Cheraw, S. C., is 3 feet 3 inches in diameter.

4. **Hicoria cordiformis** (Wang.) Britton [**H. minima** (Marshall) Britton]. **Bitternut Hickory, Swamp Hickory.**

THIS is a tree which is common in the mountain valleys and along streams and swamps in the piedmont and rare in the coastal plain. It is a common tree of the north and extends from Canada through all the Atlantic states as far south as northern Florida. It occurs also in Tennessee along the Cumberland River near Nashville. In North Carolina we have found it as far east as Kinston (bank of Neuse River).

Bark brown with small flaky ridges; leaves 6-12 inches long, petiole, rachis and lower surface of leaflets hairy most of the season, less so or nearly smooth in late summer; leaflets 7-9, serrate, lateral ones sessile, terminal one on a stalk up to $\frac{1}{3}$ inch long; the lowest pair ovate to lanceolate, $1\frac{1}{2}$-3 inches long, $\frac{3}{4}$-1 inch wide, upper pairs ovate to lanceolate, 3-6 inches long, 1-2 inches wide; buds and young fruits covered with small yellow scales, often not noticeable on the mature fruit; hull very thin and papery, slightly

1, Twig with leaves and a young fruit. 2, fruit.
3, cross-section of a nut. All x ⅓.

ridged or nearly smooth; nuts globose to ovate, small, about
⅞ inch long without the long beak, pale, smooth, shell very
thin, the meat highly convoluted and very bitter. Both in
its hull and nut it strongly resembles the Nutmeg Hickory,
except that the hull below is not ridged or pointed. The
largest tree we have seen is on the bank of the Cape Fear
River about six miles below Fayetteville, N. C. It was 2
feet 8⅓ inches in diameter four and a half feet from the
ground. Flowering began in Chapel Hill on May 19, 1914.

Hicoria cordiformis var. *elongata* Ashe with a more
elongated nut occurs in the mountains of North Carolina.

5. Hicoria pallida Ashe. Pale Hickory.

THIS is a scattered tree, with an open, spreading crown, which grows in the upland woods of the piedmont section, in the valleys of the coastal plain, sparingly in the mountains, from Virginia and Tennessee to Florida.

Leaflets 5-9, narrow, the terminal and upper pairs about 3-5 inches long and ¾-1¼ inches wide, lower pair smaller, rachis and midveins densely woolly with fascicled hairs, serrate, covered below with minute peltate scales which give them a silvery appearance when young; hull con-

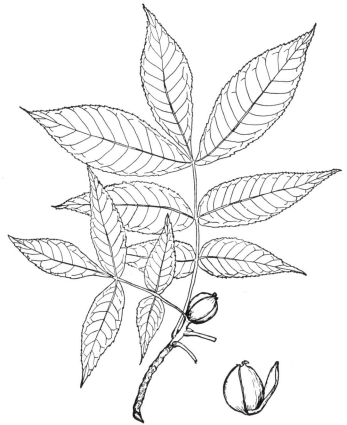

Twig with leaves and young fruit; fruit.   All x ⅖.

spicuously yellow with minute granular scales as are the
smooth buds; nut globose to ovate, small; meat sweet.
The delicate foliage and widely spreading crown of this
tree make it one of the most decorative of all our hickories.
Its shape is in strong contrast to the shaft-like habit of
most of the other species.   In Chapel Hill it reaches a
height of about 60 feet and a diameter of 2 feet 8½ inches
two feet from the ground.   Flowering from April 18 to
May 8.

Three varieties of this species have been reported from
our range, *H. pallida* var. *apposita* Ashe, *H. pallida* var.
arenicola Ashe, and *H. pallida* var. *pyriformis* Ashe.

6. **Hicoria alba** (L.) Britton.   **White-heart Hickory, Mock-
ernut.**

This is a common, tall, short-limbed hickory, which occurs
throughout our area and is highly valued for its strong
tough wood.   On the wind-swept, sandy dunes as at Myrtle
Beach, South Carolina, this tree is often found mingled
with Yaupon and Live Oak, forming the characteristic depressed and wind-shorn coverings of exposed elevations.
Behind the dunes it assumes the regular tree form but
with a more dwarfed appearance than inland.

Bark gray, ridged; leaves large, strong-scented, turning
a beautiful yellow in the fall; leaflets usually 7, the upper
three much larger than the others, about 5-8 inches long
and 2-4 inches broad, serrate except at the base, lower side
of leaflets, rachis, and petiole hairy and with yellow resinous dots; hull with yellow resinous dots, moderately thick,
splitting away from the nut, which is thick-shelled and
variable in size and shape.   The ones with the smallest nuts
have been described as the variety *albicans* and those with
the largest as the variety *maxima*.   Besides the typical
ones we have trees in Chapel Hill showing nuts of both of
these extremes, some with nuts up to 1¾ inches long and
others with nuts as small as 1 inch long.   Flowering begins
from April 5 to April 18.

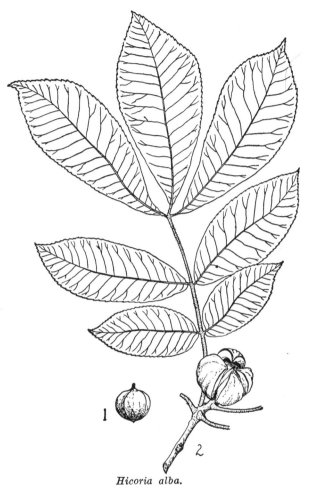

Hicoria alba.
1, Nut. 2, twig with a leaf and a fruit. All x ⅓.

7. Hicoria laciniosa Sarg. Big Shell-bark Hickory, Big-leaf Shag-bark Hickory.

THIS very large-fruited hickory, which is common in the low grounds of the central Mississippi basin, is found in our region only rarely in alluvial soil along streams in the lower mountains of North Carolina and Tennessee, and re-

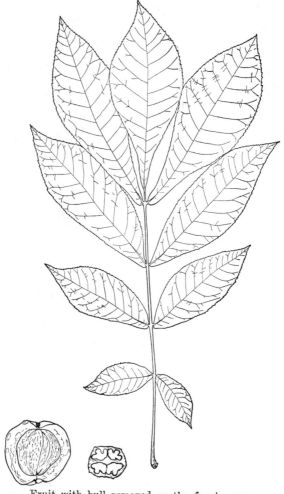

Fruit with hull removed on the front; cross
section of nut; leaf. All x ⅓.

ported by Erlanson from west of Williamsburg, Virginia,
and by Bishop and Duncan from Oglethorpe County, Ga.
(*Amer. Journ. For.* **39**: 730. 1941). Except in the mountains, we know of only one place in North Carolina where
this plant has been found. This is in Beaver Swamp in
Guilford County (E. H. Hall). It does not occur in South
Carolina or Florida.

Bark flaky; leaves very large, 1-2 feet long, usually with seven leaflets, sometimes as many as 9; the upper leaflet stalked, larger than the lateral ones; fruit resembling that of *H. ovata* in its very thick hull, but with a very much larger nut (1½-2½ inches long) and a thick, bony shell.

8. **Hicoria ovata** (Mill.) Britton. **Shell-bark Hickory, Scaly-bark.**

THIS is a well known and valuable timber tree of rich low grounds or mountain slopes (up to 4,000 feet), that is scat-

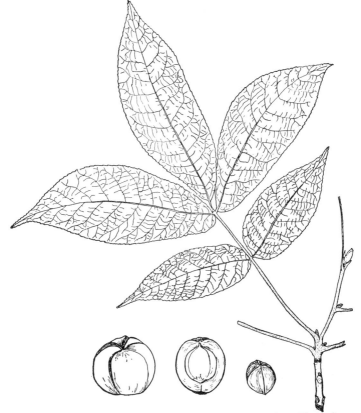

Fruit; fruit with hull removed in front; nut, twig with leaf.
All x ⅓.

tered throughout most of Virginia, Tennessee, and the Carolinas, in the northern half of Georgia, and western Florida.

Bark gray, separating into large flakes; leaves very large, about 10-17 inches long, leaflets usually 5, the terminal one usually the largest, about 4-10 inches long and 2-4½ inches broad, on a stalk up to ¾ inch long, pubescent below, serrate except near the base; petioles also pubescent; hull very thick; nut four-sided, usually flattened, with a thin shell; meat sweet. The nuts vary much in shape and quality but are always distinctly four-angled.

The following varieties have been reported from our states: *H. ovata* var. *grandis* Ashe, *H. ovata* var. *holmesiana* Ashe, *H. ovata* var. *nuttallii* (Sarg.) Ashe, and *H. ovata* var. *pubescens* (Sarg.) Sudworth.

9. Hicoria carolinae-septentrionalis Ashe. Southern Shellbark Hickory, North Carolina Scaly-bark.

THIS is a medium sized tree which is found in low grounds and sparingly on uplands in our area from North Carolina and Tennessee to northern Georgia. In North Carolina it is found from Durham County to the mountains. We have a collection from McCormick County, South Carolina, and it has been reported from Abbeville and Laurens counties in that state.

Bark gray, flaky; leaves 5-9 inches wide; leaflets usually 5, the upper three about the same size and usually 2¾-4½ inches long and 1-1¾ inches wide, lower pair 1½-3½ inches long and ½-1 inch wide, serrate except near the base, glabrous above and below, as are the petioles; fruit globose to oblong, hull thick, nut small, shell thin. This species differs from *H. ovata* in its smaller, smooth leaves and slightly thinner hull. The nut may be like that of *H. ovata* or less ridged. It has about the same shell and is of equally good quality. Boynton reports a tree near Clinton, S. C., which is 2 feet 6 inches in diameter.

Twig with leaves and young fruit; fruit; fruit with part of hull removed. All x ⅓.

Hicoria carolinae-septentrionalis var. *australis* Ashe with slightly broader leaflets replaces the typical form in the coastal plain south of Sampson County, North Carolina.

10. **Hicoria ovalis** (Wangenheim) Sudworth. [**H. micro-carpa** (Nutt.) Britton]. **Small-fruited Hickory, Red-heart Hickory, Pig-nut Hickory.**

THIS is a tall, rather narrow tree that has been reported heretofore from Virginia and Tennessee to central Georgia.

We can now extend the range to Tallahassee, Fla., from specimens in our herbarium sent us by Mr. Herman Kurz. We have many collections of this plant from North Carolina, where it is freely scattered in upland woods from Wake County to the mountains. We also have collections from trees near Myrtle Beach, South Carolina, that we are placing in this species with some hesitation.

Bark gray, deeply ridged and tending to flake up; terminal bud small and ridged by 3-5 thickened scales that fall off during the winter; leaves 6-11 inches long, the glabrous rachis reddish at base, leaflets 5-7, ovate to lanceolate, finely serrate, the terminal one 5-6½ inches long and 1¾-3½ inches broad on a short stalk, upper pair about

Twig with young fruits and leaves; fruit with part of hull removed; fruit. All x ⅓.

same size as the terminal one, lower pair smaller, practically glabrous except for abundant small, resinous scales on the lower surface; hull thin, freely dehiscing, nuts oblong to obovate, usually flattened, sometimes ridged, thin-shelled, sweet, a large percentage wormy with a hole in the side. In the spring this species is easily distinguished from all others by the late swelling of the buds, which are just breaking when *H. ovata* is in flower. We have a section of the largest tree we have seen of this species. It grew in Raleigh, N. C., and is 3 feet 5½ inches in diameter some distance above the ground. Flowering April 8 to April 23.

Several varieties have been recognized: *H. ovalis* var. *obcordata* Ashe, *H. ovalis* var. *odorata* Ashe, *H. ovalis* var. *obovalis* Ashe, *H. ovalis* var. *mollis* (Ashe) Sudworth.

11. Hicoria glabra (Mill.) Britton. Pig-nut Hickory.

THIS is usually a small or medium sized upland tree of poor soil, occurring plentifully in the middle section, frequently in the coastal plain and occasionally in the mountains in our area from Virginia to Georgia and in Tennessee and with large-fruited coastal variety, *megacarpa*, extending into Florida. A specimen of the typical *H. glabra* with a diameter of 3 feet 10 inches at breast height has been reported from the Great Smoky Mountains (S. A. Cain).

Bark usually low-ridged, in some forms flaky; buds like those of *H. ovalis;* leaves with 3-7 glabrous leaflets, broader and more noticeably toothed than those of *H. ovalis* and in the typical form without glandular scales; fruit slightly flattened, ovate to nearly spherical, usually with a neck at the base, varying greatly in size from $1\frac{1}{16}$-$1\frac{3}{8}$ inches long not counting the neck, hull thin, about $\frac{1}{16}$ inch thick; not opening at all or only partially; nut somewhat flattened to nearly spherical, not ridged, with a very short beak, shell moderately thick to very thin. The smallest fruited form we have seen, with a little round nut about $\frac{5}{8}$ inch long and a hull $\frac{1}{20}$ inch thick, occurs near the Raleigh road about one mile from Chapel Hill. Flowering April 13 to May 5.

The very large-fruited coastal variety [*H. glabra* var.

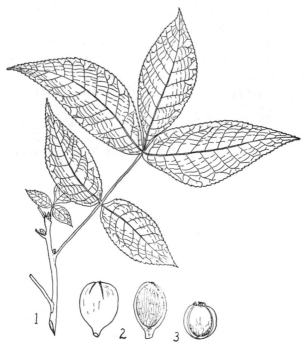

1, Twig with leaves. 2, fruits with a neck.
3, fruit without a neck. All x ⅓.

megacarpa (Sarg.) Sudworth] has abundant resinous scales on the leaflets, while another eastern large-fruited variety (*H. glabra* var. *similis* Ashe) lacks the resinous scales at maturity. A variety (*H. glabra* var. *reniformis* Ashe) with a slightly flattened fruit has been described from Chapel Hill.

BETULACEAE (BIRCH FAMILY)

CARPINUS (Tourn.) L.

1. **Carpinus caroliniana** Walt. **Hornbeam, Ironwood, Blue Beech.**

This is a small crooked tree common along streams and in rich woods in the piedmont and mountains in our states. In the coastal plain it is less common and retires to the deeper swamps. It is plentiful in bottom lands of Shelby County, Tennessee, and there it sometimes reaches a diameter of 10 inches (C. E. Moore).

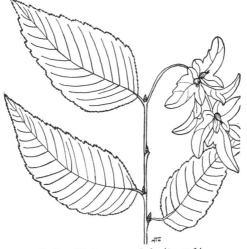

Twig with leaves and fruits, x ½.

Trunk ridged, bark dark gray, close and hard; leaves elm-like, small, blade about 1-3½ inches long and ½-1½ inches broad, doubly serrate, smooth above and with conspicuous tufts of hairs in the axils of the veins beneath; fruit a small nut attached to the base of a leaf-like bract. The wood is very hard and is used for mallets, wedges, cogs, and levers. Flowering from March 20 to May 6.

OSTRYA (Mich.) Scop.

1. Ostrya virginiana (Mill.) K. Koch. Hop Hornbeam.

THIS is a small tree found along the edges of low grounds and on rocky river banks in our area from Virginia to the western part of northern Florida, and Dr. C. E. Moore reports it as rather common on uplands in Shelby County, Tennessee. It is found throughout the piedmont and in the mountains up to 5,200 feet, but is not nearly so plentiful as *Carpinus caroliniana*. It is rare in the coastal plain but in

Branch with leaves and fruits, x ½.

North Carolina it occurs along the Cape Fear River in Cumberland and Bladen counties (H. A. Rankin).

Bark scurfy-scaly; twigs tomentose; leaves oblong-lanceolate, pointed, about 2½-4½ inches long, sharply toothed, petioles short, tomentose as are the veins of the leaf below; flowers of two kinds borne in catkins, the male developed to some size the year before maturity, as in the case of *Carpinus caroliniana* and the Hazelnuts; female flowers small, inconspicuous, borne in the axils of large thin bracts which develop at maturity into a pendent catkin that looks very much like a head of hops, each bract having at its base a small nut; fruit bracts strongly tomentose at the tip, sparsely so elsewhere. As in the Hornbeam, the wood is hard and tough and has the same uses. Flowering March 25 to April 16. Fernald (*Rhodora* **38**: 414. 1936) describes a variety *lasia* of *Ostrya virginiana* with pilose twigs, confined mainly to the coastal plain from Florida to Texas, more rarely in other sections. Our Chapel Hill plants are pilose with very few or no glands intermixed. Other collections from coastal and piedmont North Carolina, Florida, Georgia, and Mississippi are pilose without glands. One from our mountains (Polk County, N. C.) is glandular and slightly pilose on the twigs, strongly pilose with glands intermixed on the petioles. In all cases that we have seen, if the twigs are pilose the petioles are more strongly so.

BETULA (Tourn.) L.

1. Twigs with the odor of wintergreen............... 2
   Not as above................................... 3
2. Bark silvery or yellowish, peeling off in papery layers; cone bracts ciliate on the margins
   Betula lutea, Yellow Birch   No. 1
   Bark dark, cherry-like, not papery; cone bracts glabrous
   Betula lenta, Cherry Birch   No. 2
3. Bark in white papery layers
   Betula papyrifera var. *cordifolia,* Paper Birch   No. 3
   Bark falling away in brownish papery layers
   Betula nigra, River Birch   No. 4

1. Betula lutea Michx. Yellow Birch.

THIS birch is confined in our area to the high mountains from Virginia to northern Georgia.

Bark silvery or yellowish, scaling off in large, very thin, papery sheets; however, on older trunks the bark may not be papery but rough and of a darker color; leaves long-ovate, 1¾-4 inches long, the base not heart-shaped or slightly so, dull green above and hairy on the veins below; male flowers in long catkins; female flowers in cone-like clusters, the cone bracts ciliate on the margins. The bark and twigs of this tree have the wintergreen odor, but not so strong as in the Cherry Birch. This tree may attain a large size. One has been reported on White Top Mountain, Virginia, which measured 7 feet 3 inches in diameter three feet from the base (Small and Vail). The wood, like that of the Cherry Birch, is highly valued for the manufacture of furniture.

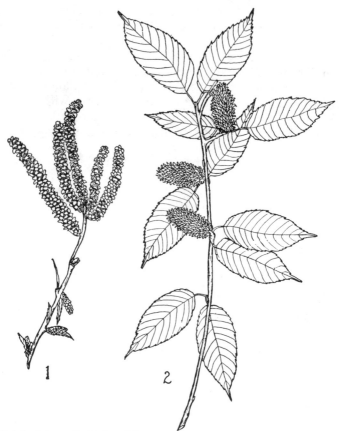

Betula lutea. 1, Twig with staminate catkins. 2, twig with leaves and fruiting cones. All x ½.

2. Betula lenta L. Cherry Birch, Black Birch.

This is a fine tall tree which in our area is confined mostly to cool rich soil in the mountains south to Georgia. Small reports it on ridges in western Florida but Harper denies its occurrence south of the mountains of Georgia and Alabama.

Bark smooth and cherry-like; twigs and bark with a strong odor of wintergreen; leaves ovate to oblong-ovate usually heart-shaped at the base, sharply serrate, bright green above, slightly hairy on the veins beneath; male

1, Twig with leaves and fruiting cone, x ½.
2, cone bract, x 2.   3, nut, x 2.

flowers in long catkins, female flowers in short cone-like clusters, cone bracts glabrous; fruit a small winged nut. This birch reaches a large size, has been reported up to a diameter of 6 feet, and around Highlands, N. C., trees 3 feet in diameter are not uncommon. The wood is strong, hard, dark in color, takes a fine polish, and resembles that of cherry. The bark and twigs of the Cherry Birch are distilled as a substitute for the true oil of wintergreen which it very closely simulates and which it has almost or quite superseded.

Trees from the banks of Dickey Creek, Smyth County, Virginia, with narrowly winged nutlets have been given the name *B. lenta* var. *uber* Ashe.

There is a tree somewhat intermediate between *B. lenta* and *B. lutea* which is considered distinct by Britton and given by him the name of *B. alleghaniensis*. Sargent considers it as *B. lenta*. Both Britton and Small think that it takes the place of true *lutea* in all our area. The leaves are mostly cordate like those of the Cherry Birch, but the cone bracts are hairy while those of the latter are glabrous. It resembles the Yellow Birch in the hairy bracts, but differs in the cordate leaves. The bark is said either to be close and furrowed or to peel off in thin, yellowish layers. If really distinct, it is difficult to determine with certainty.

3. **Betula papyrifera** var. **cordifolia** (Regel) Fern. **Paper Birch.**

This is a slender graceful tree which is an illustration of a boreal plant found in the high mountains of North Carolina, but not between there and northern New York. The Paper Birch is one of the most localized trees in North Carolina. It was reported from Mt. Mitchell and mountains near by in the Black Mountains by Ashe from 5,500 feet up, oc-

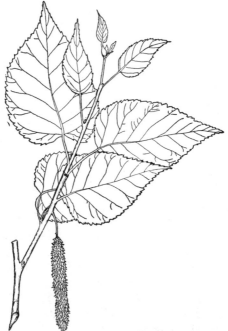

Branch with leaves and fruiting catkin, x ½.

curring in the balsam-spruce woods. We have specimens from the top of Mt. Mitchell, from Wilson Ridge on Mt.

Mitchell (J. S. Holmes), and from the Black Mountains, altitude 6,400 feet (W. W. Ashe). We may expect the Paper Birch in the Smokies, since Gattinger (1887) reported as *B. papyracea* Ait. a tree from the mountains of eastern Tennessee which is perhaps this form of the Paper Birch.

Bark very white, gray, or bronze, with many long brownish corky lenticels, easily separating into thin sheets; leaf blades 2-3 inches long, 1¼-2 inches broad, heart-shaped, long-pointed, margin irregularly serrate, hairy on the veins beneath; mature female catkins 1¼-2 inches long. The largest tree measured by Ashe was 16 inches in diameter at breast height and about 70 feet high.

4. Betula nigra L. River Birch, Black Birch.

THIS is a common tree along creeks and rivers in the lower

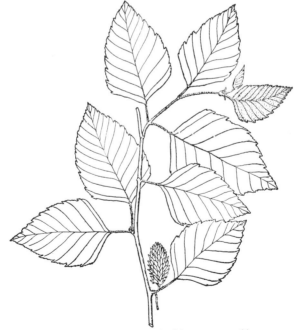

Twig with leaves and fruiting cone, x ½.

mountains and piedmont, less common in the coastal plain, from northern Florida northward throughout our area. It is plentiful in bottom lands of western Tennessee. It is the only birch of the coastal plain.

Bark reddish brown, peeling off in thin papery layers; leaves ovate with a broadly pointed base, 2-3½ inches long, serrate, at maturity dark green and smooth above; light green below, tomentose or with hairs only on the veins; flowers of two kinds, male flowers in long catkins, female flowers in short cone-like clusters, appearing before the leaves; fruit a very small winged nut. Flowering April 2 to April 17.

FAGACEAE (BEECH FAMILY)

FAGUS (Tourn.) L.

1. Fagus grandifolia Ehr. Beech.

THIS is a large tree found mostly along brooks and creeks from the coast to the tops of the mountains in all our area.

Nut; branch with leaves and fruit
All x ⅖.

Bark light, smooth, often marked with initials, hearts, and dates; buds slender, sharply pointed; leaves oblong-ovate, coarsely serrate, up to about 5 inches long, dark green and smooth above, light green and shining below, hairy along the midrib and veins; fruit a shiny, angular nut, one or two enclosed in a bur covered with recurved spines. It reaches its greatest size in the rich mountain valleys where it may be 3 feet in diameter and 80 feet high. The Beech is a beautiful, long-lived tree for lawns, and is free from disease. Flowering on April 23, 1933.

The coastal form is separated in Gray's Manual, 7th edition, as *F. grandifolia* var. *caroliniana* (Loud.) Fern. & Rehd. Sargent includes under this variety all the beech trees found south of Virginia.

CASTANEA (Tourn.) Hill.

1. Leaves glabrous beneath; more than one nut in the bur
   Castanea dentata, Chestnut   No. 1
   Leaves more or less tomentose beneath; only one nut
   in the bur...................................... 2
2. Clusters of spines densely covering the bur
   Castanea pumila, Chinquapin   No. 2
   Clusters of spines on bur more distant.............. 3
3. Low shrubs from underground runners, tomentum on
   under side of leaf thin but persistent, nearly
   glabrous
   Castanea alnifolia, Dwarf Chinquapin   No. 4
   Small trees or large shrubs..................... 4
4. Leaves narrow, more than twice as long as broad,
   uppermost leaves white-tomentose beneath, lower
   leaves nearly glabrous
   Castanea alnifolia var. floridana, Florida Chinquapin   No. 4
   Leaves mostly broad, about twice as long as broad,
   all densely white-tomentose beneath
   Castanea Ashei, Coastal Chinquapin   No. 3

1. Castanea dentata (Marsh) Borkh. Chestnut.

THIS is a large forest tree of the mountains and hills in our area from Virginia to Georgia. In Virginia Erlanson says that it occurs on uplands around Williamsburg. We have collected it at Toano in the same county. In North Carolina it is scattered sparingly over the western half of the piedmont and a few trees in the northern part of Orange County are supposed to be native.

Leaves oblong-lanceolate, blade 5-10 inches long and 1½-2 inches wide, sharply toothed, at maturity smooth on both sides, turning a bright yellow in the autumn; male flowers in long catkins borne in the axils of the leaves, female flowers in bisexual catkins borne near the base of the catkin; fruit a shiny angular nut, 2 or 3 being borne in a large spiny bur. The largest Chestnut tree now known to be standing is in the Great Smoky Mountains three miles

Branch with partly grown fruits and remains of male flowers, x ⅓.

from Crestmont, North Carolina.   It is said to have a diameter of 10 feet 7 inches seven feet from the ground.   This,
with the exception of one oak tree in California, is thought
to be the largest nut bearing tree in North America (*Journ.
Hered.* **6**: 413. 1915).   The wood is durable and is used for
cross-ties, posts, and inferior furniture.   The Chestnut
blight (caused by a fungus, *Endothia parasitica*), a virulent
disease that has practically destroyed the Chestnuts of the
northern states, has now extended southward through most
of our Chestnut territory and is destroying our trees in the
same way.   Hybrids are known between this and the Chinquapin (*Bull. Torr. Bot. Club* **49**: 266. 1922).   Flowering
in the summer.

2. Castanea pumila (L.) Mill. Chinquapin.

THIS is a small tree, usually with more than one trunk, rarely more than 20 feet high and 6-8 inches thick, sometimes having a more spreading bushy form. In our states it grows in mixed upland woods in the piedmont and mountains up to 4,500 feet (Mt. Satulah, N. C.) and occasionally descends nearly to the coast, at least in North

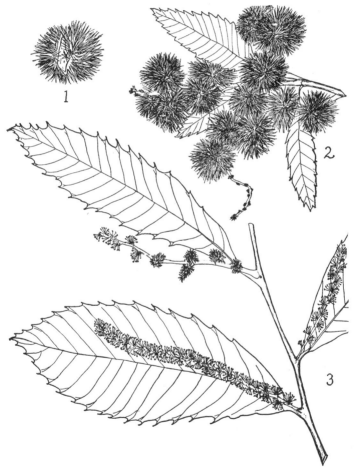

1, Mature fruit. 2, twig with half grown fruits. 3, twig with two
male catkins and one (upper) male and female. All x ½.

Carolina (Duplin and Lenoir counties) and in Virginia (Southampton County).

Twigs pubescent or nearly glabrous; leaves elliptic, about 2¾-6½ inches long and up to 2 inches broad, coarsely serrate, when mature smooth and bright green above, whitish and densely felted-tomentose beneath or varying to nearly glabrous; male and female flowers separate, the former in long, slender catkins about 2½-6 inches long which are single in the leaf axils toward the ends of the branches, simple, with a minute calyx and numerous stamens; female flowers on bisexual catkins near the very tips of the branches, several females near the base and numerous males on the more distal part, female flowers consisting of an inconspicuous calyx and a several-celled pistil, flowers usually 3, enclosed together in a prickly involucre. In the Chinquapins only one pistil in an involucre matures, the ovary forming a small, shining, reddish brown, edible nut up to ½ inch long, the involucre covered with very close-set, more or less hairy spines. The Chinquapins are preëminently plants of undisturbed upland woods with plentiful humus. They always become rapidly reduced in numbers as "civilization" advances. Flowering from May 25 to July 3.

3. Castanea Ashei Sudw. Coastal Chinquapin.

THIS small tree or large shrub was named by George B. Sudworth in honor of the late W. W. Ashe, of the U. S. Forestry Service, a native North Carolinian and close student of our southern trees. It is found on the sand dunes and in the sandy woods along the coast from southeastern Virginia to northern Florida and along the Gulf. On the South Carolina coast it is one of the most common large shrubs or small trees.

Twigs tomentose; leaves about 1½ inches broad, averaging about 3 inches long, though some leaves on vigorous shoots are up to 7 inches long with a width up to 4 inches, dark green and smooth above, whitish and tomentose below; clusters of spines on the involucre or "bur" rather distant,

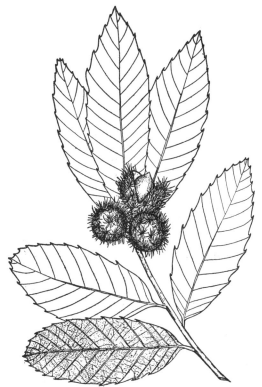

Twig with leaves and mature fruit, x ⅔.

not crowded, often leaving conspicuous bald spots on the bur; nuts ripe and being shed on September 18, 1932, at Myrtle Beach, S. C.; the same size and shape as those of *C. pumila*. Along the road from Myrtle Beach to Murrell's Inlet this tree reaches a height of 27 feet and a diameter of 10½ inches. The leaves of this species are on the average smaller and proportionately broader and the spines on the involucre less numerous than in *C. pumila*.

4. Castanea alnifolia var. **floridana** Sarg. **Florida Chinquapin.**

This is a shrub or small tree found in dry sandy soil along the coast from near Wrightsville, North Carolina, to Louisiana. Sargent says that it is a tree only on the shores of St. Andrew's Bay in Bay County, Florida.

Branchlets smooth or with only scattered hairs; the leaves 2-4 inches long, rather narrow, mostly oblanceolate in outline, and though our collections show a tomentose under surface, the tomentum is shorter and thinner than in *C. pumila* and *C. Ashei;* the clusters of spines on the "bur" even more distant than in *C. Ashei.*

The above plant is considered a larger varietal form of *C. alnifolia,* the Dwarf Chinquapin that multiplies by means of underground stoloniferous stems or "runners," found through the same region as the Florida Chinquapin and farther inland. Sargent reports *C. alnifolia* as distributed in the neighborhood of the coast from the valley of the Cape Fear River, N. C., to southern Georgia. However, we have collections from near LaGrange in the western part of Lenoir County, N. C., north of the Neuse River and from Osceola County, Florida, as well as from near Myrtle Beach, South Carolina. The Florida plants are clearly stoloniferous, but the leaves are longer and narrower than those farther north and link the var. *floridana* with the type species. The leaves of the type species are nearly glabrous beneath, but Nuttall has described a variety *(C. alnifolia pubescens)* with the leaves white-pubescent beneath.

QUERCUS* (Tourn.) L.

1. Leaves broadest at the ends...................... 2
   Leaves broadest near the middle................. 3
2. Leaves usually over 4 inches broad; acorn over ½
   inch long, in a deep cup
          Quercus marilandica, Black Jack Oak   No. 12
   Leaves as a rule 2-3 inches broad; acorn small, in a
   shallow cup
          Quercus arkansana, Arkansas Water Oak   No. 13

* The oaks are divided into two principal groups, the Black Oaks and the White Oaks, easily distinguished by the fact that the acorns in the first group mature in the fall of the second year from flower and the lobes of the leaves have bristle tips, while in the second group the acorns mature the first year and the lobes of the leaves are without bristle tips. Of the oaks here included our numbers 1-19 belong to the Black Oak group and numbers 20-33 to the White Oak group. There are 27 oaks in North Carolina, 24 trees and 3 shrubs, *pumila, prinoides,* and *ilicifolia.* For notes on hybrids, see page 158.

Leaves as a rule 1¼ -2 inches broad; acorn small, in
a shallow cup

Quercus nigra, Water Oak   No. 14

Leaves usually less than one inch broad; acorn small,
in a deep cup

Quercus myrtifolia, Scrub Oak   No. 19

3. Leaves usually without lobes.................... 4
   Leaves with lobes............................. 13

4. Leaves evergreen.............................. 5
   Leaves not evergreen.......................... 7

5. Fruits maturing the first year................. 6
   Fruits maturing the second year

Quercus laurifolia, Laurel Oak   No. 16

6. Fruits on long stalks; leaves usually whitish and
   pubescent beneath, some forms tomentose and
   some glabrous

Quercus virginiana, Live Oak   No. 20

Fruits nearly or quite sessile; leaves white-tomentose beneath; low shrubs with underground
runners

Quercus pumila, Running Oak

Fruits nearly or quite sessile; leaves whitish beneath but not tomentose

Quercus myrtifolia, Scrub Oak   No. 19

7. Fruits maturing the first year................. 8
   Fruits maturing the second year............... 9

8. Cup moderately deep, cup-shaped, scales thickened on back; leaves glabrous below except on
   the veins

Quercus Chapmani, Chapman's White Oak   No. 22

Cup as above except scales flat; leaves yellowish-
pubescent on entire lower surface

Quercus oglethorpensis   No. 23

Cup very shallow, saucer-shaped; lower leaves
tending to be lobed

Quercus Durandii, Durand's White Oak   No. 21

9. Leaves over one inch wide..................... 10
   Leaves less than one inch wide................. 11

10. Leaves pubescent beneath; base of leaf not long
    pointed; mountain plant

Quercus imbricaria, Shingle Oak   No. 17

Leaves smooth beneath, base of leaf taper pointed;
coastal plain plant

Quercus nigra, Water Oak   No. 14

11. Leaves white-tomentose beneath

Quercus cinerea, Upland Willow Oak   No. 18

Leaves not white-tomentose beneath............. 12

12. Leaves thick, nearly evergreen, smaller veins very
    prominent above

Quercus laurifolia, Laurel Oak   No. 16

Leaves thinner, not at all evergreen, smaller veins
    not markedly prominent above
            Quercus phellos, Willow Oak   No. 15

13. Lobes of leaves without bristle tips............... 14
    Lobes of leaves with bristle tips................. 22
14. Lobes mostly less than 12....................... 15
    Lobes more than 12............................. 19
15. Lobes mostly pointed, notches broad and deep;
    acorns usually less than ¾ inch long and nearly
    covered by the cup
            Quercus lyrata, Overcup Oak   No. 29
    Lobes pointed or rounded, often both sorts on the
    same leaf; notches mostly narrow and shallow;
    acorns usually over ¾ inch long, cup covering
    about ⅓ of acorn
            Quercus bicolor, Swamp White Oak   No. 27
    Lobes rounded, notches mostly broad and deep;
    acorns over ¾ inch long, cup covering ½ or more
    of acorn
            Quercus macrocarpa, Burr Oak   No. 28
    Lobes rounded; cup of acorn low 16
16. Leaves with 7-11 nearly regular lobes, whitish and
    smooth beneath
            Quercus alba, White Oak   No. 33
    Leaves with 3 shallow lobes or a few very shallow
    lobes or entire, all on the same tree
            Quercus Durandii, Durand's White Oak No. 21
    Leaves with 3-7 irregular rounded lobes........... 17
17. Leaves glabrous beneath; twigs brittle-jointed
            Quercus austrina, Bastard White Oak   No. 32
    Leaves tomentose beneath, rarely glabrous........ 18
18. Twigs glabrous, red-brown; leaves as a rule averag-
    ing less than 3 inches long
            Quercus Margaretta, Scrubby Post Oak No. 30
    Twigs tomentose, gray-brown; leaves averaging
    more than 3 inches long
            Quercus stellata, Post Oak   No. 31
19. Leaves with more than 15 shallow, regular, rounded
    lobes; fruit one inch or more long............. 20
    Leaves with more than 12 shallow, regular, pointed
    lobes; fruit less than ¾ inch long............. 21
    Leaves with 7-16 shallow or deep irregular rounded
    or pointed lobes; fruits about one inch long on
    stalks that are longer than the leaf stalks
            Quercus bicolor, Swamp White Oak   No. 27
20. Upland trees; scales of cup fused
            Quercus montana, Rock Chestnut Oak   No. 26
    Low ground tree; scales of cup separate
            Quercus Prinus, Swamp Chestnut Oak   No. 25
21. Medium sized to very large tree
            Quercus Muhlenbergii, Yellow Chestnut Oak No. 24
    Small, usually only a shrub
            Quercus prinoides, Chinquapin Oak   p. 143

22. Mature leaves green on both sides............... 23
Mature leaves pale to densely tomentose beneath.. 30
23. Cup of acorn very low, saucer-shaped............ 24
Cup of acorn deeper, cup-shaped................ 26
24. Lobes of leaf shallow; no conspicuous tufts of hairs (rarely small tufts) in the angles of the veins
    Quercus maxima, Red Oak   No. 2
Lobes of leaf deep; conspicuous tufts of hairs in the angles of the veins on the lower side of the the leaf.................................. 25
25. Acorns more than ½ inch long
    Quercus Shumardii, Swamp Red Oak   No. 4
Acorns about ½ inch long
    Quercus palustris, Pin Oak   No. 3
26. Leaf stalk less than an inch long............... 27
Leaf stalk more than one inch long............. 28
27. Leaf over 4 inches long; acorn about 1 inch long, ⅓ of the cup folded inward
    Quercus laevis, Turkey Oak   No. 5
Leaf not over 4 inches long; acorn about ½ inch long, edge of cup not folded inward
    Quercus georgiana, Georgia Oak   No. 6
28. Edge of cup not inrolled, scales loosely pressed together; circular crack around point of acorn never more than one and usually absent; leaf dark green, under side yellow-scurfy when young, but becoming smooth
    Quercus velutina, Black Oak   No. 7
Edge of cup usually inrolled, scales tightly pressed together 29
29. Most leaves cut less than half way, dull below; point of acorn not surrounded by circular grooves
    Quercus borealis, Mountain Red Oak   No. 1
Most leaves cut more than half way, shining below; point of acorn surrounded by one or more circular grooves
    Quercus coccinea, Scarlet Oak   No. 9
30. Leaves over 5 inches long; medium sized to very large trees.................................. 31
Leaves not over 5 inches long; small trees or shrubs
    Quercus ilicifolia, Bear Oak   No. 8
31. Upland tree; leaf usually with a long central lobe, base of leaf rounded on most leaves
    Quercus rubra, Southern Red Oak   No. 10
Lowland tree; leaves with long central lobes only in the tops of old trees; base of leaf pointed on most leaves
    Quercus pagoda, Swamp Red Oak   No. 11

1. Quercus borealis Michx. f. Mountain Red Oak.

THIS is one of the oaks of the far north occurring in At-

Branch with leaves and acorns, x ⅓.

lantic coast states only in northern New England, north-western New York, northern Pennsylvania, and then with certainty only in the high Appalachian Mountains of Virginia, North Carolina, and Tennessee. In North Carolina it forms the oak groves on the tops of such mountains as Cold (Haywood County), Whiteside, Short-Off, and Wayah Bald (Macon County), and Clingman's Dome (Swain County). It seems to descend to an elevation of 4,000 feet or possibly less where it meets with the larger, more common Red Oak, *Q. maxima*, and seems to intergrade with it.

Leaves large, blade about 4-8 inches long and 2½-5½ inches broad with toothed lobes which are cut ⅓ to ½ the way to the midrib, smooth and deep green above, paler, dull, or slightly pubescent and with or without inconspicuous tufts of hairs in the axils of the veins below; petioles about 1½ inches long; acorns about ⅝ inch long, with a deep cup covering the lower one-third. The main characters which distinguish this species from *maxima*, given below, are shorter acorns in a deeper cup and typically paler under surface of the leaves. However, where these forms meet there are found acorns intermediate in size and in shape of cup and this is probably another case of intergrading forms separated by a different habitat. From the northern form of *borealis,* our mountain tree differs as a rule in the larger acorns and less deeply cut leaves. For a photograph of a fine virgin forest of this oak at Frying Pan Gap, N. C., see Wells, *Natural Gardens of North Carolina,* page 170.

2. **Quercus maxima** Ashe. **Red Oak.**

THIS is the tree formerly considered as *Quercus rubra* L.

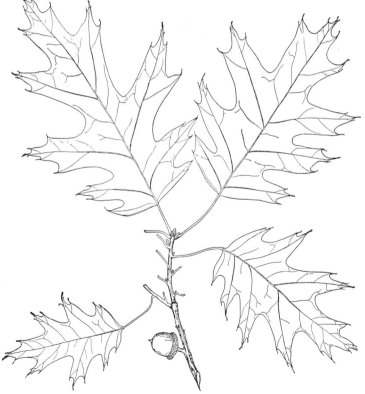

Branch with leaves and an acorn, x ⅓.

It is a fine oak found abundantly in good soil in the mountains up to 4,000 feet, not rarely near the edges of low grounds and along branches in the piedmont, and very sparingly in similar situations in the coastal plain from Virginia to Georgia. It is also reported by Small (as *Q. rubra*) from northern and middle Florida. It is plentiful in the northern states and Canada.

Leaves large, broad, smooth, dull, deep green above, with lobes which cut about 1/3 the way to the midrib, often pubescent beneath when young and with inconspicuous tufts of hairs in the axils of the veins beneath; acorns very large, up to 1¼ inches long, in very shallow cups. The cup varies to deeper in the northern states. It is a very beautiful tree for the home grounds. This is easily confused by beginners with the Scarlet Oak, but they grow in different places, the acorn cups are very unlike, and the leaves are dull beneath in the Red Oak and shining in the Scarlet Oak. It may also be confused with the Black Oak, but the Red Oak grows nearer streams, the leaves are a lighter green and tend to be more glabrous, and the acorn is larger and the cup flatter. Flowering April 16, 1916.

3. **Quercus palustris** Muench. **Pin Oak.**

THIS is a tree of swamps and low grounds which is rare and local in our area. In Virginia it is recorded on the lower Potomac River, in Caroline County, in a group of ponds and bogs at the foot of Kelly and Kennedy mountains near Stuart's Draft, Augusta County (R. S. Freer), and west of Roxbury, Charles City County, and Amelia County (J. B. Lewis). We find it abundant in Fairfax and Loudon counties, Virginia. In North Carolina it occurs along Bowlin's Creek near Chapel Hill (crossing on Route 54), in the low grounds of the Yadkin River at High Rock (Davidson County), and is reported from Biltmore, Buncombe County (House), and, according to Sargent, on "Dutchman's Creek, Forsyth County" (evidently in error for Davie County). We have no specimens of Pin Oak from South Carolina, but it is reported positively by F. H. Haskell, a well informed observer, as occurring on the Saluda

River, 12 miles west of Columbia. This area is now flooded by the Saluda dam. In Tennessee it is common in bottom lands of Shelby County (C. E. Moore). The above records are the farthest south known for the species.

Bark gray; leaves small, blade about 2-5 inches long, often cut almost to the midrib, lobes often 3-toothed with long bristle-like tips, smooth above with conspicuous tufts of hairs in the angles of the larger veins below; petioles

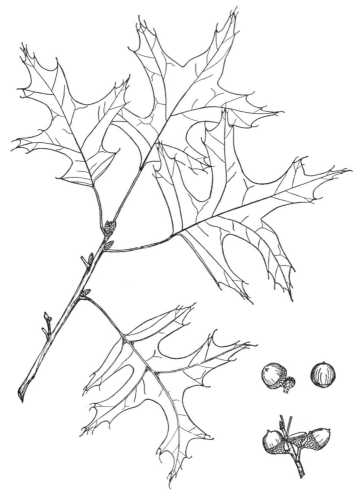

Twig showing buds and young acorn; mature acorns (separate), x ½.

slender, glabrous, ½-2 inches long; acorns sessile or on stalks up to ⅝ inch long, globose, about ½ inch long in flat cups covering about one-fourth of the nut. This oak is a tall, symmetrical, pyramidal tree, sometimes seventy feet high with many slender branches, the lower ones when not crowded drooping almost or quite to the ground, a habit which gives to the tree a striking appearance as a lawn specimen. It has also proved to be a very good.street tree.

4. **Quercus Shumardii** Buckley. **Swamp Red Oak.**

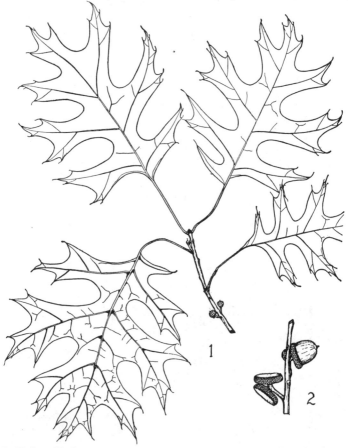

1, Twig with leaves and young acorns.   2, mature acorns.   All x ⅛.

THIS is a large tree of rich low grounds near streams with a general appearance that is much like that of the Pin Oak, but with less drooping branches. In Chapel Hill it has deeper green and more glistening foliage than that species and is a handsomer tree. The Swamp Red Oak is found sparingly from Lincoln and Davie to Craven County, North Carolina, and southward. In Georgia it extends inland to Floyd County. We have specimens from South Pittsburg, Tenn., and from Winnsboro, South Carolina.

Bark very smooth on branches, very little roughened even on the main trunk below, the central region showing a striped appearance from the cracking of the thin bark; buds much larger than in the Pin Oak, ¼ inch long, pointed and narrowly ovate, bluntly angular, grayish brown; leaves almost exactly like those of the Pin Oak in shape and texture, and with the same conspicuous tufts of down in the axils of the large veins, but averaging larger, the blade 4¾-6½ inches long and 4½-5½ inches wide on large trees; acorns much larger and of different shape from those of the Pin Oak with the stalks usually longer (⅕-⅔ inch), ovate, about 1 inch long counting the point, and nearly ¾ inch thick, nearly smooth above, slightly scurfy below; cup saucer-shaped covering about one-fourth of the acorn; inside of cup shining and nearly or quite smooth, taste of acorn flesh mildly bitterish.

5. Quercus laevis Walter (Q. Catesbaei Michx.) Turkey Oak.

THIS is a very abundant and characteristic small tree of the sand hills and other poor soil to the coast, throughout practically the entire region of the Long-leaf Pine. In North Carolina it is found as far west as Richmond and Moore counties, and extends north into Isle of Wight County (Zuni), Virginia.

Leaves rigid, with 2 or 3 long-pointed, distant lobes on each side and a long narrow central lobe, smooth on both sides; petioles very short; acorns of medium size, up to about 1 inch long, tomentose; cup covered with large scales.

Twig with leaves, a young acorn and a mature acorn, x ⅓.

the edge folded down so that the scales extend into it about half way, enclosing about one-half of the nut. A tree in the Baptist churchyard at Hartsville, S. C., is 2 feet in diameter five feet from the ground. A remarkable peculiarity of this tree is the fact that the leaves are often inhabited by a little flat sawyer beetle grub that lives inside the leaf, eating away all the tissue between the upper and lower epidermis but not breaking through and causing no swelling but only discolored spots. In some seasons every leaf of every tree seems to be attacked by several of these grubs.

6. Quercus georgiana Curtis. Georgia Oak.

THIS is a rare little tree, usually a shrub, found in a few counties east of Atlanta on granite hills as on Stone Mountain and in Jackson and Polk counties, Georgia. We have a collection from Stone Mountain, Georgia (T. G. Harbison).

Branch with leaves and an acorn, x ½.

Leaves deeply cut, sharply toothed, up to 4 inches long, in shape reminding one of *Q laevis*, at maturity smooth above and below except in some cases with tufts of whitish hairs in the axils of the larger veins; acorns about ⅓-½ inch long seated in a shallow cup. This oak may be distinguished from *Q. laevis*, by the smaller leaves and smaller acorns seated in shallow cups without inrolled edges. It is especially interesting to Carolinians because it was found by a South Carolinian, H. W. Ravenel, and named by a North Carolinian, M. A. Curtis.

7. Quercus velutina Lam. Black Oak.

This is a large upland tree found throughout our area from the mountains to the coastal plain. It is common in the mountains under 2,500 feet (ascends to 4,000 ft.), abundant in the piedmont and in the upper half of the coastal plain,

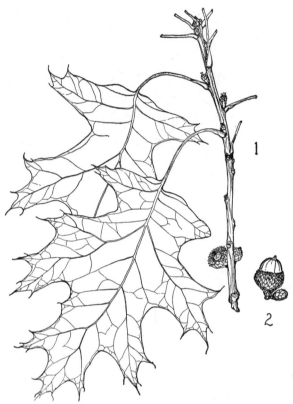

1, Branch with leaves, very young acorns and year old acorns.
2, mature acorn. All x ⅓.

and rarely extends to the coast. In Florida it is found
only in the northern part, especially in the Tallahassee
region.

Bark dark, inner bark reddish; leaves large, usually 6-8
inches long and 3½-5½ inches broad, with 5-9 (usually 7)
shallow or deep lobes, with bristle tips, upper surface
smooth or hairy, the under side yellowish scurfy when
young, becoming smooth in age; acorns large, about ⅔-⅞
inch long and ½-¾ inch thick, tomentose, about half covered by the cup. While handsome enough, the Black Oak
is more subject to breakage and decay than others of like

stature, and should not be selected for planting. In Chapel Hill this tree reaches a diameter of 3 feet 7 inches five feet from the ground and in the yard of W. J. Andrews in Raleigh, N. C., there is a tree 5 feet in diameter at the same height from the ground. It is usually called the Red Oak in North Carolina. For a hybrid between this and *Quercus marilandica*, see under hybrid oaks, p. 158. Flowering from April 5 to April 19.

At Oxford, Mississippi, on the University property Harbison found a peculiar specimen of this species in which the cup almost covered the acorn.

8. Quercus ilicifolia Wang. (Q. nana Sarg.) Bear Oak.

IN most of our range this is almost always a shrub, tending to form thickets, but in Virginia and farther north it may become a very small tree. It is partial to dry rocky hills and slopes at moderate elevations. In North Carolina it is confined, so far as known, to the tops of King's and Crowder's mountains and Moore's Knob, Stokes County. The only South Carolina record we have is the collection in the New York Botanical Garden Herbarium ascribed to South Carolina, no other data. This is the most southern record. It is not known from Georgia or Florida.

Top of tree dense, spreading; young twigs brown-pubescent, becoming nearly black the second year; buds small and either blunt or pointed; leaves numerous, small, about 2-3 inches long, usually with about 5 bristle-tipped lobes, the upper largest, angles shallow or deep, rounded; under surface densely pale pubescent; acorns ovate, nearly ½ inch long, brown and faintly streaked; cup shallow. This species has been credited with being one of the parents of several hybrids.

9. Quercus coccinea Muench. Scarlet Oak. Spanish Oak.

THIS tree, named for the scarlet color of the leaves in the fall, is the commonest oak of the mountains and is plentiful on poor rocky hills in the piedmont, extending southward to Randolph County, Georgia, and is reported as common in

Shelby County, Tennessee (C. E. Moore). In the coastal plain it is found mostly in the valleys.

Branch with leaves and acorns, x ⅓.

Leaves deeply cut and shining on both sides, blade about 3-6 inches broad and 4-7 inches long; acorns varying in size and shape but never as large as the Red Oak, borne in a fairly low cup, occasionally covering one-half the acorn, which is not flat like the cups of the Red, Swamp Red Oak, and Pin Oak. This acorn has an interesting peculiarity which makes it easy to distinguish from all others. There are one, two, or more distinct ring grooves close around the apical point. The largest tree in Hartsville, S. C., is of this species. It is 5 feet 1½ inches in diameter three feet from the ground. The commonest form in the Carolinas east of the mountains lacks tufts of hairs in the axils of the veins beneath, the leaves average larger than the mountain form, and the cups have thicker scales. This form has been given the varietal name *tuberculata* by Sargent. Our figure is of this variety. On the tops of some of the higher mountains, as Rabun Bald, Ga., occur thick stands of a dwarf form of this species, with much smaller leaves and acorns. Flowering from April 5 to April 17.

10. **Quercus rubra** L. [**Q. falcata** Michx., **Q. triloba** Michx., and **Q. digitata** (Marshall) Sudworth]. **Southern Red Oak, Spanish Oak.**

THIS is a large and very common upland tree found in our states from the low mountains (2,500 ft.) to the coastal plain. It is reported from Wakulla County, Florida (Harper), and as common in Shelby County, Tennessee (Moore).

Bark dark brownish gray with narrow, shallow ridges; leaves large, blade about 5-11½ inches long, with 3-5 sharply pointed lobes, the central lobe long and narrow and often with several lobe-like teeth near the end, upper surface lustrous, lower surface covered permanently with a yellowish gray tomentum, leaves on young trees and on sprouts wedge-shaped and three-lobed at the end; petioles up to 2 inches long; acorns small, about ½ inch long, sessile or on stalks up to ¼ inch long, scar red, cup saucer-shaped, covering about one-third of the acorn. This oak is long-lived, durable, and not easily subject to decay, and in the town of Chapel Hill reaches a diameter of 5 feet 6 inches five feet from the ground, a much larger size than given by

1, Twig with a leaf and year old acorns. 2, twig
with leaves. 3, acorn. All x ⅓.

Sargent or Britton. The large ''Rankin Oak'' four miles
northwest of Mount Holly, N. C., has a diameter of 5 feet
6 inches four and a half feet from the ground and a limb
spread of 123 feet. A tree across the street from the graded
school in Cheraw, S. C., is 5 feet 3 inches five feet from the
ground. This species has had the book name of Spanish
Oak, but in our states this name is commonly applied to the
Scarlet Oak. Flowering from April 5 to April 29.

11. Quercus pagoda Raf. Swamp Red Oak, Swamp Spanish Oak.

THIS large tree of the lowlands and swamps is distributed from southern Virginia to northern Florida and in Tennessee. It is found in the bottoms of the Apalachicola River in Florida (Harper).

Leaves, especially those from the upper parts of the old trees, much like the leaves of *Q. rubra* but whiter beneath and the base is usually pointed, though a leaf with a rather rounded base is not uncommon among the pointed based ones; leaves of young trees much broader and not so tomentose beneath; acorns small, ovate to nearly spherical, up to

Twig with leaves and several very young acorns; mature acorns (separate), x ⅓.

½ inch long, minutely pubescent, brownish buff; cup shallow, distinctly stalked. This species is amply distinct from *Q. rubra* in Durham and Orange counties, North Carolina. Only in old trees do the leaves resemble those of the latter in shape, and for at least fifteen or twenty years the leaves are shaped much like those of the Black Oak. However, as the only differences we can discover are the shape of the leaves and the habitat it is probably best to call this a variety of *Q. rubra*. The Swamp Red Oak in the swamp of New Hope Creek in Durham County, N. C., reaches a diameter of 5 feet, five feet from the ground. We have measured one near Rehobeth Church in Washington County, N. C., that is 7 feet in diameter four and a half feet from the ground.

12. Quercus marilandica Muench. Black Jack Oak.

THIS is the common, knotty scrub oak with drooping

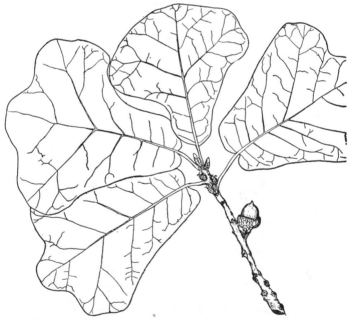

Twig with leaves, several very young acorns, and a mature
acorn, x ⅓.

branches, which is plentiful in dry or poor soil from the coast to moderate elevations in the mountains in all our area. In northern Florida it is found mostly from Leon County westward (Harper).

Leaves large, broadest at the outer end, brownish scurfy on the under surface; acorns medium sized, light brown, tomentose, with a large stalked cup covering one-half or more of the acorn. In the Carolinas this tree is usually not over 25 feet high but it may reach a much larger size. Exceptional specimens of the Black Jack Oak are handsome and quite symmetrical with dense, deep green foliage, and reach a diameter of at least 2 feet. Flowering from April 4 to April 20. For hybrids of this with *Q. velutina* and with *Q. phellos,* see under hybrid oaks, p. 158.

13. Quercus arkansana Sarg. Arkansas Water Oak.

THIS is a small tree confined in our range to a few scattered bluffs and hills in northern and western Florida and near Cuthbert, Georgia.

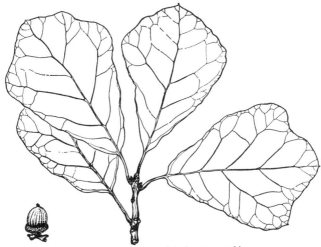

Acorn and twig with leaves, x ½.

Leaves obovate-rhombic, the base rounded or cuneate, varying to shallowly 3-lobed distally, the lobes sometimes with a minute tooth, 2-4 (-6) inches long and 1½-3 (-4½) inches wide, upper surface dark green, glabrous, lower surface paler, heavily veined, at first with scattered tufts of pale hairs all over, later becoming almost glabrous except in the vein axils. Petioles and young twigs more or less pubescent. Acorns light brown, distinctly striate, tomentose, in ours about ½ x ½ inch; cup shallow, scales closely appressed, inside silky shining except for the scar.

We have this oak from Cuthbert, Ga., from a number of places in northern Florida, and from Arkansas. Ashe first described this as *caput-rivuli* (*Rhodora* **25**: 179. 1923), later as a variety of *arkansana*. Comparing our southern specimens with Arkansas plants, the differences seem too slight to be of importance.

14. Quercus nigra L. Water Oak.

THIS is a tree which grows plentifully along streams and in low grounds in the coastal plain, extends along streams through the piedmont of all our states, and occurs in river bottoms in western Tennessee. In the mountains it is rare, but is known to occur in some places up to an altitude of 2,000 feet.

Twig with leaves and acorn, x ⅖.

Bark grayish with narrow ridges; twigs glabrous and reddish; buds small and pointed; leaves small, usually about 2½-4 inches long, in most cases broadest near the end where they are about 1-2 inches, tapering rather abruptly down to a point at the very short petiole, margin quite even all around (without teeth or lobes) or distinctly 3-lobed toward the end and with or without a sharp little point on the end of each lobe, the lower surface smooth and shining except for distinct tufts of felted hairs in the axils of the larger veins; acorns small, about ½ inch thick, minutely felted-tomentose, and more or less striate, subspherical with a flat base; cup shallow, flat, sessile, the small scales closely fused. Vigorous shoots or apical twigs often show leaves much more toothed and lobed than is typical, and they may in exceptional cases reach a length of 7½ inches and a width of 3½ inches near the end. The Water Oak holds its leaves distinctly longer than the Willow Oak and young trees in the woods are often green at Christmas. The species is distinguished from the Willow Oak by this character and by the shape of the leaves. The acorns will scarcely serve to separate them. The Water Oak is moreover a smaller and more rounded tree than the Willow Oak and is apparently shorter lived. It is popular as a street tree in the southern coastal plain, and if allowed to develop freely in good soil makes a very handsome specimen.

There has been described as *Quercus obtusa* (Willd.) Pursh a tree of the Atlantic and Gulf coastal section of the south that is supposed to differ from the Water Oak in having leaves that are broadest in the middle, tapering to each end, and typically without lobes. Leaves of this description appear on trees in the same locality with the Water Oak, and variations on the same tree may cover both kinds. Typical *Q. obtusa* from Ashe's herbarium show acorns indistinguishable from those of the Water Oak. After much collecting throughout the Carolinas, we have decided that it is impossible to separate two distinct trees from the characters given, especially in the Atlantic states. The author citation for *Q. obtusa* is erroneously given as "(Willd.) Ashe" (*Journ. Eli. Mitch. Sci. Soc.* **34:** 136. 1918) and this was copied in our earlier editions of this book and also by Rehder (*Manual,* 1940).

15. Quercus phellos L. Willow Oak.

THIS is a common tree of the low grounds and flats of the

Twig with leaves and acorn, x ⅔.

coastal plain and extends more sparingly through the piedmont in all our states. It is common in Shelby County, Tennessee (C. E. Moore).

Bark dark gray with shallow ridges; young twigs brown,
older twigs gray; leaves small, narrow, willow-like, pointed
at both ends, with a bristle on the tip, blade usually
1½-5½ inches long and ⅓-1 inch broad on a petiole up to
¼ inch long; leaves on strong shoots may be larger and
with a few lobes; acorns small, sub-globose or ovate, more
or less tomentose and striate, about ⅓ inch thick, in a
shallow flattened cup, which is sessile or on a short stalk.
The Willow Oak is related to the Water Oak, but is
of a larger size and of longer life. As an ornamental tree,
it has no superior. In the town of Chapel Hill it reaches a
diameter of 4 feet 3 inches five feet from the ground and
has a spread of 72 feet. The largest we ever saw is 5 feet
10 inches in diameter and stands in the yard of Mr. T. S.
Lucas in Society Hill, South Carolina. The common name
of this tree is badly confused. In the Carolinas it is more
often called Water Oak and Pin Oak than Willow Oak.
Both of these names properly belong to entirely different
trees and the name Willow Oak should be used. Flowering
begins from March 25 to April 19. For a hybrid between
Q. phellos and *Q. marilandica,* see under hybrid oaks,
p. 158.

16. Quercus laurifolia Michx. Laurel Oak.

THIS is a beautiful nearly evergreen oak occurring in moist woods and along streams in a rather narrow strip along

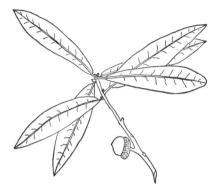

Twig with leaves and acorn, x ⅖.

the coast from Williamsburg, Virginia, southward. In South Carolina it is found inland to twelve miles north of Hartsville on a sandy bluff. It is more widely distributed in the coastal plain of Georgia and in Florida.

Leaves thick, elliptic to oblong-obovate, usually without lobes, sometimes with a few notches, about 1½-3 inches long and ⅓-1 inch broad, at maturity glabrous above and glabrous or slightly puberulous below, evergreen in large part, some falling from the periphery of the tree during the winter; petioles short; acorns ovoid, about ⅓-½ inch long, slightly pubescent and obscurely striate, in a shallow flat saucer-shaped cup, much like those of *Q. nigra*. In appearance the Laurel Oak is intermediate between *Q. phellos* and *Q. nigra*. This oak has been very popular as an ornamental tree and is much used as a street tree in our eastern towns. However, this popularity is scarcely warranted as it is much shorter lived than the Willow Oak and shows signs of dissolution in forty or fifty years. There is a very large Laurel Oak in Highlands Hammock, Florida. Measured by Mr. J. B. McFarlin in 1935 it was found to have a diameter of 7 feet 10 inches four feet from the ground. In middle South Carolina it is called the Darling-

ton Oak and is sold by some nurseries under that name
(Coker, *Journ. Eli. Mitch. Sci. Soc.* **32**: 38. 1916).   In
sharp contrast to the Willow Oak, this tree produces acorns
in greatest abundance, almost never missing a crop.   On
this account it spreads very rapidly in congenial soil.

17. **Quercus imbricaria** Michx. **Shingle Oak.**

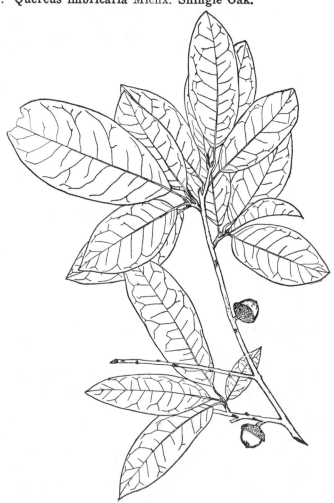

Quercus imbricaria
Branch with leaves and acorns, x ⅓.

THIS is a rather small oak occurring along streams and in good soil in the mountains from Virginia to Georgia. In North Carolina it is found as far east as Burke and Wilkes counties.

Leaves oblong-lanceolate, usually about 3-6 inches long, entire, deep green and shining above, pale green and pubescent below, larger and broader than those of *Q. phellos* and *Q. nigra;* acorns about ½ inch long and broad with a cup covering one-fourth to one-third of the acorn, top of cup inrolled.

Leaves of hybrids of *Q. phellos* with other species sometimes resemble the leaves of the Shingle Oak, and are easily mistaken for it. These hybrids are not rare in the lower piedmont and coastal plain.

18. **Quercus cinerea** Michx. [**Q. brevifolia** (Lam.) Sarg.]
Upland Willow Oak, Blue Jack Oak.

Twigs with leaves and an acorn, x ½.

THIS is a common small tree of the sandhills through the drier pine flats of the coastal plain to the seashore, where it is a minor element in the dwarfed and sheared vegetation of the exposed dunes. It is found from southeastern Virginia (Nansemond and Southampton counties; see Fernald in *Rhodora* **41**: 540. 1939) to Florida and westward.

Leaves small, usually about 2-3 inches long but up to 4¼ inches long by 1⅝ inches wide at times on vigorous trees, long-elliptic and with an abrupt little mucro, entire and decidedly whitish tomentose beneath; acorns small, up to ½ inch thick, somewhat flattened, gray-brown, pulverulent, set in a shallow cup which usually covers about one-third of the nut. This species and *Q. laevis* and in places *Q. Margaretta* make up most of the smaller tree growth of the sandhills.

19. Quercus myrtifolia Willd. Scrub Oak.

THIS is an evergreen shrub or small tree occurring in southern coastal South Carolina and westward into Florida.

Leaves thick, very small, resembling miniature forms of Water Oak or Laurel Oak, usually ¾-1½ inches, rarely up

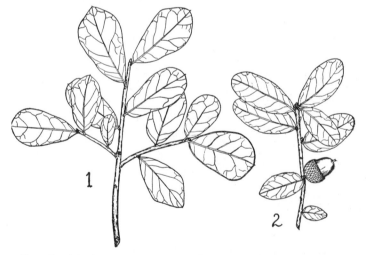

Branch with obovate leaves. 2, branch with ovate leaves and an acorn. All x ⅗.

to 2 inches long, nearly smooth, shining above, margin nearly even or undulate, sometimes with a few lobes, revolute; acorns without stalks or with very short ones, ovate to elongate, with a prominent mucro, $\frac{7}{16}$-$\frac{9}{16}$ inch long, the cup covering about one-half or somewhat less of its length, scales of the cup with ciliated edges.

20. Quercus virginiana Mill. Live Oak.

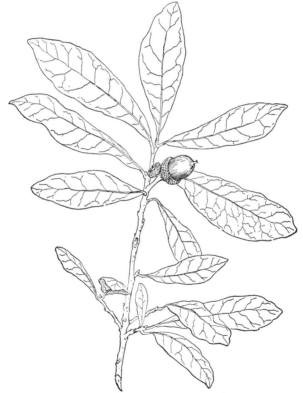

Branch with leaves and an acorn, x $\frac{1}{2}$.

THE Live Oak occupies a strip of country mostly along the coast from Virginia to Florida and is plentiful only south of Cape Hatteras. F. H. Haskell thinks it is native inland as far as lower Sumter County, South Carolina.

Leaves evergreen, thick, about 1½-4 inches long and ⅓-2½ inches broad, usually without teeth or lobes, occasionally toothed near the end, margins revolute, pale and pubescent or practically glabrous below; acorns oblong, dark blackish brown in the exposed part, pale yellowish in the cup, about ¾ inch long, cups deep, covering one-third to one-half the acorn, borne on short or long stalks. One of the largest specimens of this oak is the "Middleton Oak" in the Middleton Garden, near Charleston, S. C., which has a diameter of 8 feet 9 inches. The large Live Oak in the cemetery of old Midway Church, Liberty County, Ga., is 7 feet 5 inches in diameter three feet from the ground and 6 feet 10.6 inches five feet from the ground and has a spread of 144 feet. On the Dorchester road and only about one-fourth of a mile from this last there is an oak that measures 7 feet 6.4 inches three feet from the ground, but is slightly smaller than the one near the church at five feet from the ground and the spread is considerably less. The Live Oak makes a fine ornamental tree in cultivation and is hardy and thrifty at least as far west as Greensboro, North Carolina, but in exposed situations in severe winters (such as 1935-36) loses its leaves even on the coast of North Carolina. Contrary to the general opinion the Live Oak in rich soil is a fast growing tree. One in Mr. King's yard on Colonel's Island, Liberty County, Ga., trimmed up with a pocket knife in 1872 by J. A. M. King and now certainly not over sixty-seven years old measures 4 feet 6¾ inches in diameter three feet from the ground and has a spread of 120 feet. The "Secession Oak" at Bluffton, S. C., should be mentioned in any reference to notable specimens of the Live Oak. It was under this tree that, according to citizens of the section, the first large gathering of people to discuss seriously the advisability of secession was held. Wade Hampton was one of those present. Measured by us in 1934, the diameter was found to be 6.38 feet four and a half feet from the ground. The age that the Live Oak may attain is a subject of much discussion. In *Plant Life of Highlands Hammock*, Florida, by C. S. Donaldson *et al.*, it is estimated that a tree there would now (1944) be about 970 years old. Many other popular guesses make them even much older than that, but Mr. W. R. Mattoon of the United States Forest Service, after some experience, decides that "It seems likely that the oldest living live oaks are not more than two to three hundred years old" (*Amer. Forests* 37: 742. 1931). The wood is very tough and is valued in ship building. Of the acorns Lawson (p. 156) says: "The Indians draw an oil from them as sweet as that drawn from the olive. . . ." Individual trees with acorns as sweet as Chinquapins are reported to be near Beaufort, S. C., and in Allen Park, Augusta, Ga. (Willett, *Science* 67: No. 1743, 1928. Also in a private letter.)

In sprouting, the acorn of *Quercus virginiana* forms a distinct tuber near the surface of the ground. This is illustrated by Sargent (*Silva* 8: pl. 394) and also by Coker (*Journ. Eli. Mitch. Sci. Soc.* 28: 34, pl. 2. 1912).

A number of varieties or forms of Live Oak have been described. Several of them are essentially shrubby. One of these, *Q. virginiana* var. *geminata* Sargent (*Q. geminata* Small), which may become a large tree, is reported from the southeastern counties of North Carolina and southward to Florida near the coast. We have specimens from Myrtle Beach, S. C., with conspicuously reticulated veins and strongly revolute margins, which may be referred to this variety. The Live Oak group is so variable that we find it impracticable to define the varieties clearly.

21. **Quercus Durandii** Buckl. (**Q. breviloba** Sarg. in part). **Durand's White Oak.**

THIS is a rather large tree occurring near Augusta (Richmond County) and in Sumter and Dougherty counties, Georgia, and westward. It is abundant around Albany, Georgia.

Bark grayish white, scaly; twigs gray-brown, hairy early in the season, becoming glabrous; leaves obovate to elliptic with a wedge-shaped base, entire or 3-lobed toward the end or irregularly lobed on the sides, all forms appearing on the same tree, those at the top of the tree simplest, white and pubescent below, ½-1½ inches broad and 2½-3

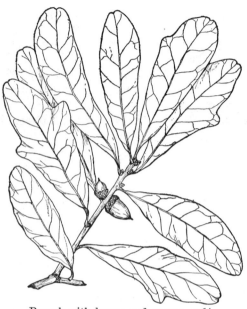

Branch with leaves and acorns, x ½.

inches long, those on lower branches usually green and glabrous below, often lobed, rarely 3½ inches broad and 7 inches long; petioles glabrous, short, rarely over ¼ inch long; acorns short-stalked or nearly sessile, ovoid, pointed, chestnut brown, shining, about ½ inch long and ¼-⅓ inch thick, seated in a very shallow, thin-walled cup with a pointed base. The general appearance of the leaf resembles the Water and Laurel oaks, but the plant is in the White Oak group and the acorns, though small, are of the White Oak type and mature the first season. It is closely related to the Live Oak and forms a handsome rounded tree, taller and less spreading than the Live Oak. From the latter it differs further in smaller acorns borne on shorter stalks, and in broader leaves which have a greater tendency to lobing and which are not evergreen. Some authors have considered *Q. Durandii* the same as *Q. sinuata* Walter. The latter has also been considered the same as *Q. austrina* and as a hybrid. Walter's type has been lost, and there is so much confusion about it that we are not including that species among our oaks.

22. Quercus Chapmani Sarg. Chapman's White Oak.

THIS is usually a shrubby oak, sometimes becoming a small tree, that occurs in sandy barrens from the coast of South Carolina to Florida. It is reported from Bluffton, Beaufort County, South Carolina, and on Colonel's Island, Georgia, and it is abundant on the western coast of Florida. We have collections from Colonel's Island, Georgia,

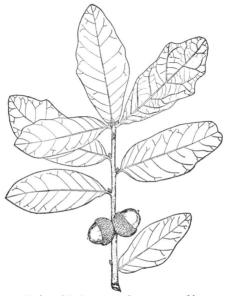

Twig with leaves and acorns, x ½.

and from Old Town, Lafayette County, and Oak Hill, Volusia County, in Florida.

Leaves obovate or oblong, 2-4 inches long and about ¾-1¼ inches wide, glabrous and dark green above, light green and pubescent on the midribs below, margins practically entire, wavy or lobed on the upper half; petioles short; acorns sessile, ½-⅝ inch long, with the cup covering about one-half of it. Harbison reports one large tree in Orange County, Florida, with an exceptional height of 50 feet. Flowering at Oak Hill, March 22, 1913.

23. Quercus oglethorpensis Duncan.

THIS tree of medium size, reaching a diameter of about two

feet and a height of 80 feet, is found in better drained bottomlands of Wilkes, Elbert, and Oglethorpe counties, Georgia.

Bark light gray or nearly white, appressed-scaly; twigs pubescent when young, then glabrate; leaves deciduous, about 2-5 inches long and ¾-1½ inches broad, entire, elliptic to ovate, base rounded or acute, tip acute or obtuse, glabrous above, velvety below on entire surface with light yellow stellate hairs; petiole short and stout; acorn cup sessile or short-stalked, turbinate, covering about one-third or more of the acorn, cup scales flat, appressed-pubescent, tan with a brown margin, acorn ovoid, gray-brown, appressed-pubescent, about ⁷⁄₁₆ inch long.

This species has been published rather recently (*Amer. Mid. Nat.* **24:** 755-756. 1940), and our description is adapted from the original one.

24. Quercus Muhlenbergii Engelm. [Q. acuminata (Michx.) Houba]. Yellow Chestnut Oak.

THIS is a large rare tree that is said to occur in limestone soil throughout our range. In Virginia we have collected it in Montgomery County, and we have specimens collected by Small on the Holston River in Smyth County. In North Carolina it is very rare. Ayers and Ashe report it along the larger mountain streams of the southern Appalachian mountains, and Michaux reports a single tree found by him on the Cape Fear River a mile from Fayetteville, North Carolina. It has been collected at Biltmore and at Farmington, Davie County, North Carolina (Biltmore Herbarium). It is found in central and eastern Georgia, and Small, Harper, and Harbison say that it occurs in dry woods in western Florida. A handsome specimen of this tree stands on the front lawn of Mt. Vernon.

Leaves lanceolate or obovate, about 2-8 inches long, usually narrower than others of this group, with many shallow lobes or teeth, smooth above, the under side whitish pubescent; acorns nearly or quite sessile, only about ⅔ of an inch long, with cups covering about one-half of their length.

Quercus prinoides Willd. is a shrubby species closely

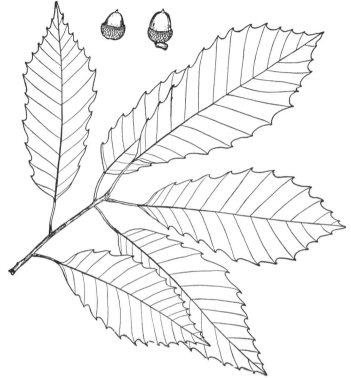

Quercus Muhlenbergii. Twig and acorns, x ½.

related to this, with smaller leaves on short petioles and deeper acorn cups with thicker scales. In our specimens the length of the acorns varies greatly. We have collections from Gaston and Stanly counties, and Harbison reports it from Buncombe County, North Carolina.

25. Quercus Prinus L. (Q. Michauxii Nutt.) Swamp Chestnut Oak, Cow Oak.

This is a fine large tree of the low grounds of the coastal plain in all our area, and extends inland well into the piedmont to Davie County, North Carolina, and Clarke County, Georgia (Athens, J. Miller). Dr. C. E. Moore reports it from the bottoms of Wolf River in western Tennessee.

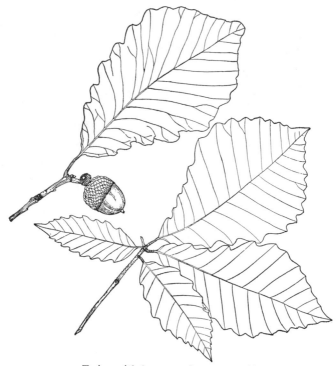

Twigs with leaves and acorns, x ⅓.

Bark dark gray, flaky; young twigs tomentose or smooth; leaves large, the blade about 4½-9 inches long, broadest above the middle where they are about 2¾-4¼ inches broad, softly pubescent beneath and with many shallow, rounded lobes, the margins narrowly inrolled; petioles short or moderately long, tomentose or hairy; acorns large, up to 1½ inches long, the cup, with large, pubescent, abruptly pointed *separate* scales covering about one-third to one-half the acorn. Near Chapel Hill some trees reach a diameter of 4 feet 11 inches five feet from the ground, but the largest tree of this species that we have measured is much farther from the coastal plain. It is the "Wiley Bailey Chestnut Oak," four miles southwest of Mocksville, Davie County, North Carolina, in the low grounds of Hunting Creek. This fine tree, saved by Wiley

Bailey for staves when the ground was cleared some time before the Civil War, is now about 85 feet high and measures 6 feet 2 inches in diameter five feet from the ground. James Henry Rice, Jr. (Colleton County, S. C.), says of the Cow Oak that it "meets every requirement of the White Oak with the additional advantage of resisting soil decay longer than the Post Oak. It is a noble and beautiful tree and might be termed majestic with no violence to the language" (letter of July 11, 1931). See *Q. bicolor* for a comparison with that species.

26. **Quercus montana** Willd. (**Q. Prinus** of authors). **Rock Chestnut Oak.**

THIS is an attractive oak, much smaller than but closely related to the Swamp Chestnut Oak and very similar in appearance. Unlike the other, it is a piedmont and mountain plant confined to upland soils and preferring rocky ridges and bluffs. It occurs in the Cumberland mountains

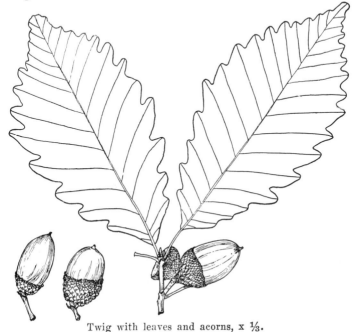

Twig with leaves and acorns, x ⅓.

of Tennessee and from the mountains as far east as Wake, Harnett, and Lee counties in North Carolina and south to Atlanta, Georgia, growing scarcer as it descends into the piedmont. In Virginia it is reported as far east as Williamsburg. In Chapel Hill it is rare except on the north slope of bluffs. Some of the largest specimens of this oak are found in our mountains, where it is one of the most abundant trees.

In addition to its size and habitat, the Rock Chestnut Oak is distinguished from the Swamp Chestnut Oak by the much less pubescent leaves and by the scales of the acorn cup which, instead of being separate when dry, are strongly fused together both when fresh and when dry. The bark of the Rock Chestnut Oak is of value in tanning and the trees are being felled in great numbers for this purpose. A section of this oak in the museum in Raleigh from Haywood County, N. C., has a diameter of 4 feet 5½ inches. Flowering in April.

We have interesting hybrids between *Q. montana* and *Q. alba* from Highlands, Macon County, and from Yadkin College, Davidson County, N. C., showing strongly *Q. montana* relationship, but the leaves have deeper lobes that are often less in number than in typical *Q. montana*. The acorns and cups are intermediate in appearance between the two species. Schneider has called this widely distributed hybrid *Q. Saulii* (Saul's Oak). For a study of the seedlings of *Q. Saulii* from a tree in Clarendon, Va., see Allard (*Bull. Torr. Bot. Club* **59**: 267. 1932).

27. **Quercus bicolor** Willd. (**Q. platanoides** Sudw.) **Swamp White Oak.**

THIS is a large tree of stream borders and swamps that is more common in the northern and central states, generally credited as far south as the District of Columbia and along the mountains to West Virginia, though the first edition of Sargent's *Manual* under the name *Q. platanoides* extended it along the Appalachians to northern Georgia. We have recently found in the Ashe collection specimens from Person and Davie counties, North Carolina, under the name *Q. macrocarpa* that will have to be referred to *Q. bicolor*,

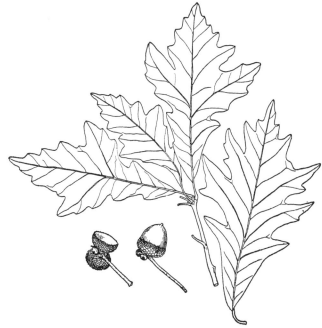

Branch with deeply lobed leaves; acorns. All x ⅓.
Tree from Granville County, N. C.

and we also have collections from Granville County, North Carolina, from the Falls of the Potomac, Fairfax County, and from Loudoun County, Virginia.*

Bark in old trunks light gray, broadly ridged or checked; leaves 3-7½ inches long, 2-5½ inches broad, obovate to oblong-ovate, with apex rounded or pointed, base wedge-shaped and entire, margin with 7-16 shallow or rarely deep irregular pointed or rounded lobes and usually ending in short glandular teeth (see the two illustrations for extremes), green above, white to tawny and velvety tomentose below, petioles short, ⅓-¾ inch long; acorn ovate with a broad base, ¾-1¼ inches long, ½-¾ inch thick; cup about one-third as long as the acorn, scales separate when dry, the lower ones thickened, tuberculate, the upper ones some-

* On seeing the Ashe specimens T. G. Harbison remarked that they suggested the answer to the riddle as to the plant that the first edition of Sargent's *Manual* reported as *Q. macrocarpa* from Caswell County, North Carolina, and that more recent manuals omit as unauthoritative.

Branch with shallowly lobed leaves and very young acorns, x ⅓.
Tree from Person County, N. C.

times forming a fringe at the edge approaching that of the
Mossy Cup Oak *(Q. macrocarpa)*, on long slender stalks,
1-4 inches long.

This tree grows in situations similar to those of the
Swamp Chestnut Oak *(Q. Prinus)* and is closely related to
that species. Young leaves of the Swamp Chestnut Oak
are tomentose beneath and on some leaves this downy tomentum persists through the season though it is usually
much less pronounced than in the Swamp White Oak. The
Swamp Chestnut Oak leaf also has a more regular edge
with lobes that are usually rounded, rarely pointed, and
that extend nearly to the base, making more lobes than is
usually found in the Swamp White Oak; both species may
have short glandular points on the lobes, but they are more
abundant in the Swamp White Oak; petioles of the Swamp
Chestnut Oak are sometimes short, but they are mostly
longer than the stocky fruit stalks, often fruit practically
sessile, while in the Swamp White Oak the fruit stalks are
slender and are always longer than the petioles. Some
forms of the White Oak have fruit stalks up to 2 inches

long, but the leaves are never velvety below as in the Swamp White Oak. We have found a peculiarity in the leaves of this oak that should be mentioned. A fine tree of the species on the campus of the University of North Carolina, planted about 25 years ago, shows the leaves on the lower part of the tree to be bright green beneath, while those on the upper part are decidedly whitish. Both types are equally soft-pubescent to the touch.

28. **Quercus macrocarpa** Michx. **Burr Oak, Mossy Cup Oak.**

THIS is one of the finest of the oaks, reaching a height of over 150 feet and a diameter of at least 6 feet. It grows in rich swamps and bottom lands from Montgomery County, Alabama, and Tennessee northward and westward. The Alabama record is given by Harper (*Jour. Eli. Mitch. Sci. Soc.* **58**: 60. 1942). For an erroneous record of this species from North Carolina, see under *Q. bicolor.*

Leaves varying greatly. On the same twig it seems to be the rule for the lower leaves to be much smaller than the apical ones, about 3½-12 inches long and 3-6½ inches broad; lobes broad, sinuses deep, sometimes extending to the midrib itself, the lower lobes simple, the upper ones broad and themselves lobed more or less deeply toward their ends; at times the leaves are much less cut (as shown in one of our figures); pubescent when young, when mature glabrous and shining above, pale below and covered with a dense velvety pubescence, as are the short petioles; twigs of the year reddish brown and more or less pubescent. Acorns remarkably variable, oval to subglobose, about ¾-2 inches long counting the cup, which covers from one-half to nearly the entire acorn, cup scales heavily tuberculate, tips free, the marginal ones extending their tips into a long, threadlike fringe, highly characteristic of the species.

This oak is easily distinguished by its remarkable, heavily fringed acorn cups (sometimes fringed in *Q. bicolor*), and the great variation in the acorns. See Harper in *Journal of the Elisha Mitchell Sci. Soc.* **58**: 60, 1942.

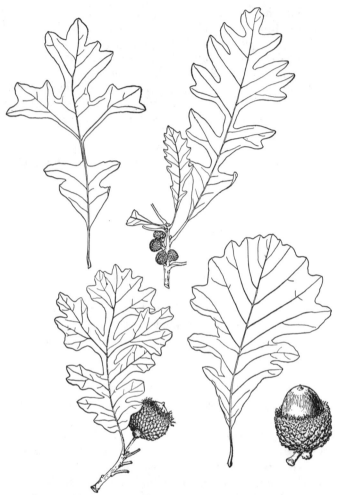

Quercus macrocarpa. Twigs, leaves, and acorns, showing
variations, x ⅓.

29. Quercus lyrata Walt. Overcup Oak.

THIS is a medium sized tree confined to river bottoms and
rich low grounds. It is plentiful in all the deeper swamps
of the coastal plain and extends for some distance into the
piedmont from Virginia to Florida. In North Carolina it
is found inland to Anson, Chatham, Guilford, Orange, and

Twig and acorns, x ⅓.

Nash counties. In South Carolina it follows the larger streams as far as the sandhills—probably farther--and James Henry Rice, Jr., wrote us that it is abundant in the swamps and bays of Colleton County. In Georgia it is distributed inland into Carroll, Gwinnett, and Clarke counties. In Florida it is found in the bottoms of the Chipola, Apalachicola, and Suwannee rivers (Harper). In Tennessee it is reported from the bottoms of Wolf River in Shelby County (C. E. Moore), and from middle Tennessee (Gattinger). We have it from Greensville County, Va.

Bark gray; twigs hairy when young, soon becoming glabrous; leaves oblong-obovate, narrowed toward the base, with 5-9 sharp-pointed, rarely rounded lobes (without bristles), separated by broad, shallow sinuses, blade about 3-7½ inches long and up to about 4¾ inches broad, smooth above and tomentose or glabrous below; petioles

short, about ¼-1¼ inches long, glabrous or hairy; acorns
sessile or borne on stalks up to ⅞ inch or more long, ovoid
with a broad flat base, ½-⅞ inch long and up to 1 inch
broad; cup thin, covered with tomentose, broad scales, with
sharp ridges on the back and free tips, remarkable in covering nearly all (at times quite all) the nut, which remains
in it permanently.

30. **Quercus Margaretta** Ashe. (**Q. stellata** var. **Margaretta**
Sarg.) **Scrubby Post Oak.**

THIS relative of the Post Oak is a small southern tree, often
only a shrub, occurring in dry sandy soil from the sandhills
to the sea and extending as far north as the James River
in Surry County, Virginia, and southward in our area to
central and western Florida.

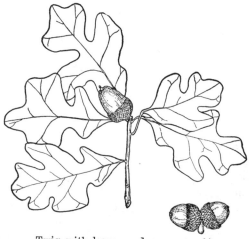

Twig with leaves and acorns, x ½.

Crown spreading; bark rough; buds small and blunt,
they and the slender twigs reddish and glabrous; leaves
small, 2-3½ (rarely 4½) inches long with 5-7 (rarely 3)
blunt broad lobes with broad or narrow, shallow or deep
sinuses, acute or often rounded or truncate, sometimes unequal at the base, upper surface glabrous, lower densely
tomentose with yellow, fascicled hairs, becoming at times
more or less glabrous toward midsummer except for the

veins, but usually remaining densely tomentose throughout
the summer; petiole short, ⅛-⅓ inch long, tomentose or
becoming glabrous; acorns oblong, ⅜-⅞ inch long, gray-
brown, tomentose or glabrous below; cup sessile or with a
short stalk up to ⅜ inch long, covering about one-fourth
or more of the nut, finely pubescent, with small, closely
fused scales. There are forms of this oak, e.g. at Bainbridge, Ga. (W. L. Hunt, coll.), in which the acorn cup is
nearly as long as the acorn, leaving only an apical disk
exposed. This oak is one of the three that are conspicuous
in the sandhills. One specimen we have seen, in rich sandy
woods, Myrtle Beach, S. C., is 27 feet high and 1 foot thick
three feet from the ground; another on Witherspoon Island,
Darlington County, S. C., is 2 feet 5½ inches thick four
and one half feet from the ground and about 60 feet high.
Britton gives the acorns and cups as smaller in this oak
than in the Post Oak, but in some of our Post Oaks, which
in Chapel Hill are very large trees, the acorns and cups
are smaller than is the rule in *Q. Margaretta.* According
to our observations in the field and on herbarium specimens,
the Scrubby Post Oak is easily distinguished from the Post
Oak, from which it differs mainly in the smaller size,
smaller leaves, and most obviously in the reddish brown,
glabrous or nearly glabrous, slender twigs. The dense
pubescence on the lower side of the leaves cannot be relied
on, as it may disappear in large part during the summer.

Sargent has described from Alabama and farther west
a variety *araniosa* of *Q. stellata,* with floccose, persistent tomentum on the lower surface. In this respect it agrees
with our collections from Myrtle Beach, South Carolina.
Ashe pertinently says that it should better be considered a
variety of *Margaretta,* as the twigs are slender, yellow or
reddish, and usually glabrous (*Journ. Eli. Mitch. Sci. Soc.*
34: 137. 1918). Sargent's figure of *Q. Margaretta,* considered by him a variety of *Q. stellata,* does not represent
the true *Q. Margaretta* but evidently belongs to the variety
araniosa. Sargent described from Alabama a shrubby
form of *Q. stellata Margaretta* (f. *stolonifera*) with smaller,
narrower leaves. This forms thickets by means of underground runners. Ashe considers it a variety of *Q. Mar-*

garetta (*Q. M.* var. *stolonifera*), and says that the same or a closely related variety grows along the Pee Dee River in Anson and Richmond counties, North Carolina. Beadle has described from rocky soil in Georgia and Alabama a small oak as *Q. Boyntonii.* He says that this shrub differs from *Q. Margaretta* in the "more lobed leaves with shorter bases and the more slender and glabrous or nearly glabrous shoots." We have from Southampton County, Va., a specimen which seems to be a hybrid between *Margaretta* and *alba.*

31. **Quercus stellata** Wang. (**Q. minor** Sarg.) **Post Oak.**

THIS small, medium sized, or sometimes very large tree with a rounded crown is found in all our states from the lower mountains to the coast. It is plentiful in the piedmont where in rich soil it is often large, as in Chapel Hill where individuals reach a diameter of 4 feet 3⅗ inches five feet from the ground. Although it does best in rich soil, it is not averse to poor soil and is one of the common trees of the sandhill region.

Bark dark gray, rather finely checked, in old trees frequently showing long horizontal fissures; twigs minutely and densely tomentose; leaves coarse, with five large truncate or blunt main lobes which are usually broadest near the ends, separated by large broad sinuses, under side light green, minutely and rather sparsely tomentose with yellowish, fascicled hairs, the upper side roughish; acorns sessile, often crowded on the ends of the twigs, small, short-oblong, blunt except for the sharp little beak, from ½-¾ inch long and ⅓-½ inch thick, tomentose or nearly glabrous; scar bright orange when fresh, soon fading to practically white; cup covering about one-fourth to one-third the nut, scales very small and closely appressed, very finely pubescent. Flowering from April 1 to April 20.

There is a peculiar tree in Chapel Hill in which the leaves have very dilated middle lobes and very small lower lobes, giving the whole leaf a 4-lobed appearance. Trelease has given the form name *Q. stellata* f. *quadrata* to this tree.

Quercus stellata. Branch with leaves and acorns, x ⅓.

32. **Quercus austrina** Small. **Bastard White Oak.**

THIS is a rather large tree found mostly near streams and in rich soil in the coastal plain from the neighborhood of Charleston, South Carolina, to central Florida and westward. In Georgia it is known from Dover, Scriven, McIntosh, Sumter, and Decatur counties.

Twigs reddish brown to gray-brown, brittle-jointed; leaves obovate with a wedge-shaped base, usually with 3-5 shallow (rarely deep) rounded lobes, sometimes with indis-

Twigs with leaves and acorns, x ½.

tinct lobes; blade 3-6½ inches long and 1-4¾ inches broad, at maturity dark green and shining above, paler and glabrous below; petioles short, usually about ¼ (rarely ½) inch long; acorns nearly sessile or on short thick stalks, ovoid, about ½-¾ inch long and ⅓-½ inch thick, in a thin-walled cup covering about one-third of the nut. This oak is closely related to the White Oak but differs in that the leaf has fewer lobes, the cup of the acorn is thinner, and the twigs are very brittle-jointed.

33. Quercus alba L. White Oak.

THIS is a fine large spreading tree which occurs in all our states. It is abundant in the piedmont and lower mountains, but in the coastal plain it is usually confined to the neighborhood of creeks and rivers. As a small tree or shrub it ascends to about 4,500 feet, as on Mt. Satulah in

Twig with leaves and acorns, x ¼.

North Carolina. In Florida it is found in the middle and western part.

Bark light gray, ridged or flaky; leaves light green, oblong-obovate with 7-11 regular rounded lobes, glabrous, pale below; acorns sessile or on long stalks, long-ovate, chestnut brown, about ¾-1¼ inches long and ½-¾ inch thick, in a deep saucer-shaped cup with thickened scales. In Chapel Hill the White Oak reaches a diameter of 5 feet 8 inches five feet from the ground, and another tree of the same size is standing in the yard of C. W. Johnson in Chatham County, North Carolina. We have measured the ''Old Sheek Oak'' at Smith's Grove in Davie County, N. C., and find it to be 7 feet 6 inches in diameter three feet from the ground, 6 feet 4 inches five feet from the ground, with a spread of 133 feet. This is considerably larger than the ''Cornwallis Oak'' at Guilford Battle Ground near Greensboro, North Carolina. In Mingo County, West Virginia, there is a very large White Oak which is claimed by several observers to be the largest of its kind in the world. Taking the entire bulk into consideration, this may be true, as it is 4 feet in diameter at the first limb which is sixty-six feet from the ground. At four and a half feet from the ground it is 5 feet and 10½ inches in diameter, which is not so large as the largest North Carolina ones mentioned above. Mr. Richard Huff of Mars Hill reports a White Oak in the Murray Gap section of Madison County, N. C., that is 8½ feet in diameter at breast height, 150 feet high and 80 feet

to the first limb. The wood of this species is very strong
and tough and is highly valued for many purposes. Flowering from April 1 to April 21.

In the fall of 1942 during a very wet spell in October
we noted that White Oak acorns on several trees in Chapel
Hill were sprouting while still on the tree, the radicles
reaching ½ inch or so in length. The root tip was covered
with an obvious layer of jelly.

A remarkable form of this tree with very scaly bark, as
conspicuously so as in the Scaly-bark Hickory, occurs in
the grove at Elon College, North Carolina. We pulled from
this tree a slab of bark at least 2½ feet long and 6 inches
wide in places. A form of the White Oak (*Q. alba lati-
loba* Sarg.) with much broader and fewer lobes, which is
common in the north, occurs in our mountains. The lobes
are not only broader but often notched at the ends. This
tree is sometimes mistaken for Post Oak. We have collected
it at Highlands, North Carolina.

Hybrid oaks are often met with and it is sometimes hard to
recognize the parents. Many of them occur in our states but we do
not have the space to refer to them. Trelease, in his recent monograph on oaks, lists 58 hybrids. In Chapel Hill we have found a
tree, which we take to be a cross between *Q. phellos* and *Q. rubra*,
and another a cross between *Q. phellos* and *Q. marilandica*. Both are
now destroyed. From the last hybrid we planted many acorns in our
propagating grounds and secured about 75 trees. This hybrid oak
was named *Q. Rudkini* by Britton (*Bull. Torr. Bot. Club* 9: 13, pls.
10-12. 1882). Sargent also illustrated it (*Silva* 8: pl. 437). It was
later found and discussed with illustrations by H. A. Allard (*Bull.
Torr. Bot. Club* 59: 270. 1932). Mr. Allard in a letter of May 30,
1943, says that he has grown hundreds of seedlings of this hybrid
and has ''gotten all the variants you sent me, even almost typical
willow oak segregates. . . .'' Ours varied extremely not only in
leaf character but also in growth habit. In some the leaves almost
duplicated the one parent, in some the other parent, while others
showed many forms between. Some were poor and stunted, others
vigorous and handsome. Outgrowing their place, most of them were
thrown away; some of the best were planted along the road to the
Country Club and farther out. See *Q. montana* for a description of
Q. Saulii, evidently a hybrid between *Q. montana* and *Q. alba*. On
our campus we have two specimens which we take to be hybrids between *Q. velutina* and *Q. marilandica*. This hybrid has been named
Q. Bushii by Sargent (*Bot. Gaz.* 65: 453. 1918).

ULMACEAE (ELM FAMILY)

ULMUS (Tourn.) L.

1. Flowers appearing in the fall, a rare tree found in
   our range in Tennessee and northwestern Georgia
   Ulmus serotina, Red Elm   No. 1

   Flowers appearing in the spring.................. 2
2. Leaves averaging less than 2½ inches long
   Ulmus alata, Winged Elm   No. 2

   Leaves averaging more than 2½ inches long....... 3
3. Leaves soft-velvety below, rough above; wing of
   fruit not hairy; winter buds brown-tomentose
   Ulmus fulva, Slippery Elm   No. 3

   Leaves smooth or nearly so above, smooth or tomentose below, wing of fruit hairy; winter buds not
   tomentose
   Ulmus americana, White Elm   No. 4

1. Ulmus serotina Sargent. Red Elm.

THE Red Elm is a cork-winged elm which has a very limited
and local distribution. In our range it is found only on
banks and bluffs in northwestern Georgia and Tennessee.
Gattinger reports it from Nashville in Tennessee. We have
specimens from the cliffs of the Coosa River near Rome,
Georgia. A collection by Rugel in 1842 on the French Broad

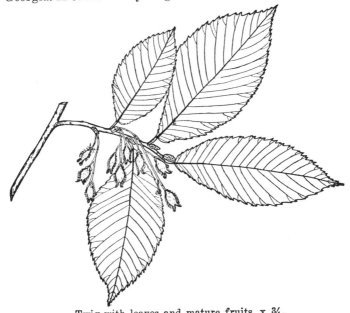

Twig with leaves and mature fruits, x ¾.

River is referred by Mohr to North Carolina, but there seems to be no evidence that this plant was not collected on that river in Tennessee, where it is known to occur.

Bark brown, with large, flat scales; twigs usually with corky wings, leaves oblong-elliptic, pointed, the base oblique, unevenly (doubly) serrate, blade 1½-3½ inches long and ¾-1½ inches broad, at maturity glabrous above, hairy on the midrib and veins beneath; petioles short; flowers appearing in the fall on long pedicels in a many-flowered raceme; fruit maturing in November, oblong elliptical, about ½ inch long, with the margin fringed with long white hairs. This tree is very much like *Ulmus alata*, except for the autumnal flowers on a long raceme and the larger scales of the bark.

Ulmus alata. 1, Twig with mature fruits. 2, twig with leaves and showing cork wings. All x ½.

2. Ulmus alata Michx. Winged Elm, Wahoo.

THIS common elm of the piedmont is found throughout our range except in the higher mountains. In northern Florida it is rare (Harper). It is named for the corky wings along many of the branches.

Leaves small and nearly or quite smooth above, minutely velvety below on the veins, margins serrate; fruit flat, winged, covered with hairs. When in fruit it can be distinguished from the Slippery Elm and usually from the White Elm, even at a distance, by the reddish color given the tree by the fruits in contrast to the light green color of the other two. However, an occasional White Elm also has reddish fruits. The Winged Elm is much inferior to the White and Slippery Elms as an ornamental tree, as it is smaller and shorter lived. It propagates quite readily from the seeds and must constantly be removed from borders, fences, and rock walls. It is one of the few trees that lightning does not kill. Flowering from January 12 to March 17.

3. Ulmus fulva Michx. Slippery Elm, Red Elm.

THIS is a medium sized tree found chiefly in the low grounds or near the foot of hills in the piedmont and sparingly in the lower mountains and coastal plain of all our states, except in Florida where it is found only in the northern part and very rarely there (Harper).

Bark dark brown, the inner bark mucilaginous; young twigs hairy; outer bud scales hairy, the inner with long tufts of brown hairs; leaves ovate-oblong, about 2½-6 inches long and 1¾-3 inches broad; margins doubly serrate; upper surface harshly hairy, lower surface densely velvety and with conspicuous tufts of white hairs in the axils of the primary veins; flowers in ample fascicles appearing before the leaves; fruit (a samara) round or wedge-shaped, flat, winged, hairy immediately over the seed cavity; the outer part of the wings and their margins smooth. Flowering from February 21 to March 18.

Ulmus fulva. 1, Twig with leaves. 2, twig with flowers.
3, mature fruits and bud. All x ½.

4. Ulmus americana L. White Elm.

This is a large and beautiful tree that is plentiful in low
grounds, preferring the neighborhood of rivers and extending throughout the coastal plain and into part of the piedmont of all our states except Florida, where it is uncommon,
occurring along the Chipola and Apalachicola rivers (Harper). In North Carolina it extends as far west as Guilford
and Mecklenburg counties. In Virginia it extends into the

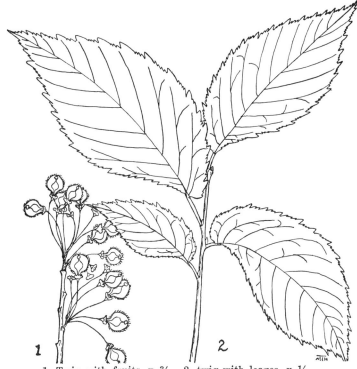

1, Twig with fruits, x ¾. 2, twig with leaves, x ½.

mountains, and we have collected it in Giles County at an elevation of 2,500 feet. Dr. C. E. Moore reports it as common in Shelby County, Tennessee.

Very young twigs usually pubescent, soon becoming glabrous or nearly so; leaves obovate-oblong, up to about 6 inches long, not so fuzzy as those of the Slippery Elm, slightly roughish above, minutely soft-velvety or smooth below, margins doubly serrate; flowers in ample clusters; fruit flat, winged, margins hairy, points of wings incurved. This elm gets to be one of the largest trees in the eastern states. There is one standing at Wethersfield, Connecticut, which is 8 feet 10 inches in diameter four feet from the ground (*Journ. Hered.* **6**: 415. 1915). A section of this elm, in the museum in Raleigh, from Columbus County, N. C., has a diameter of 3 feet 4 inches. The White Elm is one of the most popular shade and lawn trees in the south, as well as in the north, due to its plume-like form, hardiness, and longevity. The elm leaf beetle, *Galerucella xanthomelaena,* that has injured or destroyed so many of the fine elms in the north is present in our area, but does very little damage except to the few English Elms that are cultivated. Occasionally an individual White Elm seems unusually susceptible and suffers considerably every year. If this near immunity of the southern form to the beetle persists in the north, it would seem that future plantings in the north should be obtained from southern stock. Tests should be made. Flowering January 12 to March 26.

A very near relative of the White Elm, and probably only a variety, has been named *U. floridana* by Chapman. It is a swamp tree, somewhat smaller than the White Elm and distinguished from it by the glabrous twigs and slightly different fruits (samaras). Ashe reports it as common in swamps around New Bern, N. C., which seems to be the most northern station known. It extends southward through coastal South Carolina to Florida. We have it from a swamp near Savannah, Georgia.

PLANERA J. F. Gmel.

1. Planera aquatica Gmel. Water Elm, Planer Tree.

THIS is a peculiar slender tree found in swamps (often in water) along the coast from lower North Carolina (Cape Fear River) southward, extending inland to the sandhill region (Cheraw, S. C.). It grows along the Apalachicola and Suwannee rivers in northern Florida (Harper), and ascends the Mississippi through Tennessee.

Bark light brown or gray, separating into scales several inches long; young twigs puberulous; leaves varying greatly, up to 3¼ inches long and 1¾ inches broad in the sterile shoots to much smaller, 1⅙ inches long to almost bract-like in the fertile shoots, elm-like, base oblique, margins coarsely serrate, pale beneath, finely roughened at maturity on both sides; the short petioles slightly hairy; flowers very small, inconspicuous, of three kinds, male, female, and perfect on the same tree; the male flowers in

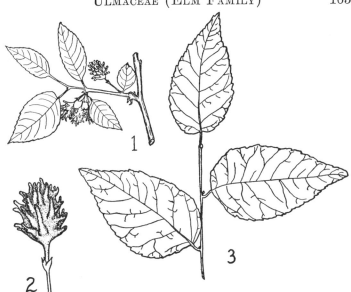

1, Twig with leaves and fruits, x ½. 2, fruit, x 2. 3, large leaves, x ½.

little dense clusters in the axils of the small leaves, female flowers also clustered; fruit a very peculiar drupe about ⅓ of an inch long, the outer part covered with curious plates and processes. In their manuals, both Sargent and Britton say that the flowers appear with the leaves, and Sargent's figures show well developed leaves with the opened flowers. In the southern states flowers appear well before the leaves, and this is stated by both Curtis and Chapman. Plants from Lynche's River, Lee County, S. C., April 1, 1941, in our herbarium show open flowers and no sign of leaves. A tree in a swamp near Cheraw, S. C., measured 1 foot 10⅞ inches in diameter two feet from the ground.

CELTIS* (Tourn.) L.

1. Leaves ovate-lanceolate to oblong-lanceolate, entire or toothed

Celtis laevigata, Hackberry   No. 1

Leaves ovate.................................. 2

2. Leaves usually over two inches long, smooth

Celtis occidentalis, Hackberry   No. 2

Leaves usually not over two inches long, rough above

Celtis georgiana, Hackberry   No. 3

* The genus *Celtis* is a very confusing one, and it is impossible to make any considerable number of specimens agree with the species descriptions.

1. Celtis laevigata Willdenow (C. mississippiensis Bosc). Hackberry, Sugarberry.

THIS tree of medium size is found growing in wet swampy places or along streams of the coastal plain from Virginia to Florida, and near the Mississippi River in Tennessee. We have collections from Davie and Lenoir counties, North Carolina, and Berkeley County, South Carolina, and Colonel's Island, Liberty County, Georgia.

Bark light gray, cracked into scales, and very often with prominent irregular warts; twigs glabrous; leaves prevailingly ovate-lanceolate with long acuminate tips, margins entire or with a few teeth near the end, majority 2-3¼ inches long, both surfaces smooth; flowers perfect or with male and female flowers on the same tree, both on slender glabrous pedicels in the axils of the leaves, male flowers

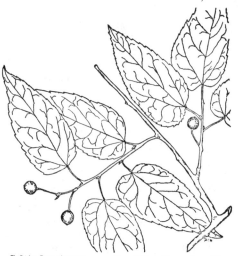

Celtis laevigata var. *Smallii*. Branch with leaves and fruit, x ½.

clustered, female flowers one or two, calyx greenish, 4- or 5-lobed, deciduous, ovary capped with a short style bearing

Various authors also disagree greatly in their concepts. The species as a rule are poorly separated. The margin of the leaf, whether toothed or even has almost no value as a distinguishing character since all or nearly all the species may have entire or toothed margins. The drupe size is also a poor characteristic to go by, although they seem to run a little larger in the *occidentalis* group than in the *laevigata* group. What we are calling *C. laevigata* var. *Smallii* is called by some a species. We are simply calling the variety *Smallii* all plants with toothed leaves but otherwise similar to *C. laevigata*.

two stigmatic lobes; male flowers bearing 4 or 5 stamens, which shed pollen later than the maturity of the stigmas; drupe light orange to orange-red, nearly globose, about ¼ inch thick, the pedicel ¼-½ inch long, usually as long as or longer than the petioles.

Celtis laevigata var. *Smallii* Sargent is like the species except that the leaves are strongly toothed from the tip to or below the middle, often more so on one side than on the other. This variety is much more common in the Carolinas than the typical species. We have collections of this form from Orange, Durham, Bladen, Davie, and Davidson counties in North Carolina and from Darlington County, South Carolina. A tree in Cheraw, S. C., is 3 feet 8 inches in diameter five feet from the ground. This Hackberry has been extensively planted as a street tree in Columbia, S. C., and it still remains there in considerable numbers. It has some good qualities to recommend it to cities as a street tree. It grows rapidly and has light, attractive foliage, but it is not long-lived in such situations and its superficial root system makes it easily uprooted by storms. Flowering April 3, 1933.

2. Celtis occidentalis L. Hackberry, Sugarberry.

THIS tree of medium size is found mostly in rich soil along streams in the mountains south to North Carolina and Tennessee. In Virginia we have collected it at the Falls of the Potomac in Fairfax County and it is reported from the bank of the Chickahominy River near Lanexa and in North Carolina it is found east as far as Orange County.

Leaves ovate with a more abruptly contracted point and varying to much broader than in *C. laevigata*, majority about 2-3¼ inches long and 1¼-2 inches broad, margins strongly toothed to near the base, smooth on both sides; twigs, petioles, and peduncles in our specimens pubescent; drupes about ¼ inch thick, nearly spherical, usually darker than in *C. laevigata;* peduncle ⅜-⅝ inch long; distinctly longer than the petioles. Ayers and Ashe say that in the Appalachians this tree may reach a height of 90 feet and a diameter of 2 feet.

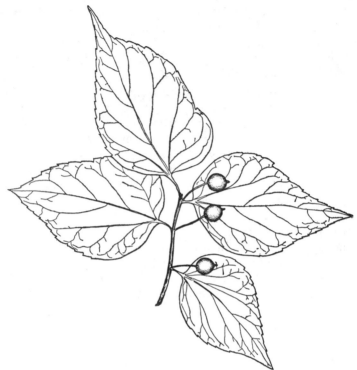

Celtis occidentalis. Twig with leaves and mature fruits, x ½.

A shrubby form of this species occurs on rocky hillsides or bluffs at Chapel Hill and in Yancey County, North Carolina. It cannot be distinguished otherwise from the tree forms. It is not *C. georgiana*. This is something we have not seen described anywhere.

Celtis occidentalis var. *crassifolia* A. Gray is scarcely distinguishable from *C. occidentalis*, except for the very rough upper surface of the leaves and the hairy veins beneath; twigs, petioles, and peduncles pubescent; drupes in our specimens yellowish brown, length of peduncles and petioles as in *C. occidentalis*. We have this plant from Lenoir County, North Carolina, and from Giles County, Virginia. According to Sargent this is the southern form of *C. occidentalis*, the typical form not coming as far south as North Carolina, but we have the typical form at Chapel Hill with leaves quite smooth above. The distinctions between the type and variety are to us unsatisfactory. In our collections the leaves with larger teeth are smooth above, while those with fewer small teeth are rough above, the opposite of the characters given.

Another variety, *C. occidentalis* var. *canina* Sarg. (*C. canina* Raf.) with distinctions very obscure in the descriptions, is said to occur in northwestern Georgia and thence northward and westward.

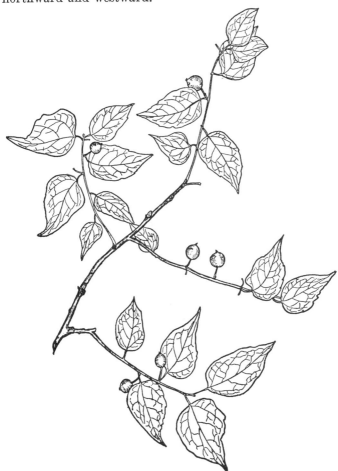

Celtis georgiana. Branch with leaves and mature fruits, x ½.

3. Celtis georgiana Small. Georgia Hackberry.

THIS shrub or irregular small tree is found in all our states mostly on hills in the piedmont and lower mountains. In the herbarium of the University of Tennessee there are specimens from five counties in Tennessee, from Davidson County eastward.

Very young twigs often pubescent, older twigs of the year obscurely hairy or glabrous; leaves ovate, abruptly long-pointed, toothed, particularly when young, or nearly even, small, mostly about 1¼-2 inches long and up to 1⅜ inches broad, rough above, slightly hairy on the veins beneath; petioles and pedicels more or less pubescent; drupes globose, about ¼ inch thick, pedicel short, ³⁄₁₆-¼ inch long, usually longer than the short petioles. A tree in Chapel Hill is 17 feet high and 11 inches in diameter one foot above the ground where it branches into two trunks which are 5 inches in diameter.

MORACEAE (MULBERRY FAMILY)

MORUS (Tourn.) L.

Leaves more or less tomentose below, harsh above; fruit
    purple or nearly black
               Morus rubra, Red Mulberry   No. 1
Leaves smooth on both sides; fruit white or pink
               Morus alba, White Mulberry   No. 2

1. Morus rubra L. Red Mulberry.

THIS is a small rather scarce tree of fertile valleys and hillsides found throughout our states. In the Carolinas it is most often found near the coast and in the middle section. and occasionally in the low mountains.

Leaves ovate, hairy, rough above and soft tomentose below (the leaves on young plants may be very large and variously lobed); flowers dioecious, male flowers in light green spikes, female flowers in a short inflorescence that becomes the so-called "berry," which is not a berry but a

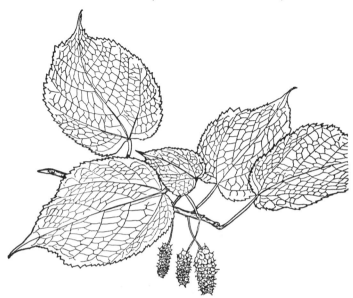

Twig with leaves and nearly mature fruits, x ½.

multiple fruit as in the pineapple; petals absent, one pistil
to a flower, the ovaries developing into small dry pods. The
edible part is the calyx lobes of the flower. A section of
this mulberry tree in the museum in Raleigh from Davidson
County, N. C., has a diameter of 1 foot 1½ inches. Flowering from April 3 to May 4.

2. Morus alba L. White Mulberry.

THE White Mulberry, a native of China, is naturalized in a number
of places in our states. It is an attractive small tree with smooth
shining leaves and whitish to pink or mottled fruits. As in the case
of the Paper Mulberry and the Sassafras the leaves are peculiar in
frequently being of two distinct shapes on the same tree or twig.
The first leaves of the year's growth are often strongly lobed, the
later ones only toothed. This tree is desirable for narrow streets and
lawns, but only male trees should be planted on streets as the abundant fruits are a nuisance under foot. The fruits are attractive to
birds, and one or more female trees somewhere about the place are
appreciated by them. Flowering in late March and early April.

   Morus nigra L., a native of Eurasia and much like *M. alba* but distinguished from it by having black fruits, is reported as sometimes
spontaneous in our states.

Morus alba. Leaf; twig with leaves and fruit. All x ⅖.

BROUSSONETIA L'Her.

1. Broussonetia papyrifera (L.) Vent. Paper Mulberry.

THE Paper Mulberry, a native of China and Japan, sprouts freely from the roots and when once planted often spreads as a troublesome weed. It is a small tree with greenish bark, hairy twigs, and leaves that are rough above and velvety beneath. As in the case of the White Mulberry the leaves are of two distinct forms, strongly lobed or without lobes. The multiple fruit is spherical, about ¾ inch thick, arising as in the true mulberry from many separate individual flowers closely packed together. At maturity the red drupes project visibly beyond the calyx lobes. Nearly all the trees in the Carolinas are male, but there are a few female trees in some places on the South Carolina coast as on James Island. The male trees seem hardier than the females (see *Science*, Jan. 12, 1944, p. 40).

MACLURA Nutt.

1. Maclura pomifera Schn. Osage Orange.

THE Osage Orange, said to be native only west of the Mississippi, has escaped sparingly. It is a thorny tree (rarely thorns absent on practically all branches) with shiny, ovate leaves and large, yellowish green fruits on the female trees. The Indians are reported to have eaten the fruit but it is a very inferior food. Squirrels tear up the fruit for the seeds. In April 1933 we found a tree with three large shoots, two of them about 1½ feet in diameter, in a swamp in Dooly County, Georgia. From our observations of the Osage Orange this tree must have been at least fifty years old. Is it not possible that it may be native in a few swamps in Georgia and the Gulf States? The heart wood is a bright orange yellow color and very hard and durable. About fifty years ago this plant had a great though short vogue as a hedge fence tree. The Osage Orange is related to the Breadfruit and Jackfruit of the tropics, both highly prized for their edible fruits. Flowering May 10, 1916.

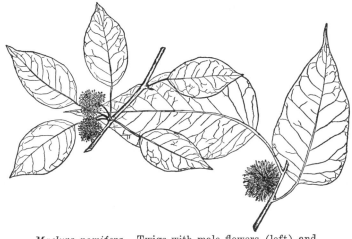

Maclura pomifera. Twigs with male flowers (left) and female flowers (right), x ⅓.

MAGNOLIACEAE (MAGNOLIA FAMILY)

MAGNOLIA* L.

1. Leaves evergreen................................. 2
   Leaves deciduous................................. 3
2. Leaves more than 6 inches long, rusty pubescent or green beneath
   Magnolia grandiflora, Magnolia   No. 3
   Leaves less than 6 inches long, white beneath
   Magnolia virginiana, Sweet Bay   No. 4
3. Leaves less than 6 inches long.................... 4
   Leaves over 6 inches long........................ 5
4. Flowers white
   Magnolia virginiana, Sweet Bay   No. 4
   Flowers canary-yellow
   Magnolia acuminata var. *cordata.*
        Yellow-flowered Magnolia   No. 2
5. Leaves eared at the base........................ 6
   Leaves not eared at the base.................... 9
6. Leaves over 14 inches long...................... 7
   Leaves less than 14 inches long................. 8
7. Fruit nearly spherical
   Magnolia macrophylla, Large-leaved Magnolia   No. 8
   Fruit more elongated
   Magnolia Ashei, Ashe's Magnolia   No. 9
8. Leaves averaging not over 8 inches long, more angular than in the following; petals about 3 inches long; fruits 2-2½ inches long
   Magnolia pyramidata, Southern Cucumber Tree   No. 7

* In all magnolias the seeds when mature are red and hang out from the cone on delicate white strings. They have a soft covering with a strong aromatic taste and are eaten by birds.

Leaves averaging more than 8 inches long; petals
about 5-6 inches long; fruits 2½-3½ inches long
Magnolia Fraseri, Mountain Magnolia   No. 6
9. Leaves averaging over 12 inches long
Magnolia tripetala, Umbrella Tree   No. 5
Leaves averaging less than 12 inches long
Magnolia acuminata, Cucumber Tree   No. 1

1. Magnolia acuminata L. Cucumber Tree.

THIS is a large tree which in one form or another extends
from southern Canada to Alabama and westward to Illinois, occurring in our territory in or near the mountains.
The typical form is described as having large greenish yellow flowers, as found in its northern range, and this is
generally cited as extending all the way south to Alabama.
Ashe has given the varietal name *aurea* to the tree in the
southern mountains that differs from the northern form in
having smaller and more yellow flowers (*Bull. Charleston
Mus.* **13**: 28, 1917; *Torreya* **31**: 37-38, 1931). This is what
Small (Fl. SE. U. S., p. 451) referred to as *M. cordata.*

Twig with leaves and fruit, x ⅓.

Until more collecting is done in our mountains we cannot be sure whether the northern large-flowered form occurs in the south, since all the flowers we have seen (as at Highlands, N. C.) are of the small yellow variety. So far as we know, there is no difference except in the flowers and perhaps in smaller more knotty cones of the southern trees. The following description refers to our southern form.

Leaves smaller than in the other mountain magnolias, about 6-12 inches long and 3-5 inches broad, whitish pubescent beneath; flowers about 1¾-2 inches high, sepals three, small, unequal, green with yellow tint, outer petals same color but slightly more yellow inside and toward the tip, inner petals clear golden yellow tinted with green only toward the base; fruits narrow, red, 1-3 inches long, resembling a cucumber; often quite knotty in appearance, as those little fruit pods of the cone that do not develop seeds remain small; seeds bright red, flattened obovate. A section of this tree in the museum in Raleigh from Macon County, North Carolina, has a diameter of 3 feet 10½ inches. The largest tree of this species yet known seems to be one reported by Prof. S. A. Cain from the Great Smoky Mountains that was 5 feet 9 inches in diameter at breast height. The Cucumber Tree is handsome in cultivation.

2. **Magnolia acuminata** var. **cordata** Sarg. (**M. cordata** Michx.) **Yellow-flowered Magnolia.**

SINCE its discovery by Michaux over one hundred years ago there has been in cultivation in the United States a small magnolia up to 25 or 30 feet high with yellow flowers that until recent years has been lost in the wild state. In 1913 L. A. Berckmans rediscovered the plant in two places near Augusta, Georgia. It has usually been considered as occurring only in the lower piedmont and upper coastal plain of South Carolina and Georgia. Its distribution has been imperfectly known and in the study of this subject by Coker (*Journ. Eli. Mitch. Sci. Soc.* **59**: 81. 1943) the range is extended into central South Carolina, several counties in eastern Georgia not mentioned in our second edition, and as far north as Moore and Anson counties in North Carolina.

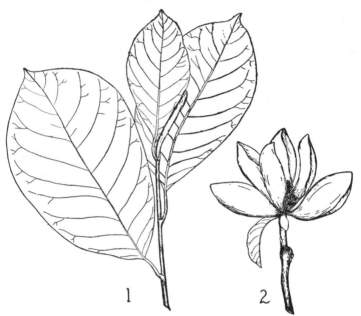

1, Twig with leaves. 2, flower. All x ⅓.

Ashe reported this species from Alabama but later (*Torreya* **31**: 37. 1931) considered these trees as *M. acuminata* var. *alabamensis.*

Leaves oblong-obovate to elliptic, blade usually 3½-6 (rarely 7) inches long and 3-4¼ inches broad, smooth above and pubescent below, usually pointed at the apex, the base rounded or cuneate; petioles pubescent, about ¼-¾ inch long; twigs pubescent; flowers up to 2 inches high, petals six, inner petals clear golden yellow, outer petals paler, about citron yellow; sepals three, membranaceous, up to ½ inch long; fruit a cylindrical or usually knotty cone, up to 1½ inches long.

Magnolia acuminata var. *cordata* differs from var. *aurea,* so far as we have yet found, only in the smaller size of trees (rare exceptions), pubescent twigs, somewhat smaller and more broadly ovate leaves, and in geographical range. For a fuller discussion of these forms, see article by Coker cited above.

3. **Magnolia grandiflora** L. [**M. foetida** (L.) Sarg.]. **Magnolia, Bull Bay.**

This is a large tree found in swamps and along streams

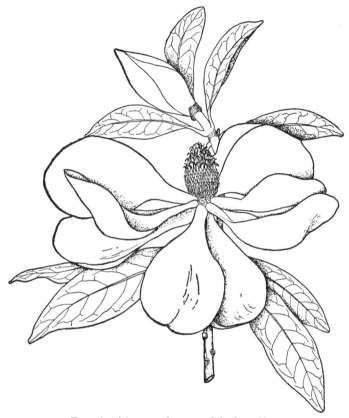

Branch with open flower and bud, x ¼.

from the southeastern corner of North Carolina southward
near the coast through Florida and westward. According
to our observations, the tree is scarce from Charleston northward. At Gause's Landing, Brunswick County, North
Carolina (7 miles from S. C. line), H. A. Rankin reports
two or three good sized trees in a swamp right on the
sound. Mr. Lionel Melvin reports that good sized trees
also occur in a swamp in northeastern Bladen County,
N. C., but we have not been able to check this. Well developed specimens may be seen near Murrell's Inlet on the
road to Myrtle Beach.

Leaves long-elliptic, pointed at both ends, the even,

more or less wavy margin slightly revolute, thick, evergreen, shiny, dark green above and rusty pubescent to
quite smooth and green beneath, 5-10 inches long, very
variable on different trees in width in proportion to length
of the blade, e.g., 3 inches wide, 6¾ inches long, 1⅜ inch
wide, 9¾ inches long; flowers large, white, fragrant, sepals
3, petals usually 6, rarely 9 or 12; fruits reddish (dull
grayish red to bright red), 3-4½ inches long. This magnolia is common in cultivation in the south and is probably
the finest of all broad-leaved evergreen trees. The tree is
very variable in both leaves and habit, and some forms are
much handsomer than others. It is planted as far north as
Washington, D. C., but is not fully hardy there. Near
Chapel Hill young seedlings are not rarely found in the
woods. We saw fair sized cultivated trees in flower about
five miles west of Brevard, N. C., on September 3, 1932.
The largest specimen we have seen is the old ''Waddell
Magnolia'' at Como, Hertford County, North Carolina.
This tree measured 5 feet 2½ inches in diameter four and a
half feet from the ground and had a limb spread of 82 feet.
It begins to flower in Chapel Hill about May 21.

Ashe has described a form of this species with slightly
different leaf characters (*Torreya* **31**: 37. 1931) from
Okaloosa County, Florida, under the name *M. foetida*
forma *margaretta*.

4. **Magnolia virginiana** L. (**M. glauca** L.) **Sweet Bay.**

THIS is a small tree found in swamps or near the water in
the coastal plain in all our area, often extending inland
for some distance. In North Carolina it is found sparsely
in the middle district as far as Moore and Durham counties and, strange to say, occurs much farther west in Iredell, Yadkin, Surry, and Polk counties. In South Carolina
it is found inland to Richland County and in Georgia to
Carroll County. It is reported in Madison County in western Tennessee.

Leaves small, averaging less than 5 inches long, white
beneath, evergreen or partly so; flowers white, smaller than
those of any other American magnolia and very fragrant,

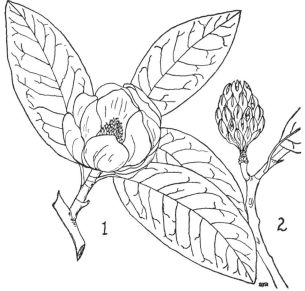

1, Branch with leaves and a flower. 2, twig
with a fruit. All x ½.

petals usually 8; fruits small, 1½-2 inches long, dull or
brownish red or nearly green at maturity. The Sweet Bay
blooms for an extended period, mostly in June, but as early
as April 29, 1941 (cultivated in Chapel Hill). Late flowers were seen in Horry County, S. C., on July 14, 1932,
and ripe fruit with seed exposed were collected the same
week in the same county. Even in Chapel Hill, ripe cones
were found in the Arboretum on July 22, 1932.

The southern form of Sweet Bay, said to reach a height
of 90 feet (*Bot. Gaz.* **67**: 231. 1919), with narrow leaves,
tomentose peduncles and branchlets has been given the
name *M. virginiana* var. *australis* by Sargent and the name
M. australis by Ashe (*Torreya* **31**: 39. 1931), who does not
mention Sargent's variety. However, the last-mentioned
form overlaps with the typical more northern broad-leaved,
smooth-peduncled form in South Carolina and Georgia.

Ashe has described from Florida as *M. australis* var.
parva (*M. virginiana* var. *parva* Ashe) a shrubby plant not
over three feet high. We have a specimen from Columbus

County, N. C. (J. S. Holmes coll.), which has leaves only 2-2⅔ inches long and petals 1⅜-1¾ inches long. This is very close to or the same as Ashe's plant. We suspect it of being a form produced by fires.

5. Magnolia tripetala L. Umbrella Tree.

THIS is a small tree found near streams and in damp rich soil in Virginia, the Carolinas, Tennessee, and western Georgia. It is most frequent in the piedmont and rare in the mountains, but is usually much scattered and is absent over considerable areas. In most of the coastal plain it is confined to the neighborhood of a few rivers. The station for *M. tripetala* that is nearest the coast, so far as our records go, is on the bluffs of the Savannah River near Two Sisters Ferry, Effingham County, Georgia (Dr. Francis Harper, in

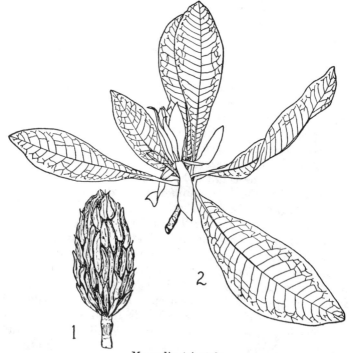

Magnolia tripetala
1, Fruit, x ⅓. 2, twig with leaves and flower, x ⅑.

letter of June 4, 1940). The highest stations we have for it are Valley River Mountains south of Andrews, Cherokee County, near Bryson City, North Carolina, and on Big Stony in Giles County, Virginia. This magnolia is as plentiful around Chapel Hill as anywhere we know of. In certain well drained branch flats here there are hundreds of young trees in small areas.

Bark gray, smooth, leaves large, 10-23½ inches long and 3½-9 inches broad, glabrous above and tomentose or nearly glabrous below; sepals 3, long and narrow, greenish white; petals creamy white, 6 or 9, up to 6 inches long, with a very disagreeable odor; fruits oblong, less than 5 inches long, red at maturity, nearly as handsome as in *M. Fraseri*. Flowering April 15 to May 3.

6. Magnolia Fraseri Walt.   **Mountain Magnolia, Ear-leaved Cucumber Tree.**

THIS is a small tree found in cool soil throughout the moun-

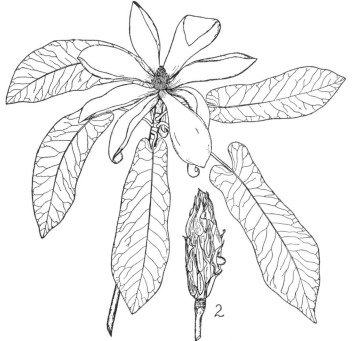

1, Branch with flower, x ⅙. 2, fruit, x ⅓.

tains, rarely in other locations, in our area from Virginia to Georgia. According to Sargent, it extends as far east as Aiken County, South Carolina. We have collected it in North Carolina as far east as the bluffs along the Pacolet River between Saluda and Tryon in Polk County. In Virginia we have seen it only in the Blue Ridge Mountains. Cocks reports *M. Fraseri* from Louisiana, but a good collection we have from him shows it to be *M. pyramidata*. It has also been reported from Mississippi but investigation by Harbison has shown that report also to be based on *M. pyramidata*.

Bark brown, smooth; leaves large, about 8-12 inches long, obovate-spatulate, auricled at the base, glabrous, clustered at the ends of the branches as in the Umbrella Tree; flowers large, petals 6 or 9, averaging 5-6 inches long, creamy white, fragrant, not fetid, the odor resembling that of *M. grandiflora;* fruit red at maturity and shaped like a cucumber, about 2½-3½ inches long; seeds dull red, flattened obovate, suspended on white strings. The large, well-formed and brilliant scarlet cones of *M. Fraseri* are the most beautiful of any of the genus. They are far finer than the much smaller knotty cones of *M. acuminata*. They show almost full color by early August and retain this color well into September. The cones of *M. grandiflora* and *macrophylla* are larger, but the color in both is much duller. Sargent gives the upper dimensions of this tree as 18 inches in diameter and says that the largest trees are probably found on the upper Savannah River in South Carolina. However, in the Primeval Forest in Macon County, N. C., there stands a tree that is 22⅖ inches in diameter at four and a half feet from the ground. It is interesting to note in Walter's *Flora Caroliniana* (1788), in which it was first described, there is a good colored plate of this species. In full bloom at Caesar's Head, S. C., on May 19, 1935, altitude 2,800 feet.

7. **Magnolia pyramidata** Pursh. **Southern Cucumber Tree.**
THIS is a small tree which is very similar to *M. Fraseri* in general appearance and often mistaken for it. It takes the place of the latter in the coastal region, rarely lower pied-

1, Twig with leaves. 2, mature fruit. All x ⅓.

mont (Macon County, Ga.), from central South Carolina
through southern Georgia and northwestern Florida to
Louisiana (see under *M. Fraseri*). The South Carolina station is on the LeConte plantation about ten miles east of
Columbia (Coker, *The State*, Columbia, May 25, 1937).
Bartram (*Travels*, p. 277 of 1928 ed.) mentions a magnolia
on the banks of the Altamaha River which he compares
with *M. auriculata* [*M. Fraseri*] but it is probably *M.
pyramidata*. We have specimens of this tree from Gadsden County in northwestern Florida and from Louisiana
(Cocks, Ashe). We have found a tree at Tallulah Falls,
Georgia, that we are placing in this species with some
hesitation. The fruits are typical and the leaves practically
so, but some are rather large. We have not seen the flowers from this locality and they are needed for a certain
identification. Dr. Julian Miller says that this magnolia

is native in Mobile, Ala., and Harbison has found it at Elba Junction (Coffee County) and at Selma, Alabama.

Leaves obovate-spatulate, auricled at the base, tips usually bluntly pointed, as a rule not over 8½ inches long and 4½ inches wide, pale beneath; flowers creamy white, petals up to 3¼ inches long; fruit oblong, rose colored, 2-2½ inches long, seeds ovoid, red. *Magnolia pyramidata* differs from *M. Fraseri* in the smaller leaves, flowers, and fruits, and in the more rhombic and abruptly pointed leaves. For a good figure of this species see Sargent's *Trees and Shrubs*, Part III, plate 51, 1903.

8. Magnolia macrophylla Michx.   Large-leaved Magnolia.

This is a rare and very local tree, which is found in rich valleys from North Carolina to western Florida and westward. For details on the distribution see below.

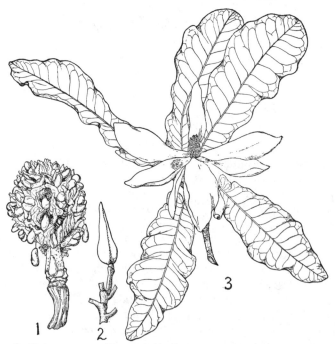

1, Mature cone with hanging seeds, x ⅓.   2, twig with bud, x ½₁₂.   3, twig with leaves and open flower, x ½₁₂.

Leaves very large, 20-32 inches long and up to a foot wide, narrowed and heart-shaped at the base, white and pubescent beneath; young twigs, petioles, and pedicels also softly whitish pubescent; flower bud up to 9 inches long, pointed, the three wrapping sepals green, turning dull yellowish in the open flower; flowers large, up to 18½ inches across, creamy white, petals 6, the 3 inner narrower than the outer and with a diffuse purple blotch near the base, the outer in our flowers without any sign of such a blotch; odor of flowers rather pleasing to some, to others scarcely so, about intermediate between that of *M. grandiflora* and *M. tripetala;* fruit an ovoid to globose cone, up to 3 inches long, rose colored when mature; seeds bright orange red, triangular-elliptic, about ½ inch long and ¼ inch broad. The flowers of the specimens we describe above are much larger than those given in the manuals. However, Weatherby (*Rhodora* 28: 35. 1926) refers to Ashe's observations and herbarium specimens which approximate the sizes we give. Michaux in the *North American Silva* says: "sometimes 8 or 9 inches in diameter." Sargent gives them as 10-12 inches and Britton up to about 12 inches. There is a strange discrepancy in the description of the flowers of this magnolia and the flowers of the Statesville tree described above. All the sources available to us except Miss Eaton's painting (see reference below) state either explicitly or by implication that all the petals are blotched near the base. Michaux says that the blotch is purple. Britton says that the petals are purple or rose-colored within. In our flowers the diffuse blotch was purplish and only the inner petals showed any trace of it. Dr. Charles Raynal of Statesville, N. C., reports (letter of May 31, 1937) that the purple blotch is very variable and says: "In some flowers it is large, deep and even. On others it is small and pale. On still others it is entirely absent." See also his article with photographs in *American Forests* 44: 204, 1938. The figure shown in Britton's *Trees* and Britton and Brown's *Flora* gives a very erroneous appearance of the sepals. The sepals, in fact, are very long, in ours almost exactly 6 inches long and about 1½-1¾ inches broad in the middle, from thence narrowing upwards to a slightly rounded point. For a photograph of the flower and leaves see *Nature Magazine* 11: 184, 1928; for a colored plate by Miss Mary Eaton of leaves, flower, and fruit see *Better Homes and Gardens*, page 11, September, 1933. Flowering at Statesville, N. C., on May 24, 1932, and fruits mature on September 4 of same year.

Michaux discovered this tree near Charlotte, N. C., in 1789. Curtis says: "It is a rare product east of the Alleghanies, having been found only on the Chattahoochie in Georgia, in Middle Florida, and in Lincoln County of this State [N. C.]. . . . In Lincoln it occurs in several places not far from the road between Lincolnton and Tuckaseegee Ford, as near Smith's, the Moore Mine, and Huntersville, 6, 10, and 18 miles from the former place." J. H. Redfield (*Bull. Torr. Bot. Club* 6: 332. 1879) reports it from near Statesville, N. C. In 1932, accompanied by Dr. Charles Raynal, we visited the location near Statesville. Here it is found along Fourth Creek and its tributaries, often in dense groves, in a narrow strip near the creek for several miles toward the Rowan County line. Some of these trees are up to 50 feet in height and one foot in diameter. A fine lot of flowering branches from this place sent to us by Dr. Raynal showed flowers up to 18½ inches across. House (*Woody Plants of Western N. C.* 1913) says that *M. macrophylla* also grows along the French Broad and Pigeon rivers in North Carolina. Hunter (*South Atlantic* 3: No. 2, 1878) reports it as found in Gaston County, North Carolina. He is in error in thinking that Thomas Nuttall first discovered the tree. The occurrence in Gaston County has recently been confirmed by Dr. H. L. Blomquist who found it near the Charlotte-Gastonia highway about one mile east of the Gastonia Country Club (specimens in Duke Herb.), and by Dr. Dorisse Howe who collected it on the south side of Spencer Mountain six or seven miles east of Gastonia (U. N. C. Herb.). There is in the Duke Herbarium a specimen of *M. macrophylla* collected by R. K. Godfrey at Lake Johnson, Wake County, N. C., far out of its presently known range. We assume that this was wild but there is no note on the label to this effect.

9. **Magnolia Ashei** Weatherby. **Ashe's Magnolia.**

THIS small tree up to 25 feet high or a large shrub, named for W. W. Ashe by C. A. Weatherby, has been found in western Florida along Rogue and Rocky creeks in Okaloosa County and in Walton and Santa Rosa counties. It is also reported from Texas. We have some of the type specimens in the Ashe Herbarium.

Leaves large, obovate-spatulate, auricled at the base, blade up to 22 inches long and to 12½ inches broad, at maturity dark green and smooth above, whitish and sparingly pubescent below; petiole pubescent, up to 3 inches long; flowers creamy white, petals up to 5¾ inches long, the three large ones up to 3 inches broad and the three small ones up to 2¼ inches broad; fruit ovoid-cylindrical, 2-4½ inches long and 1-2 inches broad, seeds flattened, about ¼-⅓ inch long and ³⁄₁₆-¼ inch broad. In bloom on April 26, 1925, and fruits mature on June 6, 1925, in Oka-

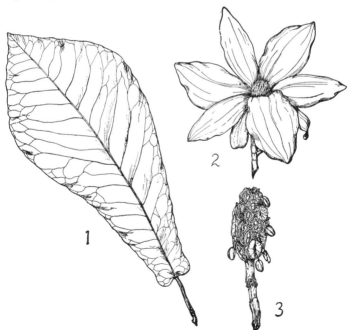

1, Leaf, x ⅙. 2, flower, x ⅙. 3, fruit, x ⅓.

loosa County, Florida. For a photograph of shrubby plants in flower in Florida see *Bull. N. Y. Bot. Gard.* **34:** 150, 1933. This is closely related to *M. macrophylla*, but differs from that species in that the leaf is less pubescent below, the flower is much smaller, the fruit is smaller, more elongated, and with much smaller beaks on the pods (carpels), and the seeds are smaller and thinner. *Magnolia Ashei* has larger leaves and flowers and the beaks of the pods of the fruit are less prominent than in *M. pyramidata*.

LIRIODENDRON L.

1. Liriodendron tulipifera L.   **Tulip Tree, Yellow Poplar.**
THIS large timber tree is common in rich soil throughout our area as far south as Putnam County, Florida.

Bark gray, closely ridged; leaves truncate with four lobes and shallowly notched at the end, smooth, dark green above and light green below, turning a beautiful yellow in the fall; flowers structurally as in Magnolia, tulip-shaped,

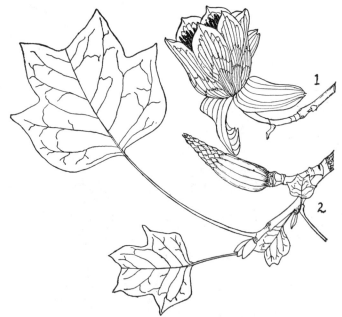

1, Flower.   2, twig with leaves and fruit.   All x ⅓.

petals light green marked with orange. The largest tree in North Carolina of which we have a record is the "Reems Creek Poplar" in Buncombe County. According to the latest measurements, this tree was 198 feet high and 10 feet 11 inches in diameter four feet above the ground (*Journ. Hered.* **6:** Sept. 1915). Sad to report, this magnificent tree, probably the largest tulip tree in the world, was burned in April, 1935, leaving only about 30 feet of the trunk standing. The tree was estimated by Harvard experts to be 1,000 or more years old. The large Tulip Tree on Sugar Camp Creek on the steep slopes of Mt. Mitchell in Yancey County is 9 feet 4 inches in diameter three feet from the ground. Other well known individual trees of this species in North Carolina are the "Wiley Bailey Poplar" in Davie County which is 7 feet 8 inches in diameter three feet from the ground, and the Battle Branch Poplar at Huntsville in Yadkin County which is 6 feet 5 inches in diameter at the same distance from the ground. The historic "Davie Poplar" on the University of North Carolina campus is this species. It was under this tree that General Davie took lunch when in 1789 he and his committee selected Chapel Hill as the seat of the University. One of the best known Tulip Trees in our whole area is the George Washington Tulip Tree at Falls Church, Virginia. According to tradition, George Washington tied his horse to a ring in this tree when he worshipped there before the Revolutionary War. This old tree has been estimated to be at least 300 years old and is over 6 feet in diameter four feet above the ground. Each year the Davey Tree Experts prune, repair, and fertilize one historic tree selected by the Daughters of the American Revolution. This tree was selected in 1932. However, a still larger poplar in Virginia is on the lawn of Westover on the James River, measured in May, 1936. It was 7 feet 1 inch in diameter five feet from the ground. The Tulip Poplar is a very fine tree in cultivation but the tender bark is easily injured and nearly all old trees are hollow. It is especially valuable for veneering as it takes a higher polish than any other American wood. Flowering begins from about April 3 to April 17.

ANONACEAE (CUSTARD APPLE FAMILY)

ASIMINA Adans.

1. Asimina triloba Dunal. Pawpaw.

This is a small tree or shrub, rarely over 15 feet high or 3 inches in diameter, which grows in rich low grounds and is of wide distribution. It is most frequent in the piedmont, rarer in the coastal plain and mountains, and extends as far south as central Florida. It is not uncommon on the Cape Fear River in Cumberland County, North Carolina (H. A. Rankin).

Leaves obovate-lanceolate, resembling those of the Umbrella Tree but smaller, 4-12 inches long, and alternate along the branches instead of clustered at the ends, giving off a distinctively fetid odor when bruised; flowers a peculiar reddish brown color, about 1¾ inches broad with 3 sepals and 6 petals in two rows; pistils several and separate, ripening into 1-5 clustered fruits which are greenish yellow, short, thick, reminding one of a short irregular banana.

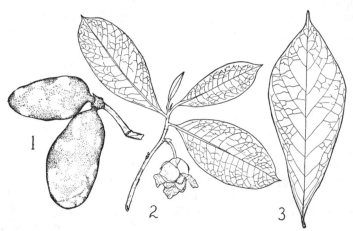

1, Fruits, x ⅓.   2, twig with flower, x ⅓.   3, leaf, x ⅙.

It is the only representative in temperate America of the large family of tropical trees producing highly valued fruits as Sweetsop, Soursop, Cherimoya, Custard Apple, etc. The fruits of the Pawpaw are also edible and much liked by some. It is a handsome tree in cultivation. The flowers are open in infancy while still very small and green, as is the case of the Snowdrop Tree, Sparkleberry, and Squaw Huckleberry. Flowering from April 8 to May 7.

Several other shrubby pawpaws occur in our territory. *Asimina parviflora* extends at least as far north as Orange County, N. C., the others being confined to Florida and southern Georgia. For good photographs of pawpaws and hybrids, see *Journal of Heredity* **32:** 83, 1941, and for named varieties, see U. S. Department of Agriculture Leaflet No. 179.

LAURACEAE (LAUREL FAMILY)

PERSEA (Plum.) Gaertn. f.

Twigs tomentose; peduncles usually 2-3 inches long
Persea palustris, Red Bay No. 1
Twigs slightly hairy or nearly glabrous; peduncles ½-1 inch long
Persea Borbonia, Smooth Red Bay No. 2

1. **Persea palustris** (Raf.) Sargent. [**P. pubescens** (Pursh) Sargent]. **Red Bay, Swamp Bay.**

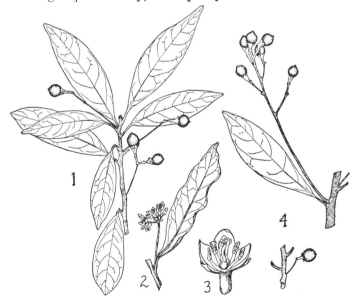

1 and 4, Twigs with mature fruits, x ⅓. 2, twig with flowers, x ⅓.
3, section of flower, x 2.

THIS is a small evergreen aromatic tree which is found in the eastern swamps of the Carolinas, western Georgia, and throughout most of Florida.

New twigs and leaf stalks rusty tomentose; leaves elliptic to lanceolate, 3-6 inches long and 1-1¾ inches wide, velvety beneath, margins entire; flowers small, several (up to 20) clustered on a common peduncle which is usually 1½-2 inches long, some much shorter (down to ⅝ inch long) on the same tree, sepals 3, small, greenish, petals 3, creamy, stamens 9, peculiar in having four window-like openings in the anther; fruit a dark blue berry about ⅜ inch long. This is the common Red Bay throughout most of the coastal plain. Flowering in cultivation at Chapel Hill June 22, 1932.

Fernald (*Rhodora* **44:** 399. 1942) reports a glabrous form of *P. palustris* which he names *laevifolia,* but which is quite different from the following glabrous species, *P. Borbonia.*

2. **Persea Borbonia** (L.) Spreng. **Smooth Red Bay.**

THIS is a small tree similar to the above, which inhabits

Branch with leaves and mature fruits, x ½.

swamps near the sea but it is much less common in its typical form than the Red Bay and apparently more nearly confined to a narrow coastal strip from Virginia to Georgia, but more widely distributed in Florida.

Twigs slightly hairy or nearly glabrous; leaves thick, rather narrow, 2-4 inches long and pointed at both ends, shiny green above, pale and nearly smooth beneath; flowers small, creamy, several on a common peduncle that is usually not more than an inch long; fruit a dark blue berry, oval to subglobose, minutely pointed, about ⅜ inch long, with one large seed.

Our Red Bays are universally treated as two species but the distinctive characters are vague and unsatisfactory. The differences emphasized are long peduncles, smaller fruits, and the twigs brown-tomentose the first year, wearing down to a pubescence the second year for *P. palustris;* short peduncles, larger fruits, and glabrous or nearly glabrous twigs and leaves for *P. Borbonia.* None of these points is by any means consistent and only the extremes are satisfactorily separated. Both are found on the coast but *P. Borbonia* rarely extends inland except in Florida. We have a collection from New Hanover County, N. C., showing on the same branch flowers single with a peduncle scarcely ⅛ inch long and flowers clustered with a peduncle ⅝-1½ inches long; leaf blades 2-2½ inches long and ⅗-1 inch wide; twigs and leaves copiously pubescent; fruits only 5⁄16 inch long. Small has described a small tree or shrub from the eastern coast of Florida as *Persea littoralis.*

SASSAFRAS Nees.

1. **Sassafras variifolium** (Salisb.) Ktze. **Sassafras.**

THIS is a small aromatic tree which is common in dry soil, especially in abandoned fields, through our area and extends as a shrub beyond an elevation of 5,000 feet on the slopes of the mountains. In Florida it is usually a shrub (Harper).

Bark roughly furrowed; leaves thin, variously shaped, with or without lobes; flowers of two sexes borne on differ-

1, Twig with male flowers, x ⅔.   2, branch with
leaves and fruits, x ½.

ent trees, pale yellow-green, in small racemes; fruit a
berry-like blue drupe which is seated in the thickened
bright red calyx cup on a red stalk thickened at the top.
The male tree is very ornamental in flower, the female much
less so but compensates for this when in fruit. The Sassafras, in fact, is one of the most decorative trees we have.
It is long-lived and almost free from disease, deep green,
with rounded crown and could be very effectively used as a
more or less formal park or street tree. In the middle and
Gulf states the tree sometimes reaches the height of 90 feet.
A specimen at Horsham, Pennsylvania (16 miles north of
Philadelphia), is 5 feet in diameter four feet from the
ground (*Journ. Hered.* **6:** 417. 1915). In the Carolinas it
is very rarely over 2 feet in diameter. A tea made of the
root bark is often used as a spring tonic for children and
is not unpleasant, but its medicinal value is doubtful. The

oil made from the whole root is widely used as a flavoring, as in the compound syrup of sarsaparilla; the pith from the stem is used in the preparation of a soothing application for inflamed eyes. A. A. Rowell (*Bull. Charleston Mus.* **14:** 17. 1918), in describing the excavation work on an Indian burial mound in Greenville County, S. C., states that above the skeleton, supposedly of an Indian chief, they found two pieces of the trunk of a Sassafras tree that must have been twenty inches in diameter, and that most of the wood, though it had been in the mound, he estimates, for five hundred years or more ''was as sound as though it had been placed there but yesterday,'' and that ''the fragrance was so powerful that it filled the air about us with its pleasant odor.'' Flowering from March 16 to April 13.

The beautiful evergreen Camphor Tree, *Cinnamomum,* used as an ornamental in the south, is a member of the same family.

HAMAMELIDACEAE (WITCH HAZEL FAMILY)

HAMAMELIS L.

1. **Hamamelis virginiana L. Witch Hazel.**

This plant attains tree size only in the mountains where it is found up to an elevation of 4,000 feet, but as a shrub it is common along streams and moist woods through the piedmont, less common through the coastal region in all our area as far south as northern Florida.

Twigs of the year's growth rusty pubescent; leaves oval to elliptic, up to 6 inches long and 3 inches broad, unequal at the base, margins wavy or barely toothed, under surface rusty pubescent with stellate hairs when young, becoming less so at maturity; petioles also pubescent; flowers with long slender petals, varying from pale to bright yellow, the latter by far the more ornamental, appearing in late fall; fruit a scurfy, blunt pod containing two polished seeds which ripen in the summer or fall. These seeds are shot for some distance by the sudden popping of the pod. The well known extract of witch hazel is made by distilling any part of this plant. Flowering from early November to the middle of December.

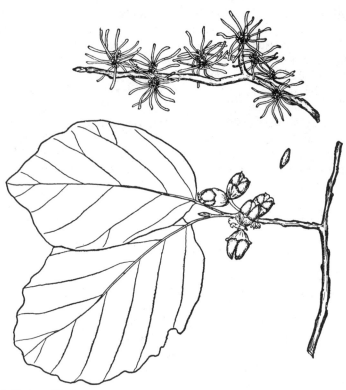

1, Twig with flowers. 2, twig with leaves and open fruits. All x ½.

The Witch Hazel found in southern Georgia, Florida, and westward is considered by some as a distinct species and is called *H. macrophylla* Pursh (see Sargent, *Journ. Arn. Arb.* 1: 246. 1920.) The main difference proposed seems to be the presence of little projections or tubercles on the under surface of the leaves to which stellate hairs were attached before falling off. This character, however, is obvious also in several of our specimens of Witch Hazel from various parts of North Carolina from the mountains and lower down. A more northern form of *Hamamelis virginiana*, the var. *parvifolia* Nutt., has been reported from southeastern Virginia (*Rhodora* 42: 453. 1940).

LIQUIDAMBAR L.

1. Liquidambar Styraciflua L. Sweet Gum.

This is a large tree which is common in the low grounds throughout our area as far south as central Florida and extends to the mountainous section, where it is found only along the larger streams at low elevations. In the piedmont it is also found in upland woods.

Branchlets winged; leaves with 3-5 sharp-pointed, serrate lobes, smooth above and below, turning many shades of red and purple in the fall; male and female flowers on the same tree, male flowers in heads on a raceme, female flowers in a single close ball-like inflorescence on a long drooping peduncle; fruits round, prickly, and polished. This tree reaches a very large size, sometimes a height of 140 feet and a diameter of nearly 7 feet (see report of a specimen near Columbia, S. C., in *Amer. Forests* **47**: 452,

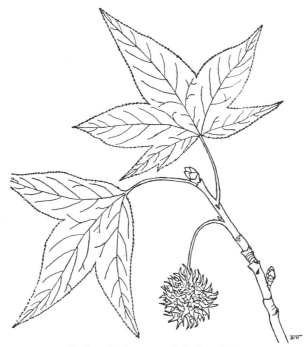

Twig with leaves and fruit, x ½.

1941). The Sweet Gum is one of our finest trees and is
suitable for formal planting, as on streets, especially in
poorly drained soil where most trees fail. The balsam from
this tree was a great favorite with children before chewing
gum became so easily available. In pharmacy this balsam
is known as American storax and is used in several phar-
maceutical preparations, notably as the expectorating agent
in compound tincture of benzoin. It is also used as a per-
fume in soaps and toilet preparations. Phillips Russell
thinks that it was the incense used by the Indians of Central America in their religious ceremonies. The wood of
this tree, under the name of Red Gum, is much used for
veneering.

A form with broad rounded indistinctly toothed lobes
found at Pinehurst, N. C., by R. E. Wicker has been
described as *L. Styraciflua* f. *rotundiloba* by Rehder (*Jour.
Arn. Arb.* 12: 70. 1931).

PLATANACEAE (PLANE TREE FAMILY)

PLATANUS (Tourn.)

1. Platanus occidentalis L. Sycamore.

THIS is a large tree which is common along streams throughout our area as far south as northern Florida and often
spontaneous in uplands. In the mountains it ascends to
about 2,500 feet. It is found along the Apalachicola River
in Florida (Harper).

Bark light gray, scaling off in thin plates; leaves large,
4-8 inches broad, with many irregular lobes and teeth, very
woolly when young, becoming glabrous except along the
veins; petioles stout, woolly, the enlarged base covering the
bud; flowers of two kinds borne in separate round heads;
fruit head brownish, composed of a compact mass of long,
hairy achenes, which separate in the spring and are carried
long distances by the wind. It is one of our largest trees
and in North Carolina often reaches a height of 110 feet
and a diameter of 5 or 6 feet. A section in the museum in
Raleigh from Edgecombe County, North Carolina, has a
diameter of 3 feet 9 inches. In the middle west it may be
much larger, sometimes with a diameter up to 15 feet.

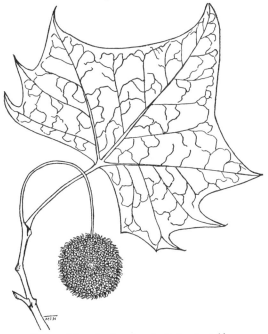

Twig with a leaf and a fruit head, x ½.

Michaux reported a tree along the Ohio River near Marietta, Ohio, which had a circumference of 47 feet four feet above the surface of the ground. The largest Sycamore known living today, which is 42 feet 3 inches in circumference five feet from the ground (diameter 13 ft. 8 inches), is on White River near Worthington, Indiana (*Journ. Hered.* **6:** Sept. 1915). This is the largest tree of any species known east of the Mississippi River. Still larger specimens now dead have been known. One near Mt. Carmel, Illinois, had a circumference of 62 feet twenty feet from the ground. Flowering from April 1 to April 27.

Many of our trees are being killed by the Sycamore anthracnose due to the fungus *Gnomonia veneta* (Sacc. & Speg.) Kleb., which attacks the leaves and twigs. For this reason the planting of the Sycamore is not advised. Several other diseases of the Sycamore that have been studied more recently seem to be even more destructive than *Gnomonia* (see Wolf, *Mycologia* **30:** 54, 1938; Walter and Mook, *Phytopathology* **30:** 27, 1940, and **31:** 349, 1941).

ROSACEAE (ROSE FAMILY)

SORBUS (L.) S. F. Gray.

1. Sorbus americana Marsh. Mountain Ash.

This is a small tree or shrub found in our area only in the mountains (from about 3,000 ft. up) of Virginia, North Carolina, and Tennessee. It is commoner near rocky summits but is also found in wet sphagnum flats as at Highlands, North Carolina (elevation 3,800 ft.).

Twig with leaves and fruit, x ⅓.

Bark smooth, gray; leaves compound with 9-17 toothed leaflets, resembling the leaves of the Sumach; flowers small, structurally resembling an apple flower, dull white, in elder-like clusters 3-5 inches across; fruits like tiny apples (but only three cells in the core), bright red, not over ¼ inch in diameter, remaining on the tree through the winter. A tree by the main trail up Mt. Mitchell and within one-fourth mile of the summit measures 1 foot $\frac{7}{10}$ inch in diameter three feet from the ground. In Canada the Mountain Ash grows in moist and rocky woods and is much cultivated but in our area it does poorly in cultivation.

MALUS (Hill) S. F. Gray.

1. Calyx externally tomentose; branches without thorns
Malus Malus, Apple   No. 4
Calyx externally glabrous; branches usually thorny   2
2. Leaves in most part not more than twice as long as broad, frequently strongly lobed; fruit large (about 1¼-2½ inches in diam.); mostly occurring in the piedmont and mountains
Malus coronaria group, Crab Apples Nos. 1 and 2
Leaves in most part much longer than broad and without lobes; fruit smaller (about 1 inch in diam.); in large part characteristic of the coastal plain
Malus angustifolia group,
Narrow-leaved Crab Apples   No. 3

1. Malus coronaria (L.) Mill. (Pyrus coronaria L.). Crab Apple.

UNTIL recent years Malus coronaria has stood as a blanket name for a highly variable consort of forms or what not of most of the Crab Apples of the eastern United States. Various authors have now separated out the more or less obvious groups of these variants and given them specific or varietal names. Most of them will be mentioned below and the most obvious one we are recognizing as a species. According to general agreement what may be considered the typical form of M. coronaria is a small tree found in our area only in the mountains as far south as North Carolina and Tennessee, where it is common in pastures and open woods. We have specimens from Macon, Yancey, Jackson and Swain counties in North Carolina, and from Giles County in Virginia. It is characterized as follows:

A small tree with a spreading crown, the flowering branches short and spur-like and a number in the form of spines; leaves ovate to triangular, sharply serrate or doubly

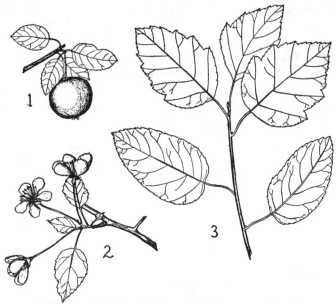

1, Fruit.   2, twig with flowers.   3, leaves.   All x ⅓.

serrate, blade thin, about 1½-3 inches long, the primary
veins arising some distance from the base, when young
floccose-tomentose, at maturity glabrous on both sides as are
the petioles and twigs; leaves of fast growing shoots may
be pubescent below and lobed as in the Red Maple; flowers
1½-2 inches in diameter, pink to white, very fragrant;
calyx glabrous, the inner surface tomentose as in all our
other Crab Apples; fruits globose with both ends depressed, ridged at the tip or scarcely so, 1-1½ inches in
diameter, yellowish green, fragrant and sour.

Malus glaucescens Rehder.

This is distinguished from *M. coronaria* by its thicker
leaves which are glaucous below. We have it from Tip
Top, Tazewell County, Virginia (Harbison), and from
Yancey County, North Carolina (Ashe).

Malus bracteata Rehder.

Typical forms of this vary from *M. coronaria* in the
strongly tomentose under surface of the leaves even at
maturity and the tomentose petioles and twigs. Numerous

collections of ours in our herbarium show no other important differences, with many intermediate forms. This goes
farther south than the typical *M. coronaria.* We have
what appear to be rather typical specimens from as far
south as Augusta, Georgia. *Malus redolens* Ashe seems to
be the same as *M. bracteata* as considered by Rehder.

Malus platycarpa Rehder.

This varies from *M. coronaria* in the larger and more
depressed fruits that are almost as much ridged as in *M.*

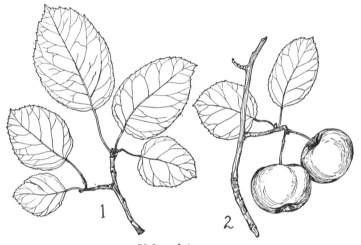

Malus platycarpa
1, Twig with leaves.   2, twig with fruits.   All x ⅓.

glabrata and reach a diameter of 2½ inches. For a time
this was considered a hybrid. We have collected it between Franklin and Wayah Bald in Macon County, North
Carolina. We also have it from Biltmore, North Carolina,
and Columbus, Georgia.

Malus elongata Ashe (*M. coronaria* var. *elongata* Rehd.).

The extreme of this is easily distinguished from *M.
coronaria* by its much narrower and long acuminate leaves.
We have collected this at Highlands, Macon County, North
Carolina, and in Giles County, Virginia, and we have it
from Scranton and Waverly in Pennsylvania and from
Canandaigua, Chapinville, and Salamanca in New York.

It has also been reported from Peak Mountain, Virginia, and from Rabun County, Georgia.

Malus cuneata Ashe.

This is the form in which the leaves have a sharply pointed base and perhaps smaller fruit. It is reported from along streams in Rabun County, Georgia, and from Oconee County, South Carolina.

2. **Malus glabrata** Rehder. **Crab Apple.**

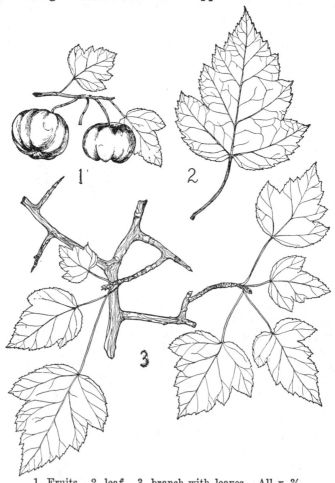

1, Fruits. 2, leaf. 3, branch with leaves. All x ⅖.

This is the most easily recognized of the variants in the *coronaria* group. Unlike the others the leaf has two large primary veins arising from the base of the blade and it is typically lobed as in the Red Maple. It is also distinguished by the fact that the much compressed apple is conspicuously ridged not only at the tip but on the sides. Outside of these characters it is like *M. coronaria*. This is a small tree that is found in the western North Carolina valleys at altitudes up to about 3,500 feet. We have specimens from Buncombe, Macon and Haywood counties in North Carolina and it has been reported from Jackson County. We also have in the Ashe herbarium a specimen from Pennsylvania, further locality not indicated, that looks like this.

3. **Malus angustifolia** (Aiton) Michx. (**Pyrus angustifolia** Aiton). **Narrow-leaved Crab Apple.**

This low, broadly rounded, thorny tree is most abundant in the flat woods and along the rivers of the lower coastal plain from southeastern Virginia to Florida. We have specimens from Lenoir and Bladen counties in North Carolina, from Cheraw, Pine Island, Kershaw and Berkeley counties in South Carolina, from Clarke, Brooks and Thomas counties, Georgia, and from near Tallahassee, Florida.

Leaves elliptic to oblong-lanceolate, rounded or pointed at the tip, characteristically small, blade 1-2 (3) inches long and ½-¾ inch wide, serrate or almost entire, thick, shining above, giving them an evergreen appearance; leaves on strong shoots may be slightly lobed; leaves on flowering shoots often rounded at the tip; leaves usually becoming brown upon drying; flowers large, about 1 inch across, pink and very fragrant; calyx glabrous on the outer surface; fruit about 1 inch in diameter, nearly globose and without ridges, fragrant, sour and yellowish green. In Chapel Hill the use of this beautiful ornamental is prohibited by the cedar-apple rust. It, with the Choke Cherry, is also preferred by the tent caterpillar, and is almost always badly attacked by it in its natural groves. Plants in the woods

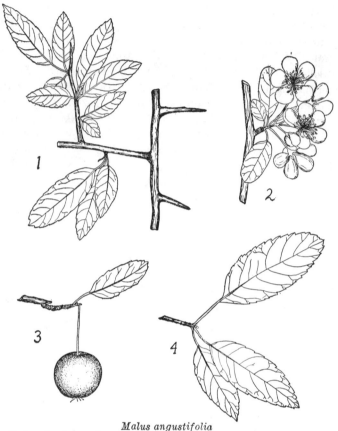

Malus angustifolia
1, Twig showing spines.   2, cluster of flowers.   3, fruit.   4, twig
with leaves.   All x ½.

in Pitt County, N. C., were just coming into bloom on
April 8, 1932, and it was in full bloom at Cheraw, S. C., on
April 3, 1933.

Malus lancifolia Rehder.

The leaves are distinctly longer in proportion to the
width and are much less lobed and have smaller teeth than
in *M. angustifolia*. The most conspicuous character is the
thin and papery leaf. When dry the leaves are much
greener than those of *M. angustifolia* which characteristically turn brown on both surfaces. This is apparently a

very thin leaved species or variety that takes the place of *M. angustifolia* in the mountains. It is known in our region only from the mountains of Virginia, North Carolina, and Georgia. We have it from Black Mountain, Biltmore, Asheville, and Swannanoa Gap in Buncombe County and from Jackson County in North Carolina, from Marion, Virginia, from Fannin County, Georgia, from Clarion, Pennsylvania, from Swope Park, Missouri, and from Lawrence County, Ohio.

Malus carolinensis Ashe.

This is very similar to *M. lancifolia* but according to Ashe may be separated by "having prevailingly oblong crenate-serrate and not lanceolate, sharply serrate leaf blades." He distinguished it from *M. angustifolia* by the "thinner leaves rounded at base and fruit usually green and slightly impressed when ripe." We have some of the type specimens from Mills River, Transylvania County, North Carolina.

4. Malus Malus Britt. (M. pumila Mill.) Apple.

THE cultivated apple, a native of Europe and Western Asia, has escaped to a considerable extent in the northern states and single seedling trees are occasionally found in upland woods in our southern area. These seedling plants tend to have smaller leaves than the cultivated ones and are sometimes mistaken for native crab apples but they can be easily distinguished from them by the woolly outer surface of the calyx, the abundant wool on the pedicels, and the absence of spines. The only crab apple in the eastern United States with a calyx that is woolly on the outside is *M. ioensis* Britt. and that is far outside of our territory.

PYRUS (Tourn.) L.

1. Pyrus communis L. Common Pear.

THE cultivated pear, a native of Europe and Western Asia, has like the apple escaped rather freely in the northern states and also like it is once in a while found wild in the woods in the south. The fruits of these seedling trees, in all the cases known to us, revert back to an inferior primitive type, which is scarcely edible except when cooked. One such seedling brought in from neighboring woods by the senior author has borne abundant fruit and is entirely immune to fire blight.

AMELANCHIER Medic.

Leaves tomentose until maturity or later; young leaves whitish green; fruit tasteless
Amelanchier canadensis, Swamp Shad Bush   No. 1

Leaves glabrous or nearly so at maturity; young leaves
  purplish brown; fruit sweet and edible
                    Amelanchier laevis, Shad Bush   No. 2

1. Amelanchier canadensis (L.) Medic.   Swamp Shad Bush.

THIS slender shrub or small tree usually grows in the low
grounds of the coastal plain and piedmont but extends into
the mountains to an altitude of about 4,000 feet. It is found
in all our states southward to western Florida.

Leaves obovate to ovate, usually slightly cordate at
the base, apex acute, margin with numerous, small, close-
set, acute teeth, lower surface densely white-tomentose
until maturity or later, whitish green from the first, not
purplish; flowers in nodding racemes, usually about 6-12,
both peduncles and pedicels closely pubescent; calyx lobes
pubescent, reflexed at the base when the petals fall, broad
and abruptly long pointed, petals white, oblong; fruit
purplish red, scarcely edible, often diseased by the attack
of a rust fungus. A form of this with pretty rose pink buds
and pink then white petals has been found in Orange
County, North Carolina. Flowering begins about March 22
to March 25.

Ashe has described a close relative of this species which
occurs in the foothills from Oconee County, S. C., to Jackson County, N. C., as *A. beata.* Ashe has since found it at
Purefoy's Mill near Chapel Hill. It is a shrub or small
tree which differs from *A. canadensis* in the acuminate leaf
blades and in long petioles. A hybrid between this and the
next species, superior to both as an ornamental, has been
produced. A form of this hybrid, named *rubescens,* is said
to be the most beautiful of all Amelanchiers.

2. Amelanchier laevis Wiegand. Shad Bush, Service Berry, Currant Tree.

THIS shrub or small tree is a rather common plant of dry
woods, hillsides, and creek bluffs and banks in the piedmont
and mountains of our states, rarely in the coastal plain as
far south as northern Georgia.

Leaves ovate to elliptic, blade about 1½-4 inches long and 1-2 inches broad, purplish brown until full maturity,

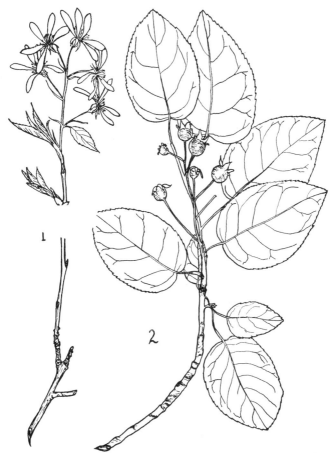

1, Twig with flowers. 2, twig with mature leaves and fruits. All x ½.

in the young stages pubescent on both sides, at maturity nearly or quite glabrous; flowers white, in many-flowered racemes; peduncles and pedicels pubescent, calyx lobes narrower and more lanceolate than in *A. canadensis;* fruit purple to nearly black, sweet and of a better quality than in *A. canadensis.* The difference between our two species in regard to the pubescence of the leaves is only a matter of degree. There is a large tree near Chapel Hill which has a diameter of 9⅓ inches and a spread of 20 feet. The time of flowering varies considerably in different plants but begins about March 1 to April 17.

The tree described above is the form occurring in Chapel Hill. The more typical *A. laevis* farther west has entirely smooth leaves at the time of unfolding. There is a big tree in the mountains, as at Highlands, N. C., which reaches a height of 60 feet and a diameter of 20 inches or more that needs further study. It may be that this tree is what has been called *Amelanchier arborea* (Michx.) Fernald (*Rhodora* **43**: 563. 1941).

A tree with very orbicular leaves occurring in our mountains has been given the name of *A. sanguinea* (Pursh) DC. Intermediate forms are said to connect this with *A. laevis*. This seems very near the plant which Ashe has named *A. laevis cordifolia* found in Lincoln County, N. C., and in Georgia.

The scientific names of the Amelanchiers have been badly confused. We are following Sargent's *Manual of Trees,* second edition.

CRATAEGUS L.

In recent years a great number of so-called species of *Crataegus* have been described, and it is now practically impossible to separate many of these with any certainty as specific entities in nature. The present taxonomic situation in the genus is one of unparalleled complexity and no two experts agree on the validity of all the species described. Sargent, Beadle, and Ashe have described in the last thirty-five years about 125 species (trees and shrubs) in the area covered by this book, and in the second edition of his *Trees of North America* Sargent includes 35 arborescent hawthorns in the same area. Of these we are describing and illustrating only 18 species (not all of them in Sargent). As for the others in Sargent we are mentioning them with only a few descriptive words in the discussion under the species that they resemble more or less superficially. In choosing the ones to be described and illustrated we are guided largely by their abundance or distinctive appearance in the areas best known to us. In a book of this nature some inconsistency in choice we hope will not be considered too great a fault. No one not an expert systematic botanist may hope to recognize anything like all the *Crataegus* species, and most of the users of this book should be content to recognize with certainty only a moderate number of the best marked kinds.

Palmer has contributed a valuable piece of work in getting together all the described species with references in the *Journ. Arn. Arb.* **6**: 1, 1925. In a more recent article of his in the same journal (**13**: 342. 1932) he discusses most helpfully and sensibly the whole situation. To the surprise of most systematists and students of heredity, it has been shown by the behavior of many thousands of seedlings in the Arnold Arboretum that, while these species are separated often by minute characters (color of anthers, color or shape of fruit), these characters are usually perpetuated in the offspring and are not simply a mercurial shuffling of unstable characters (see another case under *C. Ravenelii*). Our own observations also tend to establish the fact that a number of species once thought to be represented by a single tree or a few trees in a limited locality are found with identical characters in widely separated areas (see our notes on Haw Ridge under *C. Ravenelii*).

For interesting remarks on *Crataegus*, see R. M. Harper in *Geol. Survey Alabama, Monog.* **9**: 202, 1928. Murrill has recently described a number of new species of *Crataegus* from Florida (*Contrib. Herb. Univ. Fla.*, Nov. 1940).

KEY TO THE SPECIES

1. Fruits maturing in the spring (April and May); leaves small, spatulate, with red-brown hairs in the axils of the leaves below (for leaves with the entire lower surface reddish pubescent see *C. rufula* mentioned under *C. aestivalis*); swamp trees, often standing in water
Crataegus aestivalis, May Haw No. 1
Fruits maturing in the summer and fall......... 2
2. Fruits very small, less than ¼ inch in diameter, numerous in a cluster; strong veins, at least in

deeply lobed leaves, extending to the sinuses as
well as to the tips of the lobes................ 3
Fruits larger; the veins in the leaves not extending to the sinuses........................... 6
3. Leaf blade cut into 5-7 narrow lobes; fruit oblong
           Crataegus Marshallii, Parsley Haw   No. 2
Leaf blade toothed, often 3-lobed, sometimes
5-lobed 4
4. Tips of nutlets visible in mature fruit; leaves
truncate to slightly cordate at the base
       Crataegus phaenopyrum, Washington Thorn   No. 3
Tips of nutlets not exposed in mature fruits;
leaves tapering gradually downward (cuneate)
or abruptly pointed below..................... 5
5. Leaf blade small, spatulate, toothed, on strong
shoots often 3-lobed, gradually tapering to near
the base of the petiole
         Crataegus spathulata, Spatulate Haw   No. 4
Leaf blade wedge-shaped below, but not running
far down the long slender petiole, usually
3-lobed
         Crataegus Youngii, Young's Thorn   No. 5
6. Leaves spatulate to fan-shaped, not lobed, thick
and shining above; flowers usually numerous in
a cluster 7
Leaves lobed or deeply toothed, if not, then flowers
few in a cluster, 3-6, rarely 7 8
7. Leaves smooth above; stamens 8-12 with red
anthers
       Crataegus Crus-galli, Cockspur Thorn   No. 6
Leaves smooth above; stamens 20 with red anthers
         Crataegus limnophila   No. 7
Leaves smooth above; stamens 10-15 with yellow
anthers
        Crataegus algens, Clammy Haw   No. 8
Leaves with short harsh hairs above; stamens 8-12
with red anthers
        Crataegus torva, He Hog-apple   No. 9
8. Large trees of the coastal plain swamps (*C.
viridis* extends to Durham County, N. C.);
anthers cream colored (for anthers rose colored
see *C. arborescens* mentioned under *C. viridis*);
fruits small, ¼-⅓ inch in diameter
        Crataegus viridis, Green Haw   No. 10
Trees not growing in swamps, found in the piedmont and mountains or in sandy soil in the
coastal plain; fruit ⅓ inch or more thick...... 9
9. Petioles not glandular, not winged, very hairy;
leaves large and strongly tomentose below; fruit
very large, up to one inch (found only in Tennessee in our area)
         Crataegus mollis, Red Haw   No. 19
Petioles not glandular, winged above or nearly to
the base, blade usually over 1 inch wide, singly
or doubly toothed but not lobed; fruit large
(usually ½-⅔ inch long) red, dotted, flesh

ample and sweet; trees of the high mountains
or foothills 10
Petioles glandular and pubescent, winged; blade
over one inch wide, shining and rough above,
more or less pubescent below, sharply and doubly
toothed; trees of hills, mostly limestone (Tennessee and Alabama)
Crataegus Harbisonii   No. 20
Petioles glandular, winged or not winged, blade
usually over 1 inch wide, glabrous at maturity,
doubly toothed but not deeply lobed; flowers in
ample clusters; trees of the piedmont and foothills 12
Petioles and teeth conspicuously glandular, petioles
winged to or nearly to the base, blade usually
less than an inch wide, often 3-lobed, lower surface tomentose at least on the veins; flowers
few in a cluster, 3-6, rarely 7 14
For a number of other species mentioned by us but
not described in detail and some of them not
coming easily under the three above headings
see notes under *C. meridiana*
10. Fruits usually not over ⅓ inch in diameter;
stamens 20 with purple anthers (for *C. crux*
with 10 stamens with white anthers see under
C. Chapmanii)
Crataegus Chapmanii, Chapman's Haw   No. 11
Fruits usually over ⅓ inch in diameter........... 11
11. Leaf blades long-obovate, broadest at or above the
middle, veins conspicuously sunken above and
very prominent below; a tree of the high mountains (Va. to Ga.)
Crataegus punctata, Dotted Thorn   No. 12
Leaf blades ovate to nearly orbicular; veins
sunken above but less so than in *C. punctata;* a
tree of the low grounds of northwest Georgia
and Tennessee; stamens 20 with pink anthers
(for *C. amnicola* with whitish anthers see under
C. ingens)
Crataegus ingens   No. 13
12. Veins of leaves sunken above and very prominent
below; stamens 20 with yellow anthers
Crataegus collina, Chapman's Hill Thorn   No. 14
Veins of leaves not sunken above.............. 13
13. Stamens 10 with red anthers (see also *C. Buckleyi*
and *C. roanensis* mentioned under *C. iracunda*)
Crataegus iracunda, Red Haw   No. 15
Stamens 10 with yellow anthers (see *C. Boyntonii*
mentioned under *C. iracunda*)
Stamens 20 with purple anthers (see *C. arcana*
mentioned under *C. iracunda*)
14. Leaves on fruiting spurs small, ¾ inch or less
broad with short teeth, densely woolly when
young and remaining pubescent to late in the

season, not shining; fruit orange-yellow, pear-shaped or oval

Crataegus meridiana, Southern Haw   No. 16

Leaves about the same size as in *C. meridiana,* equally woolly but decidedly more deeply toothed

Crataegus dispar   No. 17

Leaves of fruiting spurs prevailingly larger, up to ⅞ inch broad, shining above, on strong shoots less lobed; trees much larger and usually with larger, red or orange-red fruits

Crataegus Ravenelii, Big-fruited Haw   No. 18

For other plants running to this section but not fitting well under any of the three species above see those mentioned under *C. meridiana*

1. Crataegus aestivalis (Walter) Sarg. May Haw, Apple Haw.

THIS tree is found in wet soil in the coastal region from North Carolina southward. Often it grows in shallow

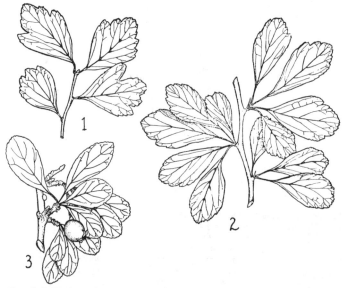

1 and 2, Twigs with leaves. 3, twig with mature fruit. All x ½.

ponds. Neither Britton nor Small extends this tree northward as far as North Carolina, but Sargent and Sudworth note it from southeastern North Carolina. H. A. Rankin reports it as abundant along South River and Black River in Sampson (near Ivanhoe) and Pender (near Atkinson) counties, North Carolina. We have specimens from New Bern, North Carolina, from Conway and near Kingstree in South Carolina, and from Meldrim and Quitman, Georgia.

Leaves oblanceolate to obovate, the blade about 1-1¾ inches long and ½-1⅜ inches wide, rounded or pointed at the tip, tapering downward nearly to the base of the petiole, finely serrate except toward the base, the teeth tipped with glands, on strong shoots more deeply and irregularly toothed and sometimes 3-lobed, at maturity glabrous on both sides except for reddish tufts of hairs in the forks of the veins in most cases (see the tomentose form below), dark green and shining above, lighter green below (in deeply lobed leaves the veins run to the sinuses); flowers 2-5 in small clusters, stamens 15-20 with pink anthers, peduncles glabrous; fruits ripening in May (just beginning to ripen at Quitman, Ga., on April 19, 1933), globose, large, up to 9⁄16 inch thick, red, dotted, succulent, and much used for jelly.

Sargent has described as *C. rufula* a tree very much like the above except for the conspicuous reddish pubescence of the leaves beneath, which is apparently persistent. We have specimens of this from along the Neuse River, south of Goldsboro, North Carolina, from Hartsville, South Carolina, and from Decatur County, Georgia.

2. **Crataegus Marshallii** Eggl. (**C. apiifolia** Michx.). **Parsley Haw.**

THIS tree is found along the borders of streams and swamps or hammocks in pine barrens through the coast region, and in both low and upland woods in the piedmont region from southeastern Virginia to northern Florida.

Leaves broadly ovate or orbicular, ¾-1½ inches in diameter, jagged-toothed, and with 5-7 deep narrow clefts; the leaves and twigs pilose-hairy when young, both sides of the leaves sometimes becoming glabrous toward the end of the summer; flowers in clusters of 10-12, stamens 20 with red anthers, the whole inflorescence, including the calyx, covered with long white hairs; fruit small, oblong, ⅓ inch long, bright red, and shining. From the other small-fruited haws this is easily distinguished by the woolly flower clusters and twigs in youth and by the deeply and amply cut leaf blades. It is also peculiar in the fact that strong veins extend to the bottoms of the notches in the leaf blades. Flowering April 26 to April 30.

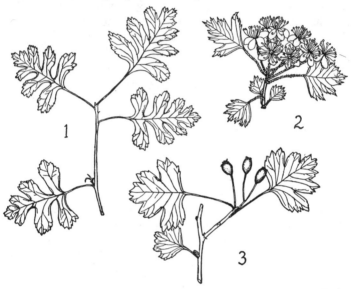

1, Twig with leaves.   2, flower cluster.   3, twig with mature fruits.
All x ½.

This plant under cultivation, taking a graceful broadly rounded form, becomes one of our most handsome hawthorns. It is very ornamental throughout the whole year. In winter its many small branches are almost lace-like; in spring it is covered with a cloud of small flowers which are very fragrant and full of bees; in summer with small deeply cut leaves and in fall with scarlet fruit; and for a hawthorn it has remarkably few thorns.

3. **Crataegus phaenopyrum** (L. f.) Medic. (**C. cordata** Ait.). **Washington Thorn.**

THIS is a handsome tree of moderate size, which is much cultivated for ornament. Until recent years it has been confused with the preceding. In our range it is found from the valley of the upper Potomac River southward through the Appalachian Mountains to northern Georgia. In our area it is apparently found more often in the lower mountains as around Asheville, North Carolina, but we now have typical specimens from as far east as Chapel Hill.

Branch with leaves and fruits, x ⅖.

Twigs slender, reddish brown with straight or slightly curved thorns 2 inches or less long; all parts glabrous; leaves more or less broadly triangular with long slender petioles, deeply and doubly toothed, many of the teeth with glands, often with three distinct lobes in addition to the teeth; leaf base nearly square (truncate) with a slight abrupt point or slightly cordate; flowers very numerous in compound clusters, stamens about 20 with rose colored anthers; fruit scarlet, usually less than ¼ inch thick, the calyx falling away at maturity and exposing to view the tips of the little nutlets. This species is distinguished from *C. Youngii*, its nearest relative, by the less obviously 3-lobed leaves, by the truncate or even slightly cordate rather than pointed base of the leaf blade, and by the exposed tips of the nutlets at maturity.

4. Crataegus spathulata Michx. Spatulate Thorn, Red Haw.

THIS is a small tree found along streams and on uplands from North Carolina to Florida. It is most abundantly distributed in the southern sections of our area but is found as far north as Davidson County, North Carolina. It is plentiful in middle and southern Georgia and northern Florida and extends nearly to the mountains around Rome, Georgia. We have specimens from along the Yadkin River in Davidson County and from Stanly County in North Carolina, from Macon, Georgia, and from dry hills near River Junction, Florida. Small extends its distribution to Virginia.

1, Twig with leaves. 2, flower clusters. All x ¾.

Twigs with slender thorns up to 1½ inches long; leaves spatulate to oblanceolate, small, ½-1½ inches long and ⅛-¾ (rarely 1) inch broad, toothed, often 3-lobed at the end, dark green, slightly hairy when young but smooth at maturity, blade gradually tapering to near the base of the petiole, the more terminal leaves with large, toothed, leaf-like stipules; flowers in a many-flowered, glabrous cluster, stamens 20 with yellow anthers; fruits globose, small, ¼ inch or less in diameter, red. This is about the latest flowering of our thorns. Near Quitman, Georgia, it was in bloom at the time (April 20) the May Haw fruits were beginning to ripen. It was in full bloom throughout southern Georgia and at River Junction, Florida, on April 20, 1933.

5. Crataegus Youngii Sarg. Young's Hawthorn.

THIS is a fair sized tree which is found from the upper piedmont to the coastal plain from Amelia County, Va.,

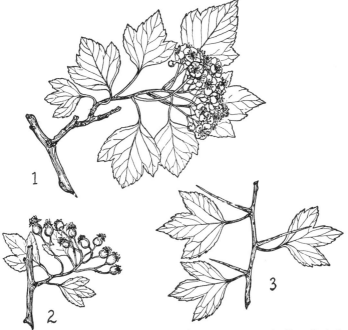

1, Branch with flower cluster. 2, twig with mature fruits. 3, twig with leaves and thorns. All x ½.

south to Florida. Sargent described this species (*Journ. Arn. Arb.* **4**: 105. 1923) from a low wet bottom at Greensboro, North Carolina, and recorded it also from Wake County, N. C., and Kershaw County, South Carolina. To these localities we can add Durham, Richmond, Montgomery, Nash and Northampton counties, N. C., York County,

Virginia, and Wakulla County, Fla. We have specimens from the type tree. In Durham County we find this species only in swamps, agreeing with the type habitat, but the Richmond County plant was found in gravelly upland soil on the edge of woods. The Kershaw specimen noted by Sargent grew on the banks of the Wateree River.

Twigs glabrous, often with slender, reddish, straight or curved thorns about 1-1½ inches long; leaf blades ¾-2 inches long and about the same width, distinctly 3-lobed as a rule and somewhat resembling a Carolina Red Maple leaf, toothed, truncate to more or less abruptly pointed below and extending some distance down the slender glabrous petiole, on strong shoots sometimes decurrent to the base of the petiole and in such cases often with toothed stipules like those of *C. spathulata;* midrib slightly elevated above; smooth except for a few white hairs along the veins on the upper surface when young or until midsummer; flowers small, numerous in dense glabrous clusters, stamens 15-20 with yellow anthers; fruits scarlet, slightly oblong, small, about ³⁄₁₆ inch in diameter or less. Flowering near Chapel Hill on May 25, 1924, and in Richmond County on May 2, 1927.

6. Crataegus Crus-galli L.   Cock-spur Thorn, Hog-apple.

THIS is a small thorny tree which is supposed to extend south to the Appalachian foothills of North Carolina and Tennessee. We can now extend its range to Orange and Durham counties, North Carolina. Northward it extends into Canada. In the mountains and upper piedmont it is found in uplands but near Chapel Hill we find it in swamps. We have specimens from Davie, Yadkin, Orange, and Durham counties in North Carolina.

Bark dark and scaly; twigs stout, reddish, glabrous, and with many stout, curved, very long (usually 2 inches or more) thorns; leaves small, mostly 1½-2 inches long, obovate or spatulate, thick, glabrous on both sides, upper side shiny, the broad end toothed and often rounded; flowers about ⅔ inch broad, numerous in glabrous clusters, stamens about 10 with pink anthers; fruits hanging on late,

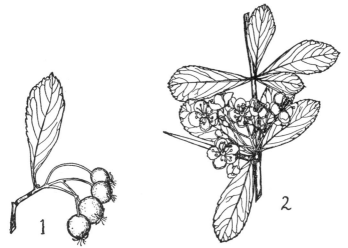

1, Twig with mature fruits.   2, flower cluster.   All x ⅝.

dull red or greenish red, about ½ inch in diameter, with
1-3 (usually 2) large nutlets. This is one of the better
trees for planting. Its spreading crown, deep green shining leaves, and ample flowers recommend it for ornament.
Like all the others, however, it is subject to rust and like
C. torva badly attacked by the cottony scale.

A number of trees closely related to *C. Crus-galli* have
been given specific names. Among these we would mention
C. Mohrii Beadle from western Georgia, easily distinguished when in flower by its 20 stamens with yellow
anthers; *C. macra* Beadle in northwestern Georgia with
small flower clusters, smaller fruits, and 10 purple anthers
(what we are calling *C. Crus-galli* may possibly include
this species); *C. regalis* Beadle in northwestern Georgia
with 10 yellow anthers, very similar to *C. algens; C. pyracanthoides* Beadle, with 7-12 stamens with purple anthers,
in the swamps of western Florida.

7. **Crataegus limnophila** Sarg.

THIS is a fine spreading tree up to about 20 feet high and
11 inches thick growing in damp or wet soil along swamps
and streams of the southeastern coastal plain section from

South Carolina to Florida (Wakulla County). We have specimens from near the Mulberry Castle estate, Berkeley County (about 40 miles from Charleston), and Dorchester County in South Carolina, and from Glynn (near Thalman), Perry, and Dooly counties in Georgia.

Bark of trunk checkered; twigs red-brown, glabrous; thorns usually very few, sometimes almost none, 1½-2½

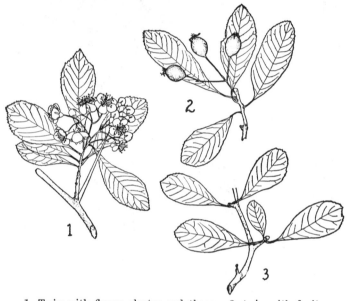

1, Twig with flower cluster and thorn. 2, twig with fruits.
3, leaves. All x ½.

inches long; leaves long-obovate, about 1½-2½ inches long including the petiole, rounded or pointed at the end, long pointed (cuneate) below, winging the slender petiole almost to the base, finely toothed except below, quite glabrous at all ages; flowers appearing as the leaves are nearly grown in rather small or ample clusters, about 6-15 (rarely 20), the flower stalks glabrous or sparingly hairy, calyx glabrous without, hairy within, stamens about 20 with purple anthers; fruit borne few in a cluster, usually 1-3, oblong, about ⅓ inch thick, bright red, hanging on late, still abundant on the Berkeley County specimens on October 15, 1932.

This fine tree, strange to say, has been without a name until rather recently (*Journ. Arn. Arb.* **3**: 3. 1921). In the older works it has of course been placed under *C. Crusgalli* but it easily differs from that species as now understood in its preference for swamp soil, by its 20 stamens, few thorns and geographical range. Palmer considers it a variety of *pyracanthoides*. It is one of the commonest trees in swampy soil in lower Georgia. Apparently it is confined to the coastal plain and appears most abundantly in central and lower Georgia.

8. Crataegus algens Beadle. Clammy Hawthorn.

THIS species has been in recent times separated from *C. Crus-galli*, which it resembles closely in general appearance. It is distinguished by having yellow anthers (stamens 10-

Crataegus algens.

1, Twig with leaves, thorns, and mature fruits. 2, larger fruits.
3, flower cluster. All x $\frac{2}{5}$.

15), apparently broader and more blunt leaves, and somewhat larger fruits on longer stalks. Without the stamens
its separation would hardly be possible with certainty. In
Chapel Hill *C. algens* also differs in occurring on uplands
instead of in swamps. It occurs on uplands from Virginia
to Georgia. In the North Carolina mountains it is more
common than *C. Crus-galli*. We have collections from
Biltmore (Ashe) and Orange County in North Carolina.
Flowering May 7, 1933.

9. Crataegus torva Beadle. He Hog-apple.

THIS is a broad-topped tree of upland hills with many stout
thorns 1-2 inches long. Heretofore, it has been reported
only from Georgia and Alabama but our Chapel Hill plants
agree perfectly with *C. torva* except that Beadle does not

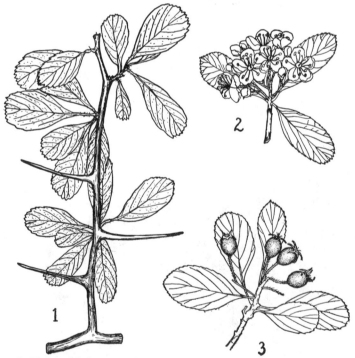

1, Twig with leaves and thorns. 2, flower cluster. 3, twig with
mature fruits. All x ½.

mention the harsh upper surface of the leaves, a conspicuous character. However, Harbison said that typical *C. torva* has this character also. Our plants answer very closely to the description of *C. berberifolia* but that is a much larger tree with yellow anthers and yellow fruit. It is known only from southern Louisiana.

Bark closely scaly, gray-brown with many large compound thorns; leaves ovate-spatulate, 3/4-2 1/2 inches long and 1/3-1 inch broad, thick, shiny, and harshly rough above with short, white, rigid hairs, softly and rather sparsely pubescent below, upper part of blade toothed, the lower half or third entire; flowers up to 3/4 inch in diameter in clusters of 7-14, stamens 8-12 with pink anthers, the flower stalk and calyx very hairy; fruit oblong, dull orange, red or greenish red with conspicuous red dots, about 3/8 inch thick, the surface slightly hairy under a lens at maturity, nutlets 2 or 3, distinctly ridged. This is called the He Hog-apple around Chapel Hill on account of the usual lack of fruit, though occasionally it bears a few fruits. The scarcity of fruits in Chapel Hill seems to be mainly due to rust. In the spring of 1933 the flower clusters were so badly rusted that very few flowers opened. This species and the Cock-spur Thorn are also seriously disfigured and injured by the cottony scale insect, more so than any of our other forms. Flowering May 1 to May 20.

10. Crataegus viridis L. Green Haw.

THIS is one of our largest haws. It grows in the swamps and on river banks in the coastal plain from southeastern Virginia to Florida and westward. We have specimens from its most northern known station in Virginia (Zuni, Isle of Wight County, Harbison), from Wayne and Pender counties, North Carolina, and from the Pee Dee Swamp near Cheraw and the Santee Swamp in South Carolina, and from Perry, Florida.

Trunk often armed with large compound thorns up to 6 inches long; twigs of the year red, then light gray, thorns few, rather small and slender; leaves oblong-ovate, rarely fan-shaped, 1-3 inches long and 3/4-2 inches broad, broadest

1, Twig with mature fruits.   2, twig showing thorn.   3, flower cluster.   All x ½.

near the middle, doubly and jaggedly toothed but not deeply lobed, pointed below and often with unequal sides, glabrous except for tufts of white hairs in the axils of the veins below, primary veins slightly depressed above; petioles slender and glabrous; flowers in ample clusters with long slender glabrous pedicels, stamens 15-20 with cream colored anthers; fruit nearly globose or slightly depressed, up to ¼ inch thick, bright scarlet, calyx lobes small. Flowering near Cheraw, S. C., on April 5, 1933.

Crataegus arborescens Ell. is a tree of similar appearance which inhabits the same swamps in the coastal plain and is distinguished from *C. viridis* by the purple anthers and somewhat larger fruits (up to ⅓ inch in diameter) of a red or orange color. We have collections of it from Georgia, near Augusta, and from North Carolina, in the swamp of Bowlin's Creek, Durham County (Emerson farm). One of the trees from the last mentioned place is one of the largest trees of this species we have seen. It is about 40 feet high and $12\frac{7}{10}$ inches in diameter. Some of the specimens listed under *C. viridis* may be this species. We cannot separate them except by the differently colored anthers. The abundant bright red and orange fruits of these two trees make them a most conspicuous element in our deeper swamps in winter.

11. Crataegus Chapmanii (Beadle) Ashe. **Chapman's Haw.**

THIS is a small tree which is found from Virginia to Georgia in rich soil at moderate elevations in the mountains. We have specimens from Biltmore (Beadle) and apparently it is not rare at similar elevations.

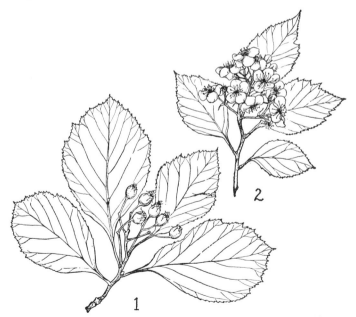

1, Twig with leaves and fruits. 2, flower cluster. All x ½.

Twigs gray; thorns few and slender; leaves ovate to ovate-lanceolate, the blade about 2-3½ (4½) inches long and 1-2¼ inches broad, not glandular, short or long pointed above, tapering down to a wing on the petiole; veins prominent below, sunken above when dry, margin with many small, rather regular teeth, lower surface persistently tomentose, the upper at first with very short appressed hairs, later becoming glabrous; flowers numerous, about ½ inch broad, borne in compound clusters, stamens 20 with purple anthers, pedicels and calyx densely tomentose as are the young twigs and petioles; fruit small, about ⅓ inch in diameter, subglobose to oblong, bright red, persistent.

This species was originally described by Dr. Chapman as *C. tomentosa microcarpa*, the type station being Silver Creek, Floyd County, Georgia. The true *C. tomentosa* L. has been recorded south to North Carolina by Beadle in Small's *Flora*, but we have no specimens and cannot substantiate its occurrence in our territory. We have specimens of it from east Tennessee (Harbison). It is distinguished from *C. Chapmanii* by the much larger dull red fruits, up to ⅝ inch long, and a more northern and western distribution.

Ashe described as *C. crux* a tree from Ashe County, North Carolina, related to *C. Chapmanii* but differing in the much less pubescent leaves and flower clusters, in having only 10 stamens with white anthers, and in the behavior of the fruit which withers and falls from the tree about the time the leaves fall. We have a specimen from the type locality (Harbison).

Another tree with nearly glabrous flower clusters, distinguished from *C. crux* by its 20 purple anthers, has been described by Ashe as *C. neofluvialis* from the mountains of Virginia, North Carolina, and Tennessee.

12. Crataegus punctata Jacq.   Dotted Thorn.

THIS is a low stout broad-topped tree with many long stout straight thorns, which is widely distributed farther north but in our states is confined to the higher altitudes, where it is common along the cold streams and around the summits of the high mountains (Virginia, North Carolina, Tennessee, and Georgia), ascending to an elevation of 6,000 feet. We have specimens from White Top Mountain, Wash-

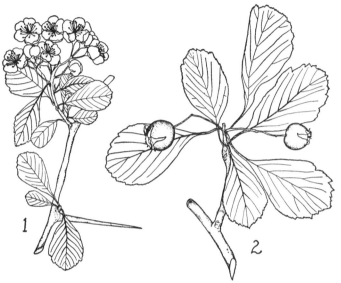

1, Twig with flower cluster and thorn.   2, twig with mature fruits.
All x ½.

ington County, Virginia, and from Craggy Mountain in Buncombe County and from Mitchell, Macon, Avery, and Watauga counties in North Carolina.

Leaves obovate, doubly serrate above the middle, scarcely serrate below, tapering downward to form more or less conspicuous wings along the petiole, blade 1½-3½ inches long and ½-2 inches wide, not glandular, hairy when young, at maturity glabrous above and with white hairs on the veins below, veins sunken above, prominent below; flowers many in a close cluster, stamens 20 with pink anthers, calyx, pedicels, and young twigs hairy; fruits short-oblong, ½-1 inch long, red or yellow, white dotted, sweet and edible.

Mr. T. G. Harbison measured a specimen of this species near the head of the Tallulah River in Georgia that was 19⅖ inches in diameter three feet from the ground.

13. Crataegus ingens Beadle.

THIS is a beautiful tree with a deep rounded crown which is found in our area only in low grounds on alluvial soil in northwest Georgia.

Twigs green; thorns stout, long, and curved; leaves approaching orbicular with rather small teeth, the blade

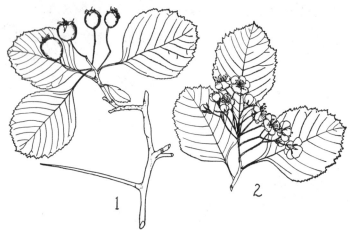

1, Twig with fruits.   2, twig with flower cluster.   All x ⅓.

decurrent almost to the base of the petiole, not glandular, about 1¾-3½ inches long, pubescent on both sides, the veins prominent below and sunken above; flowers large, in ample clusters, stamens 20 with rose anthers, calyx and flower stalks hairy; fruits large, about ⅝ inch long, subspherical to oval, red, edible.

A very closely related plant is *C. amnicola* Beadle, which grows in the same territory with *C. ingens*. It is distinguished by its whitish anthers.

14. Crataegus collina Chapm. Chapman's Hill Thorn.

THIS is a good sized tree tending to a tall, narrow shape, which is common on hillsides in the lower mountainous regions and probably also in the piedmont (as we find it in Chapel Hill) from southwestern Virginia to Tennessee and Georgia.

1, Twig with flower cluster and thorn. 2, twig with mature fruits.
All x ½.

Twigs light gray-brown; thorns stout, very long, and nearly straight, up to about 2¾ inches long; leaves broadly elliptic to broadly ovate, short-pointed, doubly toothed, about 1¾-2½ inches long and 1¼-2 inches broad, glabrous on both sides except when young, blade pointed below and decurrent down the short petiole, veins prominent below, sunken above; leaves on strong shoots with narrow, curved, highly glandular stipules; petioles and teeth glandular; flowers large, borne in ample clusters, stamens 20 with yellow anthers, calyx and pedicels pubescent; fruit nearly spherical, about ⅓-½ inch thick, red with brown dots. This species differs from *C. punctata* in the broader and more rounded leaves with glandular teeth, the yellow stamens, and the smaller fruits. It differs from *C. ingens* in the straight thorns, yellow stamens, and smaller fruits. Flowering on April 7, 1933.

15. Crataegus iracunda Beadle. **Red Haw.**

THIS is a fairly large hawthorn of rich upland woods and creek swamps. Its distribution is imperfectly known. Beadle (in Small's *Flora*) reports it only from flat woods in northwestern Georgia. Harbison said that he had found it in northern Georgia, northeastern Alabama, and through-

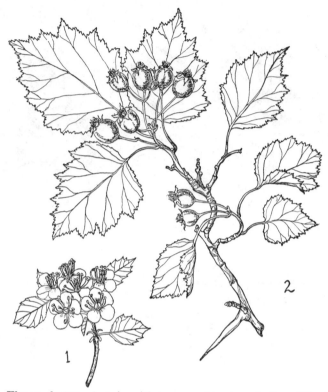

1, Flower cluster. 2, twig with leaves and mature fruits. All x ½.

out the piedmont in North Carolina. We find it one of the commonest thorns in the region of Orange and Durham counties in North Carolina.

Twigs set with conspicuous thorns; leaves broadly ovate, pointed, about 1½-2 inches long and 1-1¾ inches broad, conspicuously toothed, usually with jagged lobes, base nearly truncate or slightly acute, glabrous beneath and delicately pubescent to scabrous above, lower veins arising from the very base of the blade; petioles long, glabrous, sparingly glandular; flowers ½-¾ inch in diameter, stamens 10 with purple anthers, appearing when the leaves are very small; peduncles, pedicels, bracts, and calyx glabrous but sparsely glandular; fruit subglobose, ⅜-⅝ inch in diameter, red with small darker dots. In New Hope

Creek swamp six miles from Chapel Hill it reaches a height of 25 feet. Flowering April 8 to May 13.

This plant has heretofore been passing as *C. pruinosa* but that name is probably better confined to a close relative of this with 20 stamens occurring in a more northern latitude. *Crataegus iracunda* is separated from it by the 10 stamens and the scabrous upper surface of the leaves.

Among the numerous species made in modern days several have a very close general resemblance to *C. iracunda*. Such, for example, are *C. Boyntonii* Beadle and *C. Buckleyi* Beadle. The former differs from *C. iracunda* in the yellow anthers, the few-flowered clusters, and the somewhat pointed base of the leaf blade, while the latter has red anthers as in *C. iracunda* but is persistently distinguished from both the others by the long-stalked glands on the calyx lobes. While these plants are apparently consistent entities their distinguishing characters are so slight that their determination is impractical except for professionals. *Crataegus Boyntonii* and *C. Buckleyi* are found principally in the mountains. We also have specimens of *C. Boyntonii* from as far east as Davie County, North Carolina, and as far north as Buena Vista, Virginia.

Beadle has described as *C. arcana* a tree which is common around Asheville, N. C., and is said to differ from *C. iracunda* in having 20 stamens with purple anthers and differently shaped fruit. A similar tree with 20 purple anthers is *C. Sargentii*, found in the foothill region of northwestern Georgia and in Tennessee and Alabama.

Another tree occurring in the rather high mountains is *C. roanensis* Ashe, differing from *C. iracunda* in the more sharply cut and tapering teeth, the more ovate-elliptic and succulent fruit, and the fact that the flowers unfold when the leaves are about grown. One of these trees stands on the edge of the lake within a few feet of the Highlands Laboratory at Highlands, North Carolina. We have other specimens from Whiteside Mountain and from a field near Highlands in Macon County and from Pisgah Ridge in North Carolina.

Three other trees looking much like *C. iracunda* are *C. georgiana* Sarg., with 20 stamens with purple anthers, from near Rome, Ga.; *C. drymophila* Sarg., with 10 stamens with purple anthers, common in central and northwestern Georgia, usually growing in low damp woods; and *C. basilica* Beadle, with 15-20 stamens with purple anthers, found in open woods and fields in western North Carolina at altitudes of 2,000 to 3,000 feet.

16. Crataegus meridiana Beadle.   Southern Haw.

THIS is a rather small tree which is common throughout the sandhill country of the Carolinas, Georgia, and Florida. This haw represents a large group of so-called species that have been distinguished and named in recent years.   A

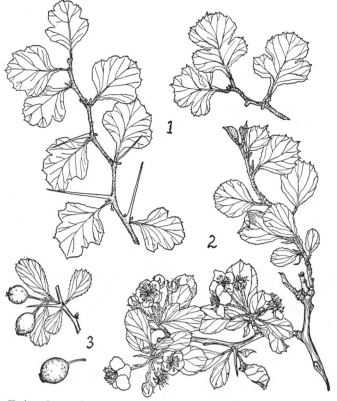

1, Twigs from vigorous young shoot. 2, flower clusters. 3, twig with mature fruits and smaller leaves. All x ½.

good many of them are shrubs. Around Augusta and no doubt at other places as well, this group runs into a profusion of forms that are baffling even to an expert. Many of these forms have never been recorded or named. Among the tree forms in this section we are including two other species that are conspicuous and easily recognized. These are *C. dispar* and *C. Ravenelii,* for which see below. We have specimens of *C. meridiana* from Cumberland and Sampson counties, North Carolina, from Chesterfield, Richland, Barnwell, Kershaw, Lexington, and Sumter counties, South Carolina, and from Augusta, Georgia.

Bark of trunk dark gray, lower part finely checkered as in the dogwood; twigs and branches zigzag, often drooping, older twigs nearly black with numerous short black thorns about ½-1⅝ inches long; leaves rather thick, obovate-spatulate to nearly orbicular, small on fruiting spurs, blade ⅜-1⅝ inches broad (on strong shoots often broader than long and tending to be distinctly 3-lobed), somewhat 3-lobed on the distal half, very conspicuously glandular all around and to the base of the petiole, upper surface when young white-tomentose, particularly on the veins, later nearly glabrous or appearing roughened under the lens, dull or faintly shining, lower surface tomentose, especially in the angles of the veins, later becoming subglabrous; flowers few, usually 4-7, in short simple clusters, stamens 20 with white anthers, pedicels and calyx cup white-villose, calyx lobes toothed and strongly glandular; fruits few in a cluster, 1-3, orange-brown or orange-yellow, oblong or subglobose, ⅓-½ inch thick, edible, ripening in October and falling soon afterwards.

The group to which *C. meridiana* belongs is called the *flava* group for an old name given by Aiton to an American hawthorn cultivated in England. Where it came from is unknown and no American tree has been found that is matched with the cultivated one with any great certainty. Beadle in Small's *Flora* draws his description entirely from a specimen cultivated in England under that name. Sargent thought that he had a tree near River Junction, Florida, which fitted *C. flava* well enough. We are not able to pass judgment on this. Both Beadle and Sargent give the stamens as having purple anthers. Beadle gives the number as 10 and Sargent as 20.

Closely related to *C. meridiana* is a smaller tree, sometimes a shrub, that seems to accompany it in all the localities where they are known to occur. It has been named *C. dolosa* by Beadle and is distinguished by the nearly glabrous leaves with smaller teeth and without lobes, the shorter petioles with less conspicuous glands, and globose not oblong fruits. The trees are more upright and the twigs less zigzag. Both have 20 stamens with white anthers.

While the *flava* group is preponderantly one of the sandhills or sandy country at the lower altitudes, some of them ascend to the mountains. Among those most common and easily recognized in the North Carolina and Georgia mountains are the following. *Crataegus pentasperma* Ashe (type locality Macon County, N. C.) is most like *C. meridiana,* which it closely resembles in the zigzag branches, small glandular leaves, and the densely pubescent flower clusters. It differs in the leaves being toothed only at the tips, the usually more numerous flowers, and the five-seeded green fruit. *Crataegus cullasagensis* Ashe (type locality Macon County, N. C.) is much like *C. pentasperma* but is almost quite glabrous throughout and has larger leaves. We have it from Turnerville, Georgia (Ashe). *Crataegus senta* Beadle (type locality Biltmore, N. C.) differs from *C. cullasagensis* in the broader, larger leaves and less jagged branches. *Crataegus aprica* Beadle (type locality Biltmore, N. C.) differs from all three above in having more ovate leaves with less jagged ends and smaller teeth which are nearly all around the blade.

Other small trees of the *flava* group recognized in Sargent are *C. visenda* Beadle with 20 stamens with pink anthers from Liberty County, Florida; *C. tristis* Beadle with 20 stamens with red anthers from around Rome, Georgia; *C. lacrimata* Small with 20 stamens with yellow anthers from western Florida; and *C. panda* Beadle with 20 stamens with nearly white anthers from Tallahassee, Florida.

Two other small trees of northern Florida coming next to the *flava* group are *C. opima* Beadle and *C. robur* Beadle.

They have rather broad, deeply toothed, glabrous leaves, few flowers (3-10) in a glabrous cluster, 20 stamens with rose anthers and small or medium sized, orange or orange-red fruits.

A most striking fruit among the haws is the large orange-red, pear-shaped one of *Crataegus colonica* Beadle. The fruit is unusually large and ripens and falls in late August. Not only are the fruits pear-shaped but can almost be said to have a neck below, a shape we have not seen in any other haw. The stamens are about 20, the color unknown. The leaves are spatulate to broadly fan-shaped, toothed above the middle and with conspicuous dark glands all around, thick, more or less shining above and pubescent below as are the petioles, fruit stalks, and young twigs. On strong shoots the leaves are pubescent above even in midsummer. This is a small tree said to be rather common around Bluffton, South Carolina, where it was collected years ago by Dr. Mellichamp. We have found in the sandhills on Route No. 1 about 16 miles northeast of Columbia, South Carolina, a tree 18 feet high with exactly such fruit and agreeing in other respects with this species. The fruits were turning orange-red on July 15, 1933.

17. Crataegus dispar Beadle.

THIS is a small tree up to 26 feet high with zigzag branches that is plentiful in the sandhills of Aiken and Edgefield counties, South Carolina, and around Augusta, Georgia. We have flowering specimens from Summerville (Augusta), Georgia (Harbison, Ashe), and Aiken, South Carolina, and leaves from Lutz Ferry, South Carolina. We have taken the fruit characters from Sargent.

Young twigs woolly-tomentose; leaves bluish green, fan-shaped, small with short petioles, blade ½-¾ inch long, deeply toothed or lobed in the upper half, strongly glandular, lower surface and margin tomentose when young, becoming much less so; petioles densely woolly-tomentose; flowers rather few, 3 or 4 to about 7 in a simple woolly cluster; pedicels ¼-½ inch long, flowers about ¾ inch broad, stamens 20; fruit red, subglobose, about ⅓ inch thick, with prominent reflexed calyx lobes.

Crataegus dispar.   Twig with leaves and flowers, x ¾.

This species is in the *flava* group, which is a very difficult and confused one.   We are including this because it is rather easily recognized and is common and conspicuous in a section of South Carolina and Georgia where it will arouse the interest and inquiries of numerous tourists.   It differs from *C. meridiana* in larger flowers and smaller red fruits, bluish green leaves with more numerous sharper teeth on the ends of the blades and with a more abruptly contracted base.

In 1900 Ashe described as *C. Cuthbertii* a haw from dry sandy soil (type locality Bladen County, N. C.) that from the description could be either *C. dispar* or *C. meridiana*. We have not been able to find any of his material of this species.

18. **Crataegus Ravenelii** Sarg.   **Big-fruited Haw.**

THIS is a handsome widely spreading tree which attains a

size of trunk rarely surpassed by any other haw. One on Haw
Ridge near McBee (Chesterfield County sandhills), South
Carolina, is 1 foot 4 inches in diameter four feet from the
ground. This large hawthorn is found in the sandhills of
South Carolina and Georgia as around McBee and Aiken,
South Carolina, and Augusta, Georgia. We have many
collections of our own from sandy soil in Lexington and
Kershaw counties, South Carolina.

Twigs reddish, strongly woolly throughout most of the
first season; thorns rather stout, about 1-1½ inches long,
straight or nearly so; leaves fan-shaped to spatulate, short-

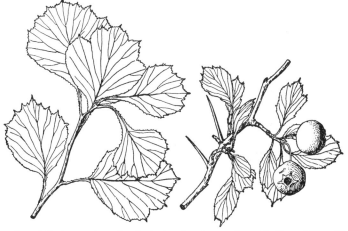

Twig of fast growing shoot; twig showing mature fruits.   All x ½.

tipped, strongly cut and serrate in the distal half, finely
serrate below, tapering down as a wing on the rather long
slender woolly petiole, upper side shining, sparsely hairy
principally on the veins, densely woolly below when young,
soon only hairy on the veins, about ¾-1¾ inches broad,
many smaller, conspicuously glandular; flowers large, few
in a cluster, stamens 20, anthers yellow, pedicels and calyx
woolly; fruit red to yellow with a red cheek, ½-⅔ inch
thick, acid-sweet, edible, variable in time of ripening. The
very large tree on Haw Ridge mentioned above ripens its
fruits late and retains them during the winter. Another
very large tree near it ripens its fruits in September and

drops them soon afterwards. On this tree the fruit is the largest known in that part of the county and is famous for its edibility.

Haw Ridge in the sandhills of Chesterfield County, South Carolina, on the Sowell farm about two miles west of McBee exhibits the most remarkable collection of haw thorns in a limited area that we have ever seen. Within 100 to 200 yards from the home of Mr. C. W. Sowell we found five species. Four of them are not before recorded from South Carolina. These are *C. aprica* (type locality Biltmore, N. C.), *C. meridiana* (type locality Ozark, Ala.), *C. dolosa* (type locality Abbeville, Ala.) and *C. abdita* (type locality River Junction, Florida). This is important evidence to show that while many of the recently described species may be separated apparently on slight differences they are nevertheless widely distributed and not confined to single individuals. In two other ways Haw Ridge is remarkable. Within a few feet of Mr. Sowell's garden occurs one of the largest hawthorns in diameter on record and very near to it is another specimen almost as large that bears the largest fruit of any known species in the area covered by this book. There are within a few hundred yards on the same ridge six or seven other trees of the same species bearing equally large fruit. It is these big-fruited haws that make Haw Ridge famous in this section of South Carolina, as they are prized for eating and the making of jelly. The fruits are nearly an inch thick and borne abundantly. The largest tree above mentioned is also *C. Ravenelii,* the fruit of which though considerably smaller is still good eating. A point worth mentioning in regard to the big-fruited *C. Ravenelii* is that the seeds come up the first spring after planting. Mrs. Sowell's sister, Mrs. Mary Huff, took seeds with her to her home in Georgia. They sprouted the following spring and are now bearing fruits just like those of the home tree. In April these magnificent trees of *C. Ravenelii* are said to produce pure white flowers in great abundance, a superb sight.

19. **Crataegus mollis** (T. and G.) Scheele. **Red Haw.**
THIS good sized hawthorn of northern distribution is found

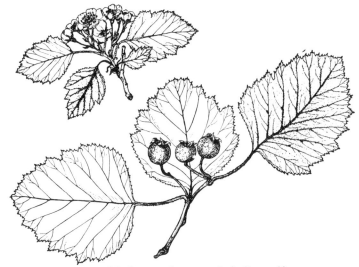

Twigs with flowers, leaves, and fruits. x ⅓.

mostly in rich woods and low grounds. It is known to occur in our area only in middle Tennessee (Davidson County); however, it will probably be found in other places farther west and north in that state.

Twigs light brown, covered at first with silky hairs; thorns few, straight, stout, about 1-2 inches long. Leaves large, long-petioled, the blade broadly ovate with base square or rounded, 2½-4¾ inches long, 1¾-4½ inches wide, doubly serrate or incised and serrate, densely soft-pubescent beneath and thinly pubescent above. Flowers up to one inch broad, in ample clusters that are densely tomentose throughout; anthers about 20, yellow; pedicels with conspicuous narrow bracts; calyx lobes narrow, abundantly set with reddish glands, as are the bracts. Fruit large, globose, up to one inch thick, bright red, edible.

20. Crataegus Harbisonii Beadle.

THIS is a good sized spreading tree, up to 25 feet high and one foot thick. It was discovered on limestone hills, West Nashville, Tennessee, by Mr. T. G. Harbison in 1899. Small reports it from Alabama; otherwise it is not known except from the type locality.

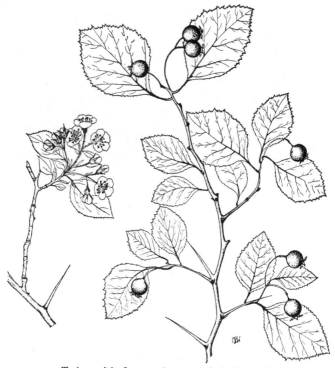

Twigs with flowers, leaves and fruits, x ⅓.

Leaves broadly oval to elliptic, unevenly and sharply toothed and pointed at each end, the blade about 1½-3 inches long and 1-2¼ inches broad, white pubescent when young, when mature thick, shining, rough above, dull and more or less pubescent below. Petioles pubescent and glandular, the glands often extending up the base of the leaf blade; stipules long and narrow, strongly glandular, deciduous. Twigs red, hairy until late in the season. Flowers about ¾ inch broad, about 10-12 in villose corymbs which are usually crowded on the ends of the twigs. Stamens 10-20 (usually 20), anthers yellow. Pedicels and base of calyx hairy; calyx lobes long, glandular, bracts large and glandular. Fruit red, large, subglobose, about ⅝ inch long, meaty, dark-dotted, ripening and falling early in October. Spines numerous, stout, straight, up to 2 inches long. For a fine painting of *C. Harbisonii*, see *Addisonia* 21: pl. 693, 1941.

PRUNUS* (Tourn.) L.

1. Fruit surface tomentose; stone pitted and wrinkled
   Prunus Persica, Peach No. 9
   Fruit surface glabrous; stone smooth............. 2
2. Fruit about ⅔-1 inch thick.................... 3
   Fruit smaller................................. 4
3. Fruit bright red or yellow, sweet and edible;
   leaves less than one inch wide
   Prunus angustifolia, Chickasaw Plum No. 1
   Fruit bright red, sweet and edible; leaves more than
   one inch wide
   Prunus Munsoniana, Wild Goose Plum No. 6
   Fruit reddish yellow, purplish, or red, bitter-sweet;
   leaves more than one inch wide
   Prunus americana, River Plum No. 2
4. Stone nearly spherical; flowers ⅝-1 inch wide;
   fruit dark red to nearly black; edible cherries
   escaped from cultivation...................... 5
   Stone elongated, flowers usually less than ⅝ inch
   wide; fruit very sour and in some also bitter.... 6
5. Fruit sweet
   Prunus avium, Sweet Cherry No. 7
   Fruit sour
   Prunus cerasus, Sour Cherry No. 8
6. Fruit bright red; a tree of the mountains
   Prunus pennsylvanica, Wild Red Cherry No. 3
   Fruit reddish purple to nearly black............. 7
7. A small tree of the coastal plain
   Prunus umbellata and variety, Black Sloe No. 4
   A very rare tree of the mountains
   Prunus alleghaniensis, Sloe No. 5

1. Prunus angustifolia Marsh. Chickasaw Plum.

This is a small, low tree with a dense, spreading top and numerous suckers which forms the "plum thickets" so common on the edges of fields and in waste places from the coast to the foothills in all our states. According to an old Indian tradition, it was brought from beyond the Mississippi.

Leaves small, narrow, 1-2 inches long, ⅓-⅔ of an inch wide, the teeth fine and close; flowers white, small, borne 2-4 in a cluster, appearing well before the leaves; fruits sweet and edible, red or yellow, the majority of the forms spherical and about ⅔ of an inch in diameter, but very variable in size, shape and quality, ripening in early summer; pedicels about ⅓ inch long. This species has given

* In Small's *Flora* and Britton's *Trees*, P. *nigra* is included from Georgia. This is an error.

Twig with leaves; fruits. All x ⅖.

rise to several cultivated plums such as the Newman and Lone Star. Flowering from February 16 to March 26.

From Lake and Polk counties, Florida, Harper has described as *P. geniculata* a plant near this species but differing in being a more diffusely branched shrub with smaller flowers and shorter pedicels.

2. **Prunus americana** Marsh. **River Plum.**

THIS is a somewhat thorny tree, reaching 20-30 feet in height, found along streams in the piedmont and lower mountains (up to 3,000 feet) and along large rivers in the coastal plain, in our area south to western Florida.

Leaves ovate to obovate, 2½-4½ inches long, 1-2 inches wide, closely toothed, smooth or tomentose below; flowers borne in umbels, nearly white to pink, very abundant and variable and in some forms rivalling the Japanese Cherry in its delicacy and beauty; fruits dull purplish red, conspicuously glaucous, ¾ inch in diameter, sweet but bitterish and scarcely edible, though making a good preserve. They begin to ripen in August and some trees still have ripening fruit in early October. The Chapel Hill plant, from which the above description is made, does not agree fully with the description by Sargent. The fruit is not orange or red and shows a very pronounced bloom. How-

Branch with leaves and fruits,
x ⅖.

ever, somewhat farther west at Asheboro, N. C., trees were found with clear red fruits. As regards suckering behavior, our Chapel Hill form is peculiar. Some of the trees sucker heavily and some do not. Some of the cultivated plums are supposed to be hybrids between this and *P. angustifolia*. Flowering March 14 to April 3.

Sargent has described a variety of the River Plum with thinner, finely serrate leaves, purple fruits, and without root suckers as *Prunus americana* var. *floridana* from the vicinity of St. Marks, Wakulla County, Florida. Harbison reported it from Tallahassee and we have collected it at River Junction. Through this northwestern part of Florida it is more common than the typical *P. americana*. The color of the fruit of our tree is more like the variety *floridana*.

On Haw Ridge, Chesterfield County, South Carolina, near where *Prunus umbellata* was found there was a small plum tree, which may be described as follows: Leaves broadly lanceolate, pointed at both ends, about 1-1¾ inches long, very finely toothed all around, bi-glandular at the base, glabrous above, midrib and larger veins tomentose below; petioles short, puberulent; twigs dark red, quite glabrous; fruit spherical or nearly so, about ⅝ inch thick, orange-yellow with a faint bloom and a red cheek flesh hardly edible, bitterish, stones about ⅓-⁷⁄₁₆ inch long, pointed at both ends, faintly pitted, ridged on one side, slightly grooved on the other, pedicels short, about ¼ inch long. This plum does not agree with any species, native or escaped, that is supposed to occur in our territory. The time of ripening indicates a possible relationship to *P. umbellata* as does the shape and harshness of the fruits. They were fully ripe and dropping from the tree on July 17, 1933. Abundant fruits on a tree of *P. umbellata* near were approaching ripeness at the same time. The latter differs in the much smaller purple fruits ripening a little later. Compared to *P. americana,* as we know it, the fruits are smaller, have a different color, mature much earlier and have a harsher taste. The leaves are not noticeably different. One will often have difficulty in finding specific names for plums found growing spontaneously near habitations. The edible ones are often hybrids.

3. **Prunus pennsylvanica** L. f. **Wild Red Cherry, Fire Cherry.**

THIS is a small tree that is common in the mountains of Virginia and North Carolina, with its southern limit in northern Georgia. In the mountains it is the first tree to reforest the burnt-over portions. At a distance the yellow-green splashes on the mountain sides, contrasting strongly with the darker green of unburnt areas, indicate the presence of this tree.

Bark on branches smooth, red; leaves oblong-lanceolate, 2-6 inches long, ¾-1¾ inches wide, finely toothed, thin, usually pubescent along most of the length of the midrib below; flowers small, white, borne in 3-5-flowered clusters appearing with the leaves; fruits red, sour, about ¼ inch in diameter.

Prunus cuneata Raf. (*P. susquehannae* Willd.) is a small shrub that has been reported by Memminger (*Journ. Eli. Mitch. Sci. Soc.* 30: 136. 1915) from Henderson County, North Carolina. The black fruit is borne in small clusters along the twigs. Memminger (*Bot. Gaz.* 13: 95. 1888) first

1, Twig with fruits. 2, twig with flowers. All x ½.

reported this (in error) as *P. pumila,* a more northern shrub. In his 1915 list he also includes *P. umbellata* but later deletes this as an error (*Journ. Eli. Mitch. Sci. Soc.* **32:** 120. 1916).

4. **Prunus umbellata** Elliott. **Black Sloe, Hog Plum.**
This is a small, spreading tree of limited range in the coastal plain and lower piedmont from North Carolina to the Everglade region in Florida. We have specimens from Anson, Stanly, and Montgomery counties in North Carolina, and it is reported from Richmond County in the same state by J. S. Holmes. According to Holmes, it

"grows on well drained old pine fields and upper slopes and tops of hills in the basin of the Pee Dee River and up to 15 or 20 miles from that river." For exact locations and other interesting information, see *Journ. Eli. Mitch. Sci. Soc.* **34**: 126, 1918. The discovery of this tree by Holmes added a new tree to the North Carolina list. It is not rare in sandy woods near the coast in the neighborhood of Myrtle Beach, South Carolina, and in that state it grows

1, Twig with flowers. 2, twig with leaves and one fruit and large stone. 3, medium sized fruit and stone. 4, elongated fruit and stone. All x ½.

certainly as far inland as the sandy ridges of Chesterfield County (as on Haw Ridge).

Twigs glabrous or pubescent in the young stages, leaves oblong-elliptic, pointed, the blade 1¼-2½ inches long and ½-1 inch broad, very finely toothed, glabrous except for the pubescent midrib; petiole pubescent, about ¼-½ inch long; flowers white, about ⅓-½ inch across, borne in 2-4-flowered clusters, sepals glabrous without and pubescent within; pedicels glabrous; fruit reddish purple (a form with red fruits is said to be common in Orange County, Fla.), flesh always very sour, sometimes bitter, on a slender stalk about ¼-⅝ inch long, variable in size and shape, e.g., nearly spherical, ⅜ inch thick, stone plump, ³⁄₁₆ x ⁵⁄₁₆ inch (tree from Anson County); fruit oblong, ⁷⁄₁₆ x ⁹⁄₁₆ inch, stone flattish, ¼ x ½ inch (tree from Stanly County); fruit nearly spherical, ⅝ inch in diameter, stone very plump, ⁵⁄₁₆ x ⁷⁄₁₆ inch (second tree from Stanly County cultivated in the Coker Arboretum). Fruits ripening at Chapel Hill on July 10, 1926, near Myrtle Beach, S. C., on July 15, 1932, and in Chesterfield County, S. C., on July 17, 1933. An excellent, tart jelly was made from the Myrtle Beach fruits by Mrs. D. R. Coker. Near Myrtle Beach this plum reaches a height of 17 feet and a diameter of 8⅔ inches three feet from the ground. This is an interesting tree which is rarely or never seen in cultivation and is little known. A plant in the Arboretum brought in from Albemarle, N. C., has grown into a small tree with a widely spreading crown. Flowering at Chapel Hill on February 24, 1933.

A form with oblong fruit, tomentose or villose twigs and tomentose leaves, which has been named *P. umbellata* var. *injucunda* (Small) Sarg., is found in several counties in central and southern Georgia, near Columbia, S. C. (Coker), and is reported from Trenton, S. C., by Boynton. He also reports a double-flowered form at Warm Springs, Georgia. Another form with oblong fruits but having glabrous twigs has been described by Beadle as *P. mitis*. It is also reported from Georgia.

5. **Prunus alleghaniensis** Porter. **Sloe.**

THIS is usually a straggling shrub, rarely a small tree, with a northern range and found in our area only in a few places in Virginia and North Carolina. We have collected it in Franklin County, Va., and it is reported from Rockbridge County, and Ashe found it on Cheat Mountain in Ashe County, North Carolina. Harbison saw it at this place and said it was rather common there. We have a specimen from him collected along Buffalo Creek in Ashe County.

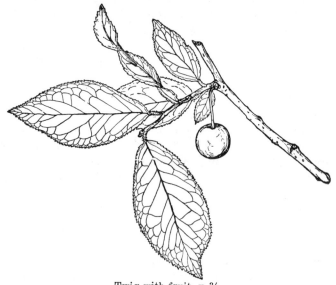

Twig with fruit, x ⅗.

Leaves lanceolate to oblong-ovate, about 2-3 inches long, glabrous or somewhat pubescent at maturity; flowers only 2-4 in an umbel; fruit up to ⅔ of an inch thick, spherical, dark purple with a bloom, flesh acid. We do not know this plant ourselves, and from descriptions we cannot find any satisfactory way of separating it from *P. umbellata* except for its very different habitat.

6. Prunus Munsoniana Wight and Hedrick. Wild Goose Plum.

This good sized tree of rich lowlands occurs in our area only in central and western Tennessee. It is often cultivated and is occasionally found spontaneous in other states. Like the cultivated cherries it suckers freely and tends to become permanent.

A tree of broadly rounded head and stout trunk. Leaves elliptic or lance-elliptic with tapering point, finely serrate, after maturity glabrous above and somewhat pubescent below. Fruit round to oval, bright red, rarely yellow, about one inch long, sweet and juicy, ripening in June and July.

There is another large plum, *P. hortulana,* of western distribution reported from northwestern Tennessee (Sargent) and Georgia (Small) that has about the same leaf, with less edible fruit which ripens in September and October.

7. Prunus avium L. Sweet Cherry, Mazzard Cherry.

This well known cultivated cherry from Europe and western Asia is frequently found escaped in hedgerows and such places. It is distinguished from the Sour Cherry below by the sweet, usually larger fruit, the glabrous leaves and much larger size of the tree (up to 40 feet or more). Both this and the next send up root suckers and when once planted tend to become permanently established.

8. Prunus cerasus L. Sour Cherry, Morello Cherry.

This is a small tree with a broadly spreading head, which is a native of Europe and western Asia. It is distinguished from the Sweet Cherry by the pubescent leaves, the usually smaller and sour fruit and the much smaller size of the tree. As in the Sweet Cherry many horticultural forms of this cherry are known. It also suckers freely and tends to become established.

9. Prunus Persica Batsch. Peach.

The Peach, a native of China, is rather frequently spontaneous particularly in hedgerows and around farms. The Nectarine, a spontaneous seedling of the Peach, has a smooth instead of a fuzzy skin. It is much rarer in cultivation and we have never seen it escaped.

PADUS L.

Leaves ovate to obovate, the teeth sharp and slender; calyx lobes not present on mature fruit
     Padus nana, Choke Cherry No. 1
Leaves oval to oblong-lanceolate, teeth coarse; calyx lobes present on mature fruit
     Padus serotina, Wild Black Cherry No. 2

1. **Padus nana** (Du Roi) Roemer. (**Prunus virginiana** of authors.) **Choke Cherry.**

THIS shrub or small tree is found in the mountains and upper piedmont of our area from Virginia to Georgia. In North Carolina it is known to occur on Cedar Cliff Mountain, Buncombe County, in Iredell County and at Tryon, Polk County (U. N. C. Herb., Peattie).

Bark grayish black, very bitter with a rank disagreeable odor; leaves obovate, blade about ¾-4 inches long and ⁹⁄₁₆ to 2 inches broad, serrate with slender, sharp teeth, thin, glabrous; petioles delicate, about ¼ inch long; flowers very small, white, borne in terminal racemes about 1¼-2 inches long counting the stalk; fruit red to blackish, said to be ¼ to ⅓ inch thick.

A variety of this species, *P. virginiana leucocarpa,* which has large yellowish edible fruits, is found in Vermont and Massachusetts.

2. **Padus serotina** (Ehrh.) Agardh. (**Prunus serotina** Ehrh.) **Choke Cherry, Wild Black Cherry.**

THIS is usually a small tree common in the middle and western parts of our states and not so common in the eastern part (except in Tennessee), extending nearly to the Everglade region in Florida.

Bark dark red-brown, smooth when young, rough in age; leaves oval to lanceolate, 2-6 inches long, rather coarsely toothed, dark green, thickish, smooth or with a conspicuous line of reddish hairs along the midrib near the base; calyx lobes present on the fruit; fruits ripening in July, small, about ⅓ inch in diameter, black, not edible,

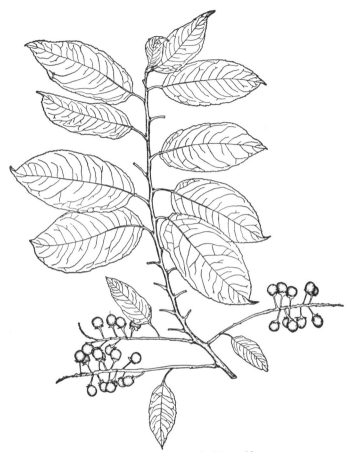

Branch with mature fruits, x ⅓.

on short stalks scattered along a common terminal fruiting axis (a raceme). In the mountains it becomes a large tree up to 100 feet high. A section in the museum in Raleigh from Transylvania County, North Carolina, has a diameter of 3 feet 1 inch. We have measured one tree 48 feet high and 2 feet 1½ inches in diameter three feet from the ground at Murrell's Inlet on the South Carolina coast, and one specimen in the Primeval Forest at Highlands which was 3 feet 9⅕ inches in diameter at four and a half feet

from the ground. Prof. S. A. Cain measured a Wild Black
Cherry in the Great Smoky Mountains that was 4 feet in
diameter at breast height. It would be a very important
timber tree if large trees were more abundant. Flowering
April 3 to April 28.

Small and Vail report *Padus serotina neomontana*
(Sudworth) Small from the balds on White Top Mountain
in Virginia. They say that it is "readily distinguished
from the species by the larger, more lanceolate and coriaceous leaves, the shorter, thicker and more divergent
racemes and the larger fruit."

A small tree first found near Augusta, Georgia, and
later reported from Upton and Meriwether counties, has
been named *Padus Cuthbertii* by Small. It is very similar
to *P. serotina*, from which it differs in its tomentose twigs
and apparently smaller size. Harper (*Geol. Surv. Ala.
Mon.* 9: 1928) is of the opinion that *P. Cuthbertii* and *P.
serotina neomontana* are the same as *Prunus alabamensis*
Mohr. He says: "I am inclined to apply them all to a
small tree with leaning or crooked trunk, differing from *P.
serotina* in these characters, and also in having blunter
leaves with rusty hairs along the midribs beneath and in
being more tolerant of fire." Harbison said that *P. Cuthbertii* and *P. alabamensis* are distinct. Small in his *Flora*
states that the fruits of *P. Cuthbertii* are red and the leaves
are blunt, and that in *P. alabamensis* the fruits are purple
and the leaves are acute or acuminate.

LAUROCERASUS Reichenb.

1. **Laurocerasus caroliniana** (Mill.) Roem. (**Prunus caroliniana** Ait.) **Carolina Laurel Cherry, Laurel Cherry,
Carolina Cherry, Mock Orange.**

THIS is a small evergreen tree. Its native habitat is probably confined to a rather narrow strip along the coast
(except in Florida) on light, fertile, well drained soil on
bluffs and banks near streams. Scattered by birds from
cultivated trees it is now spontaneous here and there as
far inland as the sandhills. Its native range is from extreme southeastern North Carolina to Florida and Texas.

Twig with leaves and fruits, x ⅖.

It forms dense thickets on Pawley's Island, South Carolina.

Leaves oblong-lanceolate, 2-4½ inches long, ¾-1½ inches wide, with a few teeth or the edges entire, thick and shiny above; flowers white, small, in short dense racemes; fruits black, oblong, about ½ inch long, hanging on the tree through the winter, not edible but popular with birds. The Laurel Cherry may reach a height of 30 feet and a diameter of one foot. It is a beautiful tree and is much used throughout the coastal plain as an ornamental and as a screen. The wilting leaves develop hydrocyanic acid, a deadly poison. Flowering in cultivation at Chapel Hill on March 23, 1933, and April 6, 1929.

Fernald (*Rhodora* **46**: 45. 1944) adds *Prunus nemoralis* Bartram (*Travels*, p. 408, 1791; p. 326 of 1928 ed.) as a synonym of this species.

LEGUMINOSAE (PULSE FAMILY)

CERCIS L.

1. **Cercis canadensis L. Redbud, Judas Tree.**
THIS is a small tree of fertile, well drained upland woods, hillsides, and valleys in all our area. It is common in the piedmont, sparingly scattered in the mountains up to 2,500 feet, and rarer in the coastal plain where it is scarcely ever found except in the vicinity of larger streams. In the

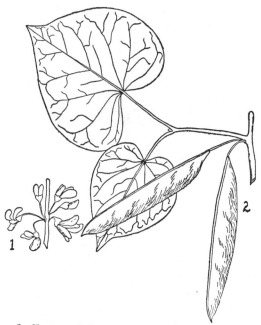

1, Cluster of flowers. 2, branch with leaves
and fruits. All x ½.

middle section of North Carolina it disappears quickly
from the highway view just east of Wake Forest and Lil-
lington though it is quite abundant from there westward.

Bark light and smooth; leaves heart-shaped, entire,
smooth above and smooth or slightly pubescent below, turning yellow in the fall; flowers rosy magenta or a duller
purple magenta, pea-shaped, borne on short pedicels in
fascicles along the twigs; fruits small flat pods bearing
several seeds, often borne in large numbers. There is much
variation in the color of the flowers. Some forms are dull,
others very pale. The brighter colored form makes a very
decorative tree for lawns, and is especially beautiful in
combination with dogwood in front of evergreen. A white
form of this species has been found several times in the
wild and has been named var. *alba*. It is now for sale by
several nurseries. A double-flowered form, var. *plena,*
found in Mississippi, is now being cultivated at the Missouri Botanical Garden. Flowering usually from March

16 to April 1, but in 1932 not in full bloom until the second week in April.

GLEDITSIA L.

Fruit 12-18 inches long, many-seeded
> *Gleditsia triacanthos*, Honey Locust   No. 1

Fruit 1-3 inches long with 1-3 seeds; a tree of the deep coastal swamps
> *Gleditsia aquatica*, Water Locust   No. 2

1. Gleditsia triacanthos L.   Honey Locust.

THIS is a rather small thorny tree of waste places, ditch

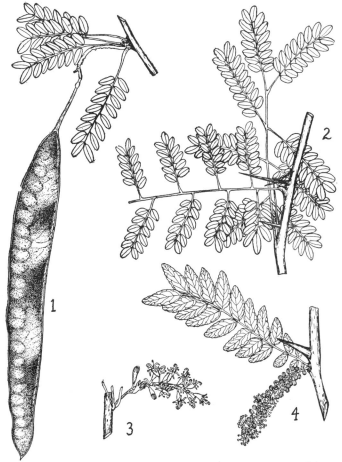

1, Twig with mature fruit, x ¼.   2, twig with thorns and leaves, x ¼.   3, female inflorescence, x ½.   4, male inflorescence, x ½.

banks, etc., throughout our area. It is said to be an introduced tree from west of the Alleghanies, but it has now
become thoroughly naturalized.

Leaves once or twice compound with many small leaflets ½-1½ inches long, acute or rounded at apex, minutely
serrate or entire, dark green above, lighter below; flowers
very small, yellowish green, male and female ones borne in
separate racemes; fruits long flat many-seeded black pods
up to 16 inches long, with a rather small amount of sweet
edible pulp. These fruits are often mixed with persimmons
to form what is known in the south as locust or persimmon
beer. The feathery foliage and spreading top give a pleasing appearance to this tree but it is rarely planted as an
ornamental, probably due to the large numbers of fruits and
rather wicked thorns dangerous to children. However, a
thornless form is known (*Bull. Mo. Bot. Gard.* 20: 101.
1932). In regard to the fruits, we have seen no reference
to the fact that individuals are often found that are almost
or entirely sterile. Two such specimens (large fine trees
but now dead) grew on Glenburnie Farm, Chapel Hill. If
this character could be combined with thornlessness, which
seems easily possible, we should have a very desirable
ornamental tree for streets and lawns. Flowering from
April 20 to May 9.

2. Gleditsia aquatica Marsh. (G. monosperma Walter). Water Locust.

THIS is a local tree somewhat smaller than the Honey Locust that occurs in the swamps of coastal North Carolina
and extends into Georgia, Florida, and westward near the
coast and up the Mississippi River and its tributaries. Heretofore it has been reported in the Atlantic states only as
far north as South Carolina, but we can now extend its
range to Sampson County, North Carolina. In Florida it is
found along the Suwannee River (Harper). We have specimens from the Santee Swamp in South Carolina, from
Hickman, Kentucky, and the New York Botanical Garden Herbarium contains collections from Santee and Summerville in South Carolina.

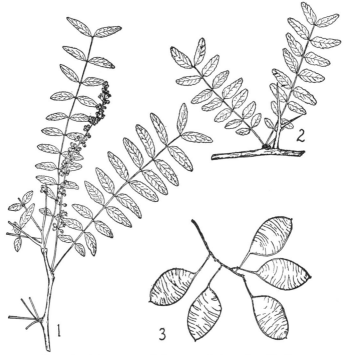

1, Branch with raceme of flowers. 2, branch with thorn.
3, mature fruits. All x ⅓.

Twigs dark gray, armed with slender sharp often compound spines, and frequently marked with many large corky lenticels; leaves 3-8 inches long, borne on knotty spurs; leaflets 12-22, ovate-oblong, ½-1 inch long and ¼-½ inch wide, crenate, smooth; flowers small, greenish, borne in long slender racemes; fruit a dark brown, flat, long-stalked pod about 1½-3½ inches long containing 1-3 seeds. This tree is distinguished from the Honey Locust by its fewer leaflets, by the more delicate thorns, by the much smaller pods containing only 1-3 seeds, and by the absence of sweet pulp.

CLADRASTIS Raf.

1. **Cladrastis lutea** (Michx. f.) Koch. (**C. tinctoria** Raf.). **Yellow Wood.**

THIS is a beautiful, rare tree which is found in our area in the high mountains of eastern Tennessee, central Tennes-

1, Twig with flowers and leaves. 2, twig with fruits. All x ¼.

see near Nashville, and in rich coves in the mountains of extreme western North Carolina. It is known from Swain, Clay, Macon, northwestern Haywood (J. S. Holmes), Cherokee (Pinchot and Ashe), and Graham counties (Ashe).

Leaves pinnately compound with 5-11 entire, alternate leaflets; flowers white, fragrant, wisteria-like in long, drooping, often compound panicles up to 16 inches long and 12 inches broad; fruit a flat pod, 3-4 inches long, containing a few flat seeds. The wood is yellow and yields a dye. The branches are thornless, by which it is easily distinguished from the Black Locust. In cultivation this is one of the most beautiful of our native flowering trees. There is a delicacy about its flower clusters that is most pleasing. Flowering at Chapel Hill about May 5 to May 26.

ROBINIA L.

Branches with short thorns; twigs and leaf stalks not sticky
   Robinia Pseudoacacia, Black Locust No. 1
Branches with or without short thorns; twigs and leaf stalks very sticky
   Robinia viscosa, Clammy Locust No. 2

1. Robinia Pseudoacacia L. Black Locust.

THIS tree is native in our states only in the mountains from Virginia to Georgia, usually ascending only about 4,000 feet. It is, however, extensively naturalized in the piedmont region, and in western Tennessee.

Bark dark, rough or ridged, thick; stipules spiny; leaves large, pinnately compound, leaflets 7-19, pubescent when young, at maturity dark green above, light green below and glabrous or with a few hairs on the midribs, turning a pale yellow in the fall; flowers pea-shaped, white, fragrant, borne in clusters like wisteria; fruit a flat brown pod bearing several seeds. A section of the Black Locust in the museum in Raleigh from Haywood County, N. C., has a diameter of 1 foot 11 inches. This tree is often cultivated in the piedmont and may be seen around deserted

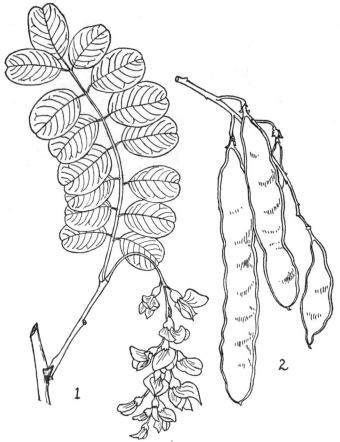

1, Branch with leaves and flowers, x ⅓.
2, fruits, x ¾.

homesteads, where it obtains possession and multiplies extensively by shoots from the roots. It is especially good for use in borders here and there, on account of its sweet flowers. For quick effect and shade it is also quite useful, as the growth is very rapid in youth. The ''locust borer'' (*Cyllene robiniae*), a large black beetle with yellow stripes, attacks the wood of the trunk and has caused the commercial planting of the tree as a supply for railroad ties and posts to be discontinued. Aside from this it is a short-lived tree in the south and reaches no great size. However, for quick results its ornamental value still remains. Flowering April 14 to May 4.

A sterile form of Black Locust called "Ship Mast" Locust occurs on Long Island and adjacent regions. The tree has a straighter trunk than the type and the wood is more durable. Dr. Oran Raber has named it var. *erectissima* (*U. S. Dept. Agric. Circ.* 379, 1936). Tradition says that the tree was brought from Virginia long ago by Capt. Sand. It is now being propagated by root cuttings and will be planted in quantity by the United States Soil Conservation Service. Many horticultural forms of *Robinia Pseudoacacia* are now in cultivation. Of these a pink form *Decaisneana* is very handsome.

2. Robinia viscosa Vent. Clammy Locust.

THIS is a small tree or shrub which is native only in the mountains of Tennessee and North and South Carolina. We have specimens in our herbarium from the following places: Mt. Satulah (alt. 4,500 ft.) and Whiteside Mountain in Macon County and Slaty Mountain on the Blue Ridge in McDowell County. Pinchot and Ashe reported it from Buzzard Ridge in Macon County and Blomquist has seen it on Mt. Pisgah and Mt. Junaluska. It occurs in great abundance on Sauratown Mountain, in Stokes County, where it varies greatly both in color and size of flower.

Twigs and petioles with viscid, glandular hairs; leaves pinnately compound, leaflets 7-21, pubescent when young, at maturity glabrous above, slightly pubescent below, dark green above, pale on the lower surface; flowers pea-shaped, rose colored, borne in wisteria-like clusters; fruit a glandular-hispid pod bearing several seeds. It is often cultivated and multiplies by suckers.

Robinia viscosa var. *Hartwegii* (Koehne) Ashe is found on Fodderstack and Whiteside mountains and on Wild Cat Ridge in Macon County, North Carolina.

Robinia viscosa.
Branch with racemes of flowers, x ⅓.

GYMNOCLADUS Lam.

1. Gymnocladus dioica (L.) Koch. Kentucky Coffee Tree.

In our area this tree is native only in Tennessee, where it occurs on the western slopes of the Smoky Mountains and also in the central part of the state. It is occasionally spon-

Seed; twig with a leaf and flowers;
fruit. All x ⅛.

taneous in neighborhoods where it is cultivated, as in Chapel Hill. It is easily recognized by its large, bipinnate leaves with oval leaflets and the large heavy brown curved pods about 6-10 inches long. The trees cultivated in Chapel Hill are all male and bear no pods.

ALBIZZIA Durazzini.

1. Albizzia Julibrissin Durazzini. "Mimosa."

THE "Mimosa" is a very attractive small tree of the legume family introduced originally from Asia (Persia to China), but now escaped and often well established in the piedmont and mountain sections

from Virginia southward. Fernald (*Rhodora* **41**: 478. 1939) reports
it along the lower James River in Virginia. Bark light, smooth;
leaves divided into 40-50 small, one-sided leaflets, that close at night,
during showers, and (while young) even if touched firmly; leaves not
casting a deep shade; flowers small, pink, thready, sweetly scented,
clustered in round heads about 2-2½ inches in diameter. The flowers
vary considerably in color from light yellowish pink to a deep clear
pink, the latter far more beautiful; fruit a flat pod about 2-3 inches
long. When all its qualities are considered it is one of the best ornamental trees in cultivation in the south, remarkably resistant to
drought, more so in our observation than any other small tree in our
area either wild or cultivated. The delicate feathery leaves and the
beautiful flowers give an unusually attractive exotic effect. It is
hardy as far north as Indianapolis and Philadelphia. Flowering begins about June 11 to June 15 and continues for a month or more.

A most destructive disease has recently attacked *Albizzia* in the
Carolinas and Georgia. A fungus, *Fusarium perniciosum*, enters the
roots and ascends the tree in the wood of the season, killing the tree
very quickly. No remedy has yet been found. This disease was first
noted in Tryon, N. C., in 1930 (*Phytopathology* **31**: 599. 1941).

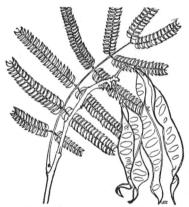

Twig with a leaf and fruits, x ⅕.

A closely related plant, a shrub or small tree, is Opopanax *(Acacia
Farnesiana)*, found in many gardens of Charleston and farther southward. It has little pompons of yellow flowers of a most delightful
fragrance and is noted with pleasure by all visitors. It blooms in
winter and early spring.

SIMARUBACEAE (QUASSIA FAMILY)

AILANTHUS Desf.

1. **Ailanthus altissima** (Miller) Swingle (**A. glandulosa**
Desf.). **Tree of Heaven, Copal.**

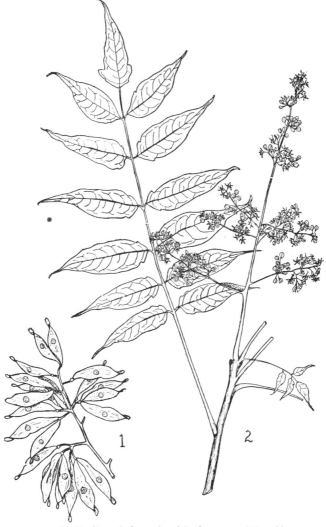

1, Fruits. 2, branch with flowers. All x ¼.

THE Tree of Heaven, a native of China, is frequently adventive in waste places, rarely in the woods. Since it suckers freely, it often forms extensive clumps. This tree is planted a good deal as a street tree in cities but it has lost most of its popularity because of the disagreeable odor of the male flowers. It is remarkable for its resistance to unfavorable conditions, and the female trees are of distinct value for planting along city streets. The large compound leaves with narrow pointed leaflets and the bad odor of the leaves when crushed easily identify this tree. Flowering May 25, 1916.

MELIACEAE (MAHOGANY FAMILY)

MELIA L.

1. Melia Azedarach L. Chinaberry Tree.

THE Chinaberry Tree, usually considered a native of India, has sparingly escaped in our area. Leaves large, twice pinnately compound, the leaflets serrate or lobed; flowers purplish, with a strong but not agreeable odor; fruit a light colored drupe with a ridged stone containing several seeds. As a rule, not all the seeds in a drupe come up the same year. A low spreading variety, called the

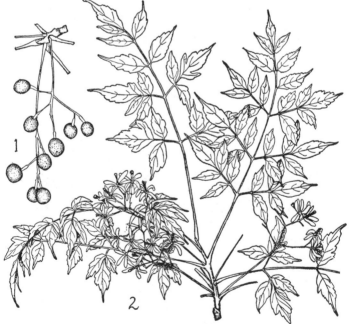

1, Mature fruits. 2, branch with flowers. All x ⅓.

Umbrella Tree, which originated in Texas, has been very popular, but in this case as in numerous other foreign introductions the tree is very inferior to a number of our own native kinds. The pulp of the fruit is an active vermifuge, is a medicine for domestic animals, and is also an efficient repellant of insects.

EUPHORBIACEAE (SPURGE FAMILY)

SAPIUM P. Br.

1. Sapium sebiferum (L.) Rox. Chinese Tallow Tree.

THE Chinese Tallow Tree, a native of China or Japan, is a good sized tree which has become rather freely naturalized near the coast of South Carolina, Georgia, and Florida and possibly to some extent in North Carolina. Twigs smooth, slender; leaves resembling those of a poplar, with a long tapering point and a long slender petiole, blade glabrous, about 1½-3 inches long and 1¼-2¾ inches wide, often

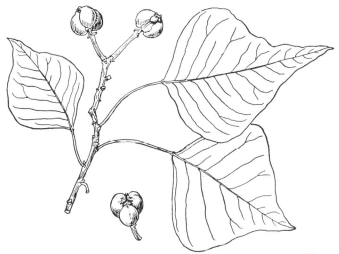

Twig with seeds left hanging after pod has fallen away, x ¾.

smaller; margin slightly wavy. Flowers male and female, both borne together in long terminal spikes; fruit a 3-lobed capsule containing 3 seeds covered with a white wax which in China is made into candles. The seed pod has the peculiar habit when mature of splitting into valves which fall away, leaving the 3 white seeds hanging from the top of a central column. The tree contains a milky poisonous juice.

2. Sapium glandulosum (L.) Morong. South American Milk-Tree.

THIS small tree or shrub from South America has become naturalized in certain places in western Florida, especially around Pensacola. The leaves are long, narrow, thick, finely toothed, glabrous on both sides, resembling those of the willow. The fruit is a brown 2-celled capsule about ⅓ inch thick, containing 2 seeds covered with a reddish wax. The white milky sap is very abundant.

RUTACEAE (RUE FAMILY)

XANTHOXYLUM L.

1. Xanthoxylum Clàva-Hérculis L. [Fagara Clàva-Hérculis (L.) Small]. Southern Prickly Ash, Toothache Tree, Hercules Club, Pillenterry.

THIS is a peculiar small tree or shrub with a short trunk and widely spreading crown which, except for a wide distribution in Florida, occurs in our area only in sandy soil near the coast, Virginia to Florida and westward, often on the dunes but never abundantly.

Leaves and branches armed with stout spines, which on the trunk and older branches become elevated on thick cushions of cork, giving the tree a very unusual appearance; leaves alternate, large, pinnately compound, leaflets 5-19, with crenulate margins; flowers small, greenish white, borne in large clusters; fruit ovoid, bearing one black seed which hangs outside the carpel at maturity. On a high sand dune about 8 miles north of Myrtle Beach, S. C., is a fine clump of this odd tree, the largest about 11½ inches in diameter two feet from the ground. On Ocracoke Island the fruit was fully ripe on September 9, 1931. The Toothache Tree is so named because the pungent bark and other parts act as a counter irritant and help to relieve toothache. Ayers and Ashe, in error, credit this to the mountains.

The only other species of *Xanthoxylum* north of Florida is *Xanthoxylum americanum* Mill. It is essentially a Mississippi valley plant but we have collected it in Giles County, Virginia, and Small extends it south to Georgia. House's list so far as we know is the only one that includes

Xanthoxylum Clàva-Hérculis.
Branch with leaves and open fruits shedding seeds, x ½.

it from the mountains of North Carolina, and it is certainly very rare in the southeastern Atlantic slope. This Prickly Ash is essentially a shrub but rarely takes the form of a small tree. The leaflets are often entire, and the small greenish flowers are borne in small axillary clusters. The flower lacks a calyx. Cultivated plants of *X. americanum* flowered in Chapel Hill on April 22, 1920. The structure of the flower and manner of flower grouping in these two species are so different that Small and some others place *X. Clàva-Hérculis* in the genus *Fagara*.

ANACARDIACEAE (SUMACH FAMILY)

RHUS L.

Twigs densely fuzzy; leaflets serrate; fruits red
Rhus typhina, Staghorn Sumach   No. 1
Twigs smooth; leaflets entire; fruits whitish
Rhus vernix, Poison Sumach   No. 2

1. Rhus typhina L. [Rhus hirta (L.) Sudworth]. Staghorn Sumach.

This is a small tree or shrub, sometimes 30 feet high, which is confined to moderate elevations in the mountains in our area from Virginia to Georgia.

Twig with fruit, x ¼.

Branches naked and thick; twigs densely fuzzy, leaves large, pinnately compound, leaflets 11-31, serrate, dark green above, pale below; flowers small, green or yellow-green, borne in dense panicles; fruit a red globose berry covered with red hairs, borne in large panicles at the ends of the branches. The wood is yellow and aromatic. Flowering at Mountain Lake, Virginia, June 28, 1936, and in cultivation at Chapel Hill, N. C., May 29, 1916.

Rhus glabra L. (Smooth Sumach) and *R. copallina* (Winged Sumach) occasionally reach the height of small trees but are essentially so shrub-like in character that they are not included here.

2. Rhus vernix L.   Poison Sumach, Thunderwood.

THIS very poisonous Sumach appears to have a rather erratic distribution.   It is not uncommon in the coastal plain bays and in the marshy open valleys of the lower mountains throughout our range.   We have never found it in the piedmont section of North Carolina.   It is often only a shrub but it frequently gets to be a little tree.   We are

Twig with leaf and fruits, x ½.

including it because so dangerous a plant should be known to everyone. Unlike all the other large sumachs the flowers and fruits are borne in long, loose, axillary panicles and the fruits are whitish, smooth, and polished instead of red and fuzzy.

Stems stout, brittle, and glabrous; buds pointed; leaves large, compound, alternate on the twig, the leaflets opposite or nearly so, about 4-5 (3-6) pairs with a single terminal one, varying much in size, usually about 2-3 inches long, elliptic, pointed at both ends, entire, quite glabrous, the leaf stalks and young twigs nearly always reddish; flowers greenish yellow, very small and numerous; fruit a little drupe with a single ridged stone, borne in large pendent panicles, smooth, shining, and whitish, subglobose (somewhat flattened), about $\frac{3}{16}$ inch thick. A very curious error in both editions of Sargent's *Manual of Trees* gives the fruit as $\frac{1}{2}$ inch long.

When driving through bays and creek swamps in the coastal plain one often sees this little tree leaning out from the edge of the woods. Even when not in fruit it is easily recognized by the large compound leaves and reddish leaf stalks and twigs. It is even more poisonous than Poison Ivy and Poison Oak and should become better known and avoided.

COTINUS L.

1. **Cotinus americanus** Nutt. (**Rhus cotinoides** Nutt.) **Smoke Tree.**

THIS is a small spreading tree found in our area only on rocky ridges and bluffs, mostly limestone, in eastern Tennessee, ranging westward and southward.

Young twigs greenish or purplish and faintly glaucous, becoming pale brownish and finally gray. Leaves very variable in size, oval or obovate, blade as a rule 2-3 inches long and 1-3 inches wide, many larger and smaller, conspicuously veined, deep green and glabrous above, paler and glabrous or in some forms moderately pubescent beneath, especially along the veins; margin even or wavy, slightly reflexed;

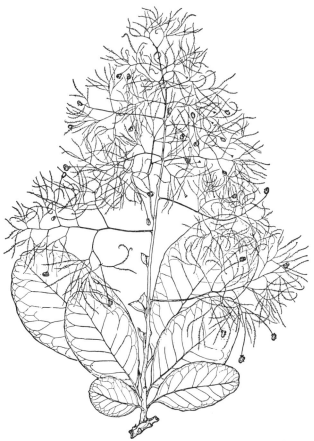

Branch with mature fruits in the inflorescence, x ⅓.

petioles also very variable in length. Flowers borne in large
open terminal panicles on slender stalks, most of which do
not produce fruits but become feathery hairy and very conspicuous and handsome. Fruits small bean-like pods with a
point on one side, very much scattered in the inflorescence.
These fruits were fully ripe on cultivated trees in Chapel
Hill about the middle of June. Soon afterward the inflorescence breaks up into a number of parts and these are
blown over the ground by the wind, scattering the little

fruits. The plant is thus a tumbler like the Tumble Grass *(Panicum capillare)*.

This is one of the most desirable ornamentals for our section. The foliage is healthy and handsome and the ample inflorescences are smoky pink, lasting a long time. The plant when cut back sprouts strongly from the stump.

CYRILLACEAE (CYRILLA FAMILY)

CYRILLA Garden.

1. Cyrilla racemiflora Walt.   He Huckleberry, Red Titi.

THIS is a shrub or small tree mostly confined to borders of streams, bays, and swamps in the coastal plain from south-

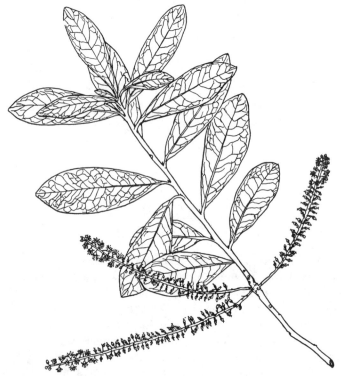

Branch with leaves and three racemes of flowers and young fruits, x ⅓.

eastern Virginia (*Rhodora* **39:** 435) to northern Florida. It extends inland to Halifax, Wake (Mitchell's Mill), and Lee (7 miles south of Sanford) counties in North Carolina, into the sandhills of South Carolina, as far up as the Pine Mountains in Georgia, and through northern Florida.

Leaves small, oblong, entire, shining, turning a fine red or mottled red and green in the fall and persisting through most of the winter; flowers small, white, in narrow, drooping racemes, fruit a dry two-celled pod (corky drupe) with two small seeds in each. It is usually not over 15 feet high (rarely up to 30 ft.) with a diameter of less than one foot. The plants can grow in water over a foot deep. In such situations the bark under the water does not decay and becomes so thick as to enlarge the circumference of the tree to 5½ feet at times. Such bark is very soft, corky, and felted with roots below the water level. The plant was seen in all the bays along the highway from Murrell's Inlet, S. C., to Wilmington, N. C., and from Wilmington to Harnett County, July 16-17, 1932, still in bloom but past its height.

Several varieties of *Cyrilla racemiflora* have been proposed. There is a shrubby species, *Cyrilla parvifolia* Raf., found from Florida to Louisiana, with smaller leaves and shorter racemes.

CLIFTONIA Gaertn.

1. Cliftonia monophylla (Lamarck) Britton. **Titi.**

THIS small tree of irregular growth reaches northward only as far as the lower portion of South Carolina near the Savannah River. It is said to be rather common in southeastern Georgia and extends into northern Florida and thence westward. We found it abundant on St. Simon's Island and in a swamp near Thalman, Georgia. Small (*Bull. Torr. Bot. Club* 24: 63. 1897) says that this "plant forms remarkably dense thickets in swamps and districts bordering streams in the vicinity of the Altamaha River, especially north of Jesup, Georgia." It is reported in Florida from Jefferson County westward (Harper).

Leaves oblong, up to 2 inches in length, smooth, even, evergreen; flowers in slender terminal racemes, small and perfect, petals white or pink; fruit a dry pod with 2-4

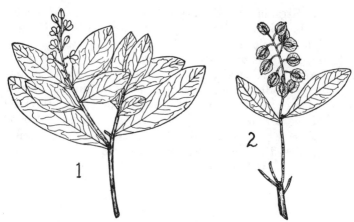

1, Twig with flowers.   2, twig with mature fruits.   All x ⅝.

wings with one seed in each of the three or four cells. According to Harper, *Cliftonia* reaches a foot in diameter and a height of 30 feet in Georgia. In Florida it is said to reach occasionally a height of 40 to 50 feet. The stems have a conspicuous pith and are of value as pipestems. This is locally called "Titi," but so are a number of other shrubs, as *Leucothoe acuminata, L. axillaris,* and *Cyrilla racemiflora.* Flowering near Thalman, Ga., on April 19, 1933.

AQUIFOLIACEAE (HOLLY FAMILY)

ILEX L.

1. Leaves evergreen 2
   Leaves deciduous 6
2. Leaves with sharp spiny teeth................... 3
   Not as above (if spiny teeth present only near the tip) 4
3. Leaves usually not over twice as long as broad
   Ilex opaca, Holly   No. 1
   Leaves usually over twice as long as broad
   Ilex Cassine, Dahoon Holly   No. 2
4. Leaves small, often linear, and with a few small sharp teeth near the tip
   Ilex myrtifolia, Myrtle-leaved Holly   No. 3
   Leaves not as above............................. 5
5. Leaves averaging less than 2 inches long, distantly crenate-serrate
   Ilex vomitoria, Yaupon Holly   No. 4

Leaves averaging more than 2 inches long, margins
entire; twigs and midribs pubescent
Ilex Cassine, Dahoon Holly   No. 2

6. Leaves obovate-lanceolate, less than one inch broad
Ilex decidua, Deciduous Holly   No. 5
Leaves ovate-lanceolate, with a long point, more
than one inch broad
Ilex montana, Mountain Holly   No. 6

1. Ilex opaca Ait. American Holly.

THIS well known tree is common in the coastal plain and
most of the piedmont in damp, well drained woods and extends sparingly into the lower mountains (up to 3,000 feet)
throughout our area. Near towns this tree is often rare,
probably due to many years of Christmas decorating.

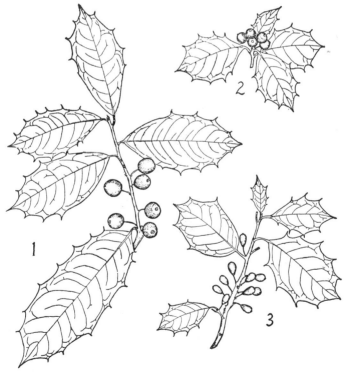

1, Twig with leaves and very large fruits. 2, twig with typical
fruits. 3, twig with elongated fruits. All x ⅓.

Bark white or pale gray; leaves thick, spiny, evergreen; flowers of two sorts, male and female, usually borne on different trees so that about one-half of the trees bear no berries; fruit a small red berry (really a drupe). Some specimens are found with leaves entirely without spines or nearly so (as from Pascagoula, Miss., U. N. C. Herb.) This has been given the form name *subintegra* by Weatherby. Forms with yellow berries (*xanthocarpa* Rehder) have often been reported. We have such from Dobson, N. C., and Eutaw, Alabama. Dr. Mellichamp mentions a form with very large yellow berries sent to him from Greenville, S. C. (*Journ. Eli. Mitch. Sci. Soc.* 27: 46. 1911). The berries vary in shape from spherical to obovate or even drop-shaped, and in diameter from ¼-½ inch. The upper limit in size of berries as given by others is too small. We have berries from woods near Tallahassee, Fla. (Kurz and Couch), which are ½ inch long and 7/16 inch thick. Even in the red-berried form the color varies from a dark red to an orange-red. This holly varies much not only in color, shape, and size of berries but in the habit of growth. They are difficult to transplant and only a very small proportion of the seeds germinate, and then frequently only after a year or so. To get the best forms and to be sure of having the berries, cuttings should be grown from the most attractive trees in the neighborhood. Cuttings will succeed if directions are carefully followed. For different horticultural varieties of holly, see *The Country Gentleman,* Dec. 1941, page 12, and for directions for propagation from cuttings, see *American Journal of Botany* 16: 556, 1929. The large holly at Hartsville, S. C., is 34 inches in diameter two feet from the ground; and it is about 48 feet in height. The American Forestry Association *Report of American Big Trees* (Jan. 1, 1944) lists a specimen on Hog Island, Virginia, that is 11 feet in circumference at four and a half feet from the ground. Flowering April 16 to May 7.

Ashe has described as *I. attenuata* a plant from Walton County, Fla., that he thinks is a hybrid between *opaca* and *Cassine.* The leaves are prevailingly without teeth and the berries are borne several on a common stalk.

2. Ilex Cassine L. Dahoon Holly.

THIS is a small evergreen tree of swamp margins and damp sand dunes near the coast of southern Virginia and southward and along the Gulf, widely distributed in Florida.

Twigs pubescent; leaves oblanceolate to oblong-ovate, about 2-4 inches long, thick and leathery, the margin smooth or more or less prickly; petioles and peduncles pubescent; berries red, about ¼ inch thick. As in the other evergreen hollies, yellow-berried forms occur. The plant is quite ornamental and worthy of cultivation.

The typical species can be easily distinguished from all its relatives by its leaves, but a variety (*angustifolia* Ait.) has small leaves approaching those of *I. myrtifolia*. The latter can be distinguished from the narrow-leaved variety of *Cassine* by the smaller, darker green leaves, much more rigid habit, and growth in damp depressions in the pine barrens farther inland, never so near the shore as to be affected by the salt. A further difference obvious with the

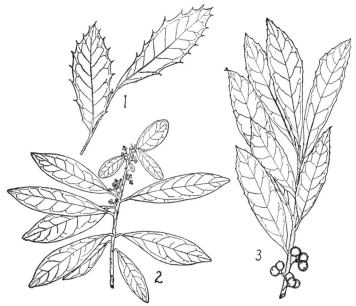

1, Twig with spiny leaves. 2, twig with entire leaves and female flowers. 3, twig with spiny leaves and mature fruits. All x ⅓.

lens is the light colored hairs along the under side of the midrib of the Dahoon Holly. We have collections of the variety *angustifolia* from southeastern North Carolina to Florida, in the same habitats as the species. Sargent says it is common in southern Alabama. Tarbox names two forms, *aureo-baccata* and *tortifolia,* of the variety.

We insert here part of an interesting and hitherto unpublished letter from Dr. Mellichamp of Bluffton, S. C., to H. W. Ravenel, dated Dec. 16, 1885 (copy in files of the Department of Botany, University of North Carolina).

"Thanks for your letter just read. I am glad that you referred to *I. Dahoon* [*I. Cassine*] & *Myrtifolia,* for it has always been one of the greatest puzzles to me that Dr. Chapman made the latter but a "variety"! To me (in my simplicity!) it seemed inexplicable! I have seen a narrow leaved form of *I. Dahoon*—but even that does not resemble (I mean in the woods!)—*I. myrtifolia*! Possibly you might like to examine *berries* (and *seeds*) and leaves of all three, i.e. the red & yellow-berried *myrtifolia* and a more narrow leaved form of *I. Dahoon,* so I send them on with this. They were all collected on the same day—some time back, and that must account for the drying and shriveling. I have never seen *I. Dahoon* & *myrtifolia* growing together. The former is found *here* on salt water usually on the edge of wet springy "salts" etc.—the latter in shallow-clay pine-barren ponds in and among Nyssa & Cypress &c.—never on salt water.

I trust that you will prevail on Dr. Chapman to separate them by a wider gap!" . . .

3. Ilex myrtifolia Walt. Myrtle-leaved Holly.

THIS is a small irregular, rigid, evergreen tree of low wet places in the pine barrens, often in shallow water, in the coastal plain from North Carolina through northern Florida to Louisiana. We have specimens from Pender, Pamlico, Onslow, and New Hanover counties, N. C., and from many places farther south. Hartsville and Orangeburg, S. C., are the farthest inland stations known to us. The species is plentiful in the swamp along the U. S. highway near Waycross, Georgia. The finest grove we have seen is on both sides of the Montgomery-Mobile highway, Baldwin County, Alabama.

Bark very pale, not cracked but often thickly set with small warts; leaves thick, evergreen, rigid, narrow, almost linear, ½-1½ inches long, usually abruptly tipped with a

1-4, Twigs with mature fruits and showing variation in leaves, x ½.

sharp mucro which is often bent downward, margin incurved, quite smooth or with a few short teeth near the end, midrib glabrous below; berries bright red, about ¼ inch thick. A yellow-berried form of this species was known to Dr. J. H. Mellichamp of Bluffton, S. C., as early as 1885. This has been named var. *Lowii* by Blake. Such a form was found near Wilmington, N. C., by Dr. T. F. Wood (*Journ. Eli. Mitch. Sci. Soc.* 27: 47. 1911). A tree between Brunswick and Waycross, Ga., is 10 inches in diameter two and one-half feet from the ground and 20 feet high. Harper reports trees in Clinch County, Ga., 30 feet tall and a foot in diameter. The typical form of this is very unlike the typical Dahoon, differing from it in the much smaller and more rigid leaves and less pubescent twigs and petioles. For a colored plate of *I. myrtifolia* see *Addisonia* **17**: pl. 564, 1932.

4. Ilex vomitoria Ait. Yaupon, Christmas-Berry, Cassine.

THIS slender small evergreen tree is confined in our area to a narrow strip along the coast from Virginia to Florida. It forms a conspicuous part of the tangled growth behind the sand dunes.

Leaves oval, small, about ½-1¾ inches long, evenly crenated, smooth; fruit a very small, bright red berry, formed abundantly on the female trees, and very ornamental. This holly does well in cultivation even as far inland as Chapel Hill. It suckers freely and is apt to be straggling in shape. The young dried leaves have been much used as a substitute for tea and are still so used in places. It is known that they contain a considerable amount of caffeine, about 0.27 per cent of the dry weight (Venable, *Journ. Eli. Mitch. Sci. Soc.* **2**: 39. 1884-85). According to Dr. G. F. Mitchell, the caffeine content in some samples may run as high as 1.6 per cent. As the name indicates, the leaves are generally supposed to have an emetic effect, and the Indians certainly used a decoction containing them to produce vomiting. It seems, however, that this effect was the result of other herbs that were added and not of the Yaupon leaves (Havard, *Bull. Torr. Bot. Club* **23**: 41. 1896). A well known and popular South American drink, *maté*, is made from the leaves of another holly closely related to this. Flowering in cultivation at Chapel Hill from April 25 to May 10. A yellow-berried form is known, and this has been given the varietal name *Yawkeyii* by Mr. Tarbox.

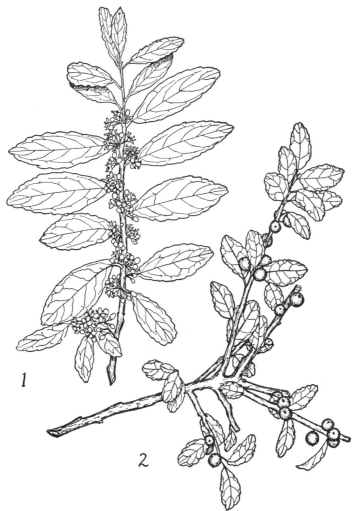

Ilex vomitoria. 1, Branch with leaves and male flowers.
2, branch with mature fruits. All x ⅗.

5. Ilex decidua Walt. Deciduous Holly.

THIS is a small tree or more often a large shrub with several stems that is common from southern Virginia and Tennessee to northern Florida on river banks, flats, and hillsides in the piedmont and extends into the mountains to an elevation of 1,500 feet. In the coastal plain it is abundant in the deep swamps of the large rivers.

Leaves small, thin, narrow, margin crenulate-serrate, not evergreen; flowers small, whitish, of two kinds on separate trees; fruits small red berries, ¼-⅜ inch in diameter, that hang on throughout most of the winter. We have specimens gathered in June which show an abundance

Branch with mature fruits, x ½.

of the preceding year's fruits. Flowering from April 14 to May 5.

In western Florida a form with exceptionally small leaves has been described by Fernald as *I. decidua Curtissii*.

6. **Ilex montana** Torr. & Gray. (**I. monticola** Gray). **Mountain Holly.**

THIS shrub or small tree of rich shady places is found from the piedmont to the high mountains (up to 5,200 ft. in N. C.) from Virginia and Tennessee to Georgia.

Leaves thin, deciduous, dark green, finely toothed, ovate-lanceolate with a long point, typically smooth on both sides, about 2½-3½ inches long and 1-2 inches broad; berries red, about ⅜ inch in diameter, on short stems. In Chapel Hill this species is a shrub reaching a height of only about 8 feet but along streams in the mountains of the Carolinas it is arborescent. It is rarely over 25 feet high and 6 inches in diameter. There is a tree near Highland Falls, Highlands, N. C., measured by us, that is 30 feet high and 4⅔ inches in diameter.

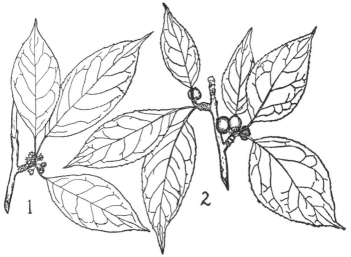

1, Twig with leaves and male flowers. 2, twig with leaves and mature fruits. All x ⅓.

There is a variant of this species occurring in the mountains and piedmont with leaves more or less pubescent beneath, otherwise indistinguishable from the typical. This has been named *I. monticola* var. *mollis* (Gray) Britton. *Ilex Beadlei* Ashe, never clearly defined, was thought by Mr. Harbison to be a pubescent shrub of dry open ridges in the mountains, somewhat resembling *I. monticola mollis* but with paler leaves and larger berries and always a shrub.

There are a number of other shrubby hollies in our states. The two Gallberries or Inkberries, *Ilex glabra* (L.) Gray and *I. lucida* (Ait.) T. & G., of the coastal plain swamps are evergreen and have black berries. The deciduous hollies, all with red berries, are *I. verticillata* (L.) A. Gray, *I. laevigata* (Pursh) A. Gray, *I. Amelanchier* Curtis, *I. caroliniana* (Walt.) Trelease, and *I. longipes* Chapman. Of these *I. verticillata* and *I. laevigata* may occasionally reach the size of small slender trees.

ACERACEAE (MAPLE FAMILY)

ACER* (Tourn.) L.

1. Leaves compound
   Acer Negundo, Ash-leaved Maple   No. 9
   Leaves simple 2
2. Flowers in terminal racemes or corymbs, appearing after the leaves or at the same time (small trees of the high mountains)......................... 3
   Flowers in lateral clusters, often appearing before the leaves 4
3. Bark striped with whitish lines; leaves with many very small teeth
   Acer pennsylvanicum, Striped Maple   No. 1
   Bark not striped with whitish lines; leaves with large teeth
   Acer spicatum, Mountain Maple   No. 2
4. Leaves green beneath 5
   Leaves pale green, glaucous or whitish beneath..... 6
5. Bark usually very white (a small tree of the piedmont)
   Acer leucoderme, White-barked Sugar Maple   No. 8
   Bark dark brown or black; leaves with very few teeth (a rare tree of the mountains)
   Acer nigrum, Black Maple   No. 7
6. Leaves deeply lobed more than half way to the middle, coarsely toothed, silvery white beneath
   Acer saccharinum, Silver Maple   No. 3
   Leaves with lobes that reach less than half way to the middle 7
7. Leaves with 3-5 lobes, which have many teeth; fruit usually red 8
   Leaves with 3-5 strong lobes, which have only 2-4 teeth or none 9
8. Leaves 3-5-lobed, smooth below
   Acer rubrum, Red Maple   No. 4
   Leaves mostly 3-lobed, tomentose below (sometimes only slightly)
   Acer rubrum var. *tridens*, Carolina Red Maple   No. 4a

* In all maples the fruit is a double samara. Each half falls away separately and is carried by the wind with a spinning motion.

9. Leaves smooth below

      Acer saccharum, Sugar Maple   No. 5

  Leaves tomentose below

      Acer floridanum, Southern Sugar Maple   No. 6

1. Acer pennsylvanicum L. Striped Maple.

Branch with leaves and mature fruits, x ⅓.

THIS is a small tree of the higher mountains which inhabits cool damp soil at elevations above 3,000 feet through our area south to northern Georgia.

Bark yellowish green or reddish green, glabrous, striped with light lines; leaves large, 3-lobed with long sharp tips, the margins serrate with many very small teeth, smooth above and below except for tufts of hairs in the axils of the veins; flowers yellow, borne in long, terminal, drooping panicles; samaras yellow or red.

2. **Acer spicatum** Lam. **Mountain Maple.**

THIS is a very small tree or shrub which grows only at high altitudes in the mountains through our states southward to northern Georgia.

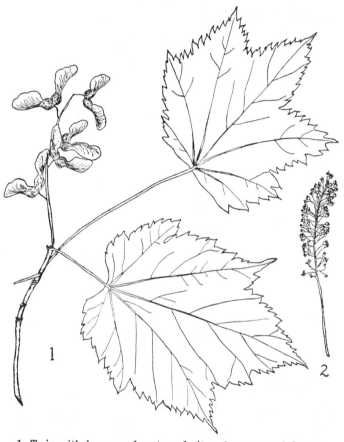

1, Twig with leaves and mature fruits. 2, raceme of flowers.
All x ½.

Bark reddish brown, smooth or with a few ridges; young twigs pubescent; leaves large, 3-lobed, the margins serrate with large teeth; flowers in upright panicles; samaras yellow or red. This tree is very much like the Striped Maple but it may be easily distinguished from it by the pubescent young twigs, the larger teeth on the leaves, the upright panicles of flowers and fruits, and the lack of stripes on the bark.

3. Acer saccharinum L.   Silver Maple.

THIS is a good sized tree which is said to occur in rich woods in the upper piedmont, at moderate elevations in the mountains, and in the valley of the Apalachicola River in Florida. It seems to be rare and local. We have collected it in the swamps of the Roanoke River, Northampton County, N. C., at the Falls of the Potomac, Fairfax County, Va., and in Anderson County, South Carolina. Dr. C. E. Moore reports it as common in Shelby County, Tennessee.

Leaves deeply cut and toothed, smooth, green above and white below; flowers yellowish green, without petals, borne

1, Mature fruit.   2, twig with leaves.   All x ⅓.

in many-flowered fascicles, appearing before the leaves; samaras large, green, ripening early and falling off in April and May. In this and in the Red Maple ("soft" maples) the seeds must germinate at once or they will die in a few days. Our other maples ("hard" maples) behave very differently, since their fruits are shed in the fall and germinate the following spring. The Silver Maple is of very rapid growth and is often planted for this reason, but its brittleness and susceptibility to scale insects make it undesirable for cultivation. Flowering in cultivation at Chapel Hill on February 26, 1931.

4. Acer rubrum L. Red Maple.

THIS is a common tree in all our area. It inhabits the valleys and hillsides in the piedmont and mountains and the swamps and low grounds of the upper coastal plain.

Twigs smooth, red; leaves with 3-5 deep lobes which are strongly and irregularly toothed, pale and usually smooth beneath, turning a fine scarlet in the autumn; petioles red; flowers of two kinds, male and female, borne on the same tree or on different trees (only a few twigs of a tree may bear fruit, the remainder being sterile), bright red or yellowish green, appearing very early before the leaves; fruits usually red, often a pale yellow-green or brown and all shades between, about 1 inch long and ⅜

Staminate flowers; leaves; fruits. All x ⅔.

inch broad, ripening in early summer. A tree in the "Primeval Forest" at Highlands, N. C., measured in the summer of 1932 was 3 feet 8 inches in diameter three feet from the ground. Prof. S. A. Cain of the University of Tennessee measured a red maple in the Great Smoky Mountains that was 5 feet 2 inches in diameter at breast height. The Red Maple is a more desirable shade tree than the Silver Maple but it is more subject to scale than the Sugar Maple. Flowering at Chapel Hill from January 9 to March 16.

The tomentose forms occurring in the mountains of North Carolina and near Augusta, Ga., are known as *A. rubrum* var. *tomentosum* Pax. The Red Maple that is common in the coastal plain, *A. rubrum* var. *tridens,* is described below.

4a. Acer rubrum var. **tridens** Wood. **Carolina Red Maple.**

The Carolina Red Maple is the common maple over the

1, Twig with mature fruits. 2, twig with leaves. All x ⅓.

greater part of the coastal plain in all our area, and extends sparingly into the mountains. We have collected it along the flats of Little Stony at an elevation of 3,150 feet in Giles County, Virginia. This striking variant of the Red Maple has been known as *A. carolinianum* Walter, but Sargent thinks that Walter's plant was not different from the typical Red Maple (Sargent, *Bot. Gaz.* **67**: 237. 1919).

Leaves usually with 3 large, irregularly toothed lobes, though often 5-lobed, thick, blade about 1½-3 inches long, dark green above with a white or rusty tomentum below, which may almost disappear in age; fruits as in *A. rubrum* or often smaller. The Carolina Red Maple may be distinguished from the Red Maple by the usually smaller, thicker, tomentose, and less lacerated leaves. In Chapel Hill we have almost the typical form of this tree growing in marshes, as in the northwest corner of Rocky Ridge farm. From our observations many intermediate forms also occur throughout the greater part of its range.

5. Acer saccharum Marsh. Sugar Maple.

This is a large tree which is scattered in our mountain valleys and slopes as far south as northern Georgia. Ayers and Ashe remark that it is "common north of the Cowee mountains, above an elevation of 2,000 feet on cold moist soil." We have collected it on the slopes along the Pacolet

Twig with leaves and fruits, x ⅖.

River between Saluda and Tryon, Polk County, N. C., at an elevation of about 1,500 feet.

Leaves large, about 4½-6½ inches long and at least as wide, some may be very small, typically with 3 large lobes above, each with two or four distant teeth, and 2 narrow tooth-like lobes at the base, deep green above, green, whitish or somewhat glaucous below, smooth except for a few tufts of hairs in the axils of the veins below; flowers greenish yellow, appearing with the leaves; fruits maturing in the summer in Chapel Hill and fall in the mountains. This maple may reach a height of over a hundred feet and a diameter of about four feet. A section of it in the museum in Raleigh from Haywood County, N. C., has a diameter of 3 feet 2½ inches. It is the finest of all our maples and very desirable in cultivation. *Acer floridanum* (see below) is very much like the Sugar Maple and is usually confused with it. Their areas approach each other closely, if they do not overlap, and observations should be made to find out if the two forms intergrade as they approach each other.

Sargent calls the form with glaucous leaves the variety *glaucum*. He states that it is the only form of *A. saccharum* that he has seen in South Carolina. We have a collection of a glaucous-leaved form from Wayah Bald, Macon County, N. C.

The Norway Maple, *Acer platanoides* L., is often planted as a street or yard tree in the upper South. One can tell it from the American maples by pulling off a leaf. If it gives off a white milk it is the Norway Maple.

6. Acer floridanum (Chapm.) Pax. Southern Sugar Maple, Florida Maple.

THIS is a close relative of the Sugar Maple that is found in Dinwiddie and Amelia counties, Virginia, and in the piedmont and coastal plain from North Carolina southward to River Junction, Florida. Just how far it extends towards the mountains has not been worked out, or whether it intergrades there with the Sugar Maple. In North Carolina we have it as far west as Chapel Hill, where it is common along creeks and toward the bases of rocky hills, and in South Carolina to Calhoun Falls.

Leaves shaped as in the Sugar Maple, with 3-5 undulate or scarcely toothed lobes, blade about 1½-3 inches long,

1, Twig with male and female flowers. 2, twig with leaves and mature fruits. All x ½.

dark green above and whitish or tawny-pubescent beneath; flowers yellowish, borne in many-flowered corymbs, appearing with or before the leaves; samaras small, hairy or glabrous at maturity, ripening in October. In Chapel Hill this tree reaches a diameter of 1 foot 8 inches. The finest specimen we have seen of this species is in the grounds of Dr. Spurgeon at Hillsboro, N. C. It has a diameter of 3½ feet four and a half feet from the ground, spread of about 70 feet, height about the same. Dr. Spurgeon says this tree is about 100 years old and almost certainly brought in from the woods near Hillsboro. The appearance and habit of the species are like that of the Sugar Maple, but it is smaller and more spreading, prefers lowlands, has smaller leaves with fewer teeth and tomentose under surfaces, and smaller fruits. Flowering from late March until April. On the University of North Carolina campus it flowered in 1933 on March 19, about two weeks earlier than the Northern Sugar Maple near it. The fall coloration takes place about two weeks later and the color is yellow, not red.

Rehder has described a variety *villipes* with "villose-tomentose petioles and usually pubescent branchlets." This is reported by Sargent (*Manual of Trees,* 2nd. edition) from near Raleigh, N. C., Calhoun Falls, S. C., several places in Georgia, in northern Florida, and westward. Both the species and the variety are planted on the streets of Raleigh. Our specimens from Calhoun Falls have the lower leaf surfaces, petioles, and young twigs copiously soft-tomentose.

7. **Acer nigrum** F. A. Michx. **Black Maple.**

THIS tree which extends far north is found in our area only in the mountains. Small and Vail record it from Hun-

Twig with leaves and mature fruits, x ⅓.

gry's Mother Creek near Marion, Virginia, and on a limestone bluff of the Holston River near Marion. They say that it is "the most conspicuous and stately tree of the region, attaining great height and development in the valleys." In North Carolina it is rare and local, being known at present only from the mountains of Ashe and Mitchell counties. In Small's *Flora, A. nigrum* is extended south to Georgia and Louisiana, but aside from our North Carolina specimens we find no authentic records south of Knox County, Tennessee (N. Y. Bot. Gard. Herb.).

Bark on old trees very dark; leaves shaped as in the Sugar Maple with three lobes, which are entire or with a few teeth, lower surface green and pubescent along the midrib; fruit smooth, the wings up to ⅞ inch long. This tree may be distinguished from *A. saccharum* by the green not whitish under surface of the leaves.

8. Acer leucoderme Small. White-barked Sugar Maple.

THIS is a small tree or only a shrub, belonging to the Sugar Maple group, the leaves resembling those of *A. nigrum*. It is known from Stanly County, North Carolina, where it grows along the falls of the Yadkin at an elevation of about 1,000 feet; from Abbeville County, South Carolina, and from Chattahoochee and River Junction, Florida. In north-

Acer leucoderme. Twig with leaves and fruit, x ⅓.

ern and central Georgia it is said to be common (Richmond, Floyd, Walker, Clarke, and probably other counties).

Bark very white; leaves small, green, and hairy below, not whitish, with 3-5 narrow lobes and few or no teeth; flowers yellow, borne in small clusters; fruit quite small, brownish red, the wings broadly spreading.

9. Acer Negundo L. Ash-leaved Maple, Box Elder.

THIS is a rather small spreading tree which is scattered in the valleys of the lower mountains, is rather common along

Fruits; leaf. All x ⅖.

sandy banks and bottoms in the piedmont, and extends along the larger rivers of the coastal plain as far south as northern Florida.

Twigs glabrous; leaves large, compound (may be small and simple near the inflorescence) with three (usually) to five leaflets resembling those of an ash, coarsely toothed beyond the middle except near the inflorescence, pubescent or glabrous except along the veins below; petioles glabrous; flowers of two kinds on separate trees, small, yellowish green, the male flowers in clusters, the female ones in drooping racemes; fruit a double samara, as in the other maples, with minutely pubescent wings, hanging in elongated racemes. This maple is widespreading and of very rapid growth. For quick shade in lawns it is much better than the more often used Silver Maple or the Carolina Poplar. Flowering from March 15 to April 15.

Acer Negundo var. *texanum* f. *latifolium* Sargent with more tomentose leaves is reported by Sargent from Virginia and along the Catawba River near Marion, North Carolina.

SAPINDACEAE (SOAPBERRY FAMILY)

AESCULUS L.

1. Fruits with prickles
   Aesculus glabra   No. 4
   Fruits without prickles........................   2
2. Flowers always red, calyx tubular, the claws of the lateral petals shorter than the calyx; primarily a plant of the lower coastal plain
   Aesculus pavia, Red Buckeye   No. 1
   Flowers usually yellow, rarely reddish, calyx campanulate   3
3. Calyx and pedicels glandular-pubescent; stamens not exserted; a tree of the mountains
   Aesculus octandra, Sweet Buckeye   No. 2
   Calyx and pedicels pubescent but not glandular; stamens exserted; primarily a small tree (or shrub) of the piedmont and coastal plain
   Aesculus sylvatica, Georgia Buckeye   No. 3

1. Aesculus pavia L. Red Buckeye.

THIS is usually a shrub, occasionally an irregular tree, spreading by underground runners. It occurs in the coastal region, usually near the sea, from southeastern Virginia to northern Florida, and in western Tennessee. Though rarely abundant, its handsome red flowers make it a conspicuous object. Some of the older botanists have reported it in the piedmont of North and South Carolina, but they may easily have mistaken red forms of *A. sylvatica* for it. The farthest inland plant we have seen in South Carolina was 34 miles north of Charleston, and in North Carolina 32 miles north of Wilmington on Route 28 to Elizabethtown. It is not scarce in wet places by road between Wilmington and Orton. We have specimens from New Hanover County, North Carolina, from Georgetown, Horry, and Colleton counties, South Carolina, from near Augusta, Georgia, and from west of Tallahassee, Florida.

Leaves with 5-7 leaflets which in shape are not noticeably different from our other species, upper surface nearly glabrous except on the midrib, the lower surface soon glabrous or in some plants remaining densely felted-tomentose; petioles nearly glabrous except at the apex; panicle usually about 4¾-6 inches long, reddish pubescent throughout, usually more open than in other species; pedicels slender, about ¼-½ inch long; calyx typically tubular, about ⅜-⅝ inch long, very minutely glandular; claws of lateral petals shorter than the calyx; stamens exserted; all parts of flower red; fruit without prickles, 1-1½ inches thick, depending on the number of seeds, which varies from one to three. We found a tree of this buckeye at Myrtle Beach, S. C., 20 feet high and 3½ inches in diameter. Mr. F. G. Tarbox, Jr., has since shown us a tree in Horry County, S. C., that is 26 feet high and 8⅓ inches in diameter four and a half feet from the ground. Later he found one still larger, 28 feet 10 inches high, and 10½ inches thick and with a spread of 27 feet. He writes: "Its shapeliness and spread make it a beautiful plant. . . . The tree is in an open field and in sandy land, the elevation being about six feet above water level in a near-by pond. The plant does not bear seed." This species should be extensively cultivated as an ornamental. It seems to be very hard to transplant successfully, however, and the best way is to plant the seeds in places where the plants are wanted permanently. In full bloom below Wilmington on April 5, 1934. From the red-flowered form of *A. sylvatica* (*neglecta* var. *georgiana*) this shrubby plant may be distinguished by the uniformly redder, longer, and more cylindrical calyx and by the claws of the lateral petals being shorter than the calyx. Speaking of *A. pavia*, Porcher says that the fruit is narcotic and poisonous. The decoction of the bark has been used for ulcers and toothache. Powdered seeds and crushed branches thrown in limited pools of water intoxicate the fish, which rise and are easily caught. The root is said to be superior to soap for washing and whitening cloth. (Will this hold for our modern highly advertised soaps?) These qualities are probably common to all buckeyes. It is said that bugs do not infest Horsechestnut bedsteads. Audubon (original folio, plate 78) has a fine colored picture of this species.

A plant closely related to *A. pavia* is *A. austrina* Small (*A. discolor* var. *mollis* Sarg.) described by Small from Louisiana. Sargent refers to this species plants from Wilmington, N. C., and Charleston, S. C., but we cannot include them as specifically distinct from *A. pavia*.

2. Aesculus octandra Marsh.   Sweet Buckeye, Horse-chestnut.

THIS tall, slender tree is found in our territory in rich soil in the higher mountains of Virginia, the Carolinas, and Georgia. We have specimens from Cherokee, Macon, and Watauga counties in North Carolina.

Leaves with 5-7 leaflets, about 3½-8 inches long, finely serrate, both surfaces woolly when unfolding and at maturity usually glabrous or nearly so except for the reddish brown pubescence along the midribs; petioles finely pubescent or glabrous; inflorescence an ample panicle 1½-2⅜ (4½) inches long, glandular-pubescent throughout as are the calyx and corolla, flowers ¾-1¼ inches long, apparently varying in size in different seasons, stamens not exserted, calyx greenish, often tinted with old rose on the upper side, petals greenish yellow, the outer ones often tinted with rose, typically four in two pairs (a fifth usually aborted), the lateral ones broader and shorter, the anterior two longer and apparently exserted between the other two, all four with distinct claws, the anterior claws quite long compared with the short blade above; fruit about 1¼-2¾ inches thick, smooth, with 1-3 seeds, which are about 1-1½ inches thick. This tree may reach a height of 90 feet and a diameter of 4 feet in the Alleghanies, according to Pinchot and Ashe. See the note under *sylvatica* for a reference to a redder form.

Sargent has given the varietal name *vestita* to the form of *A. octandra* in which the petioles, branches and lower surface of the leaves are tomentose or pubescent. He assigns to this variety specimens from Roan Mountain and Craggy Mountain in North Carolina.

The European Horsechestnut (*A. hippocastanum* L.) is often planted in this country as a lawn or street tree. It also has spiny fruits. The flowers are white, mottled with purple and yellow, and are larger and more conspicuous than in the American species. The European Horsechestnut has been hybridized with our American *A. pavia* with a number of resulting forms of different colors and habits. Some of the forms have bright scarlet flowers. The hybrids may be distinguished from *A. pavia* by the somewhat spiny fruits and the consistent tree form like the European parent.

3. Aesculus sylvatica William Bartram (**A. neglecta** var. **georgiana** Sarg.) Dwarf Buckeye, Georgia Buckeye.

THIS is usually a shrub, occurring in groups, occasionally a small tree up to 20 feet high and 5 or 6 inches thick. One tree in Oconee County, South Carolina, was 50 feet high. It is found in western Florida near Pensacola, in De Kalb, Banks, Rabun, and Habersham counties, Georgia, in Seneca, Chesterfield, and Oconee counties, South Carolina, and in Durham, Stanly, Orange, Wake and Bladen counties, North Carolina, and in Virginia. The Virginia record is based on specimens (U. N. C. Herb.) sent us by Mr. J. B. Lewis (April 1938), who says it grows in "alluvial lowgrounds along the Meherrin River and its larger tributaries in Brunswick and Greensville counties." He says further that it is always a shrub.

Leaves palmately 5-(6) foliate, leaflets lanceolate. 1½-3¼ inches broad and 3-8 inches long, acuminate at the apex, margins finely serrate, upper surface smooth, lower surface glabrous or varying in Chapel Hill plants through sparsely to densely pubescent and even felted tomentose; inflorescence an ample panicle 4-8 inches long and up to 4 inches broad; calyx and pedicels pubescent but not glandular; flowers about 1¼ inches long, light yellow or greenish yellow, varying rather rarely to dull red (about the Etruscan red of Ridgway with intermediate shades); calyx campanulate, ½ inch long or less, 5-lobed, corolla of four glandular-pubescent petals, the two upper ones smaller and

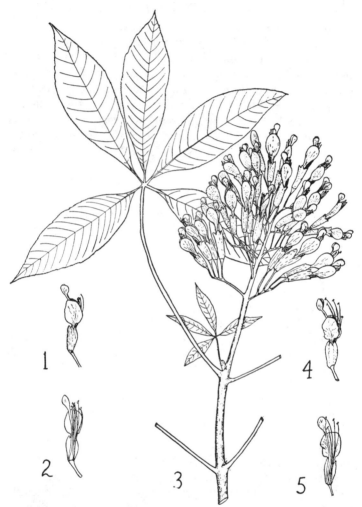

1, Perfect flower. 2, section of perfect flower. 3, branch with flower cluster. 4, male flower. 5, section of male flower. All x ½.

longer than the other two, stamens about seven, anthers usually exserted, rarely included within the corolla, pistil one; fruit a leathery 3-celled and usually 3- (sometimes only one) seeded pod 1⅛-1⅝ inches thick, without spines, opening by three valves; seeds dark brown, about ¾ inch thick,

smaller than those of *A. octandra*. The deeper red forms
may appear as seedlings from one of the yellowish forms
as proved by us in the propagating garden. Flowering
March 3 to April 27.

Fernald (*Rhodora* **46**: 47. 1944) uses the name *A. sylvatica* Bartram (*Travels*, p. 476, 1791; p. 376 of 1928 ed.)
for this plant. From the localities given by Bartram and
the description of the flowers, we do not doubt that he is
right, and we are adopting this name. The plant is characteristically a shrub, rarely a small tree, further distinguished by its distribution in the upper coastal, sandhill, or
lower piedmont regions. We are satisfied that it is a good
species.

We have a densely pubescent form from Raleigh, N. C.
(T. G. Harbison No. 14099), which is just like our pubescent form at Chapel Hill. This form has been named *A. neglecta* var. *pubescens* by Sargent (*Trees and Shrubs* **2**:
259). The same author has also named another variety
tomentosa based on plants from Oconee County, S. C. We
have plants from the type locality by the same collector and
find that they are similar to those we have from Chesterfield County, S. C., and from Stanly County, North Carolina. In Chapel Hill we have forms that are exactly like
these as well as intergrading forms to pubescent and glabrous. We have given the Chapel Hill plants much study
for a series of years and have found that these forms show
no consistent separation into true varieties. It may be that
farther southward the felted form becomes predominant
and is worthy of a varietal name. For a discussion on
Aesculus see Sargent in *Journ. Arn. Arb.* **5**: 43, 1924.

The flowers are of two kinds, perfect and male. The
perfect ones are few and are borne near the base of the
inflorescence and not rarely, apparently, the entire plant is
without any perfect flowers. At least, in several individuals none was found in a rather large number of panicles
counted, in one case as many as twelve (see table). As no
careful studies have been published on our plants, we think
it worthwhile to give in tabular form the results of counts
of many inflorescences. The counts were made by Miss
Rebecca Ward, one of our graduate students.

COUNTS OF THE NUMBER OF FLOWERS FROM ELEVEN PLANTS OF
AESCULUS SYLVATICA GROWING IN FOUR LOCATIONS IN
ORANGE COUNTY, N. C.

Number of clusters counted	Average Number per Cluster	
	Perfect flowers	Male flowers
1	0	43
3	0	54
4	0.75	64.75
4	5	31.50
7	2.71	18.29
5	1.40	19.60
14	1.57	21.71
12	0	28.33
9	0	73.33
1	3	125.00
7	15.29	47.29
Total number of flowers counted	181	2576
General average per cluster	2.7	38.45

Our Dwarf Buckeye differs from *A. octandra* not only in the shrubby habit but in the size of the flowers, which are distinctly larger, in the exserted anthers, in the absence of glands on the calyx and pedicels and in the smaller nuts. The color of the flowers is prevailingly light greenish yellow in both species but both tend through intermediate shades to a strong, dull red or more or less brick-red color. Harbison thinks that the red-flowered *A. octandra* planted by George Washington at Mt. Vernon was obtained by him from West Virginia. He has never seen such deep red flowers elsewhere, although here and there one finds a tree with pale brick-red flowers.

Sargent has given the name *A. Harbisonii* to a plant which appeared in the Arnold Arboretum from seeds of *A. georgiana* collected near Stone Mountain, Georgia. He thinks that it is a hybrid between this species and *A. discolor* var. *mollis*.

4. Aesculus glabra Willd. **Ohio Buckeye. Fetid Buckeye.**
THIS is a rather small tree and seems confined to the Mississippi valley. In our territory it occurs only in Tennessee, where it is widely scattered from the slopes of the Smoky Mountains westward and is most frequent in the valley of the Tennessee River.

The 5 (-7) leaflets on the end of a long petiole are long-elliptic or obovate, long-pointed above and narrowed down-

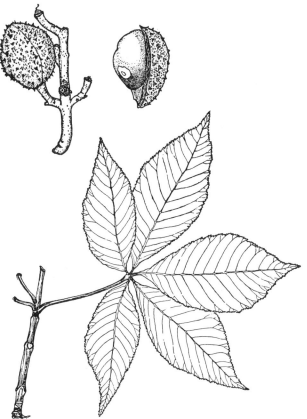

Twig with leaf and separate fruits, x ½.

ward to very short stalks, at maturity nearly glabrous or with a few hairs along the midrib below, varying greatly in size, up to 6 inches long and 2½ inches wide. Twigs reddish brown and glabrous at maturity. Inflorescence narrow, up to 5½ inches long with numerous flowers; flowers greenish yellow, pubescent, ½-¾ inch long, not including the long-exserted stamens. Fruit ovoid, usually 1½-2 inches long, armed with short scattered pyramidal prickles.

This tree is easily distinguished from *A. octandra* and the *georgiana* group by the narrow inflorescence, small flowers, and prickly fruits.

SAPINDUS (Tourn.) L.

1. Sapindus marginatus Willd. Florida Soapberry.

THIS is a small rare tree, which is reported in our area on Hurricane Island and on Colonel's Island in Liberty County, Georgia, in Alachua and Manatee counties, Florida, and from the coast of South Carolina. We have specimens from Colonel's Island.

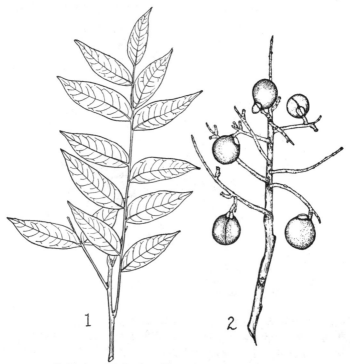

1, Twig with leaf, x ¼.   2, mature fruits, x ½.

Young twigs light grayish green, smooth; leaves alternate on the twig, very large, about 7-24 inches long, pinnately compound, leaflets 8-16, alternate or at times some opposite on the same leaf or twig, oblong-lanceolate, long pointed, glabrous, entire or nearly entire, almost sessile, on

strong shoots up to 6 inches long; leaf stalk slightly mar-
gined or only grooved, glabrous; flowers very small, reddish, borne in ample panicles, the flower stalks tomentose;
fruit a globose, light yellow, smooth berry, about ¾ inch
in diameter, with thin flesh which dries to a reddish brown,
coriaceous, translucent coat around the large, globose, dark
brown seed, which is about ⅜ inch in diameter. The fruit
is very peculiar. The ovary is 3-lobed and one (rarely 2)
of these lobes develops, the other two aborting and remaining as a sort of double keel at the base of the maturing one.

RHAMNACEAE (BUCKTHORN FAMILY)

RHAMNUS (Tourn.) L.

1. Rhamnus caroliniana Walt. **Buckthorn, Indian Cherry.**

THIS is usually a shrub, though sometimes a small tree, said
to occur along the swamps and river banks in the upper
piedmont region of our states, in western Tennessee, and in
northern Florida. It seems to prefer calcareous soil (Harper,
Sargent). Curtis says it occurs in the "Middle and Lower
Districts [of N. C.], but rare in the latter." It seems to us to
be extremely rare in the Carolinas, but we now have records
of it from Buncombe and Rutherford counties, N. C., and
from Laurens and Richland counties, S. C. In the Arboretum at Chapel Hill the Buckthorn grows very well although the soil is sour rather than calcareous.

Leaves elliptic to broad-elliptic, 2-6 inches long, 1-2
inches wide, obscurely toothed, tomentose when young, but
shining green above and smooth or nearly so when mature,
prominently veined beneath; flowers very small, greenish,
few in a cluster (sometimes single), perfect or unisexual;
fruits globose, ⅓ inch in diameter, passing through red to
black, sweet, containing 2-4 nutlets. Julian Miller says
that this species grows near Athens, Georgia, where it
reaches a diameter of 2 feet 6 inches. Flowering June 1, in
cultivation at Chapel Hill.

Rhamnus caroliniana. 1, Twig with leaves and mature fruits.
2, twig with flowers. All x ⅗.

TILIACEAE (LINDEN FAMILY)

TILIA (Tourn.) L.

The person who has only an average interest in trees
will be satisfied when he has traced this group of plants
down to the genus and knows that he has found a linden or

basswood. The cluster of flowers or fruits on a stalk that is fastened to a narrow leaf-like bract identifies the group easily. The main flower stalk (peduncle) is fastened to the top surface of the bract but the weight of the flowers or fruits is sufficient to pull down the bract, so that the top side hangs down. When the small nut-like fruits are mature the bract is blown from the tree and glides away with a whirling motion taking the fruits to some distance from the parent plant. The lindens are handsome ornamental trees and when in flower are great favorites of the bees, though the flowers of the Silver Linden are poisonous to bees. The wood is very soft and brittle and separates easily from the bark at any season. As the wood cuts easily and the internal structures are clearly outlined most teachers of botany use the twigs of the linden to teach the structure of a typical stem. The wood is used in the manufacture of cheap furniture and paper pulp. The nature lover, who wishes to know what kind of linden he has found, immediately faces difficulties. On the same tree the leaves exposed to the sun (sun leaves) may be quite different in shape, in size, and in hairiness from the shade leaves. The sun leaves may be quite hairy while the shade leaves may be smooth or if both are hairy, the hairs on the sun leaves may be quite different in length and in color from those on the shade leaves, or the hairs on the same leaves may wear down in length, change color or disappear entirely as the season advances. The twig character is just as variable, especially so as between the part of the twig grown early in the season (spring twig) and the part grown in the summer (summer shoot). The following key shows how necessary it is for one to study the whole tree carefully if he wishes to know the species of a linden. We have placed in the key thirteen species native to our region and four species that are often met with as introduced ornamentals The key also includes six native varieties that would lead to further difficulties if not treated separately from the species to which we think they belong. By some authors these varieties are considered species. The four introduced plants, *T. glabra,* the Smooth Linden, of the northern and mid-western states, *T. cordata,* the Small-leaved Linden, *T. vul-*

garis, the Common Linden, and *T. tomentosa,* the Silver or White Linden, the last three European plants (the last also found in Asia Minor), are not described further than in the key.

KEY TO THE SPECIES

1. Lower surface of mature leaves glabrous or nearly so 2
   Lower surface of mature leaves pubescent or felted tomentose 11
2. Twigs of summer shoots glabrous................. 3
   Twigs of summer shoots pubescent or tomentose... 6
3. Leaves with conspicuous axillary tufts of hairs at the base of the blade beneath; flowers without staminodia 4
   Leaves without conspicuous axillary tufts of hairs at the base of the leaf beneath; flowers with staminodia 5
4. Leaves small, averaging (excepting shade leaves) less than 2½ inches long, whitish (glaucous) beneath
   　　　　　Tilia cordata, Small-leaved Linden
   Leaves larger, averaging more than 2½ inches long, not glaucous beneath
   　　　　　Tilia vulgaris, Common Linden
5. Spring leaves practically glabrous when unfolding except for axillary tufts, summer leaves very sparsely hairy beneath, coarsely toothed; apex of bract rounded
   　　　　　Tilia glabra, Smooth Linden
   Spring leaves hairy when unfolding but soon glabrous, those on summer shoots with abundant light brown hairs beneath, coarsely or finely toothed; apex of bract often pointed
   　　　　　Tilia alabamensis, Alabama Linden　　　No. 2
6. Leaves large, averaging more than 3 inches wide, generally glaucous beneath
   　　　　　Tilia venulosa, Veiny Linden　　　No. 3
   Leaves smaller, averaging (except for shade leaves) less than 3 inches wide...................... 7
7. Leaves about as broad as long, margin with low rounded teeth (crenate) except for slender points 8
   Leaves distinctly longer than broad, distinctly toothed, except on fast growing shoots......... 9
8. Petioles mostly over one inch long; tomentum on summer shoots thick a year later; leaf base not strongly unsymmetrical
   　　　　　Tilia crenoserrata, Crenate-toothed Linden　　　No. 7
   Petioles mostly under one inch long; tomentum on summer shoots sparingly present a year later; leaf base usually much larger on one side than on the other　　　*Tilia littoralis,* Shore Linden　　　No. 8

* Not native but common in cultivation.

9. Spring leaves practically glabrous and bronze colored when unfolding; leaves on summer shoots of a more orbicular type than the spring leaves; flower cluster close; sepals, petals, and staminodia about the same length

   Tilia Ashei, Ashe's Linden   No. 11

   Spring leaves more or less tomentose below when unfolding, leaves on summer shoots not more orbicular than the spring leaves; flower cluster more open, petals about one-fourth longer than the sepals 10

10. Leaves shallowly toothed, spring leaves with axillary tufts prominent on the veins below through most of the summer; leaf base usually much larger on one side than on the other

    Tilia littoralis, Shore Linden   No. 8

    Leaves more coarsely toothed, axillary tufts not prominent on the veins, leaf base not strongly unsymmetrical   *Tilia floridana*, Florida Linden   No. 10

11. Twigs bearing long straight hairs; both simple and fascicled hairs fairly abundant under the bract

    Tilia lasioclada, Woolly Linden   No. 9

    Twigs not woolly or, if woolly, the hairs are fascicled; simple hairs not abundant under the bract except in one variety of *T. venulosa (eburnea)*   12

12. Twigs of summer shoots glabrous or very sparsely pubescent 13

    Twigs of summer shoots pubescent or tomentose... 19

13. Petioles short, mostly under 1½ inches.......... 14

    Petioles long, mostly over 1½ inches............ 16

14. Under surface of sun leaves brownish or silvery white with an abundance of close fascicled hairs; abundant fascicled hairs beneath bract; flowers small, about ¼ inch long, in large clusters of 10-25 15

    Under surface of leaves gray-green beneath with a thinner coat of fascicled hairs, leaf thin; few hairs beneath the bract; flowers about ⅓ inch long in clusters of 6-15

    Tilia heterophylla var. *tenera*,
    Thin-leaved Linden   No. 5

15. Under surface of sun leaves mostly brownish white
    Tilia heterophylla, White Linden   No. 5

    Under surface of sun leaves mostly silvery white
    Tilia heterophylla var. *nivea*, Snowy Linden   No. 5a

16. Leaves mostly finely toothed, under surface of sun leaves white or nearly so with a thick coat of fascicled hairs, axillary tufts usually lacking.... 17

    Leaves mostly coarsely toothed; tomentum on under side of leaves thinner, axillary tufts usually present 18

17. Leaves thin; flowers large, about ½ inch long
    Tilia monticola, Mountain Linden   No. 4

Leaves thick; flowers about ⅓ inch long
Tilia heterophylla var. *Michauxii*,
Michaux's Linden   No. 5

18. Leaves thick, very coarsely toothed, tending toward
lobing, white beneath or nearly so with a persistent tomentum and more or less glaucous, small
axillary tufts present but not conspicuous
**Tilia apposita, Linden   No. 6

Leaves thick, light green beneath, fascicled hairs
present but less abundant as the season advances,
not glaucous, axillary tufts usually conspicuous;
flowers about ⅓ inch long
Tilia neglecta, Neglected Linden   No. 1

19. Straight simple hairs abundant among the fascicled
hairs on the under side of bract
**Tilia eburnea (see under *T. venulosa*)

Straight simple hairs not abundant on under side
of bract (fascicled hairs may be present)......   20

20. Bracts very narrow, about ⅓ inch wide, hairs
scanty beneath
Tilia floridana var. *porracea*, Scurfy Linden   No. 10a

Bracts broader, over ⅓ inch wide, velvety beneath   21

21. Leaves about as broad as long or broader, hairs on
under surface of leaves making a thickly matted
coat that lies close against the surface.........   22

Leaves on fast growing shoots gradually narrowed
toward the apex, hairs on under surface of leaves
not thickly matted and not tightly pressed
against the surface   23

22. Twigs or young branchlets hairy for over a year;
fruit five-angled
*Tilia tomentosa, Silver Linden

Twigs soon glabrous; fruit not five-angled
***Tilia heterophylla* var. *amphiloba*, Linden   No. 5

23. Spring twigs mostly gray pubescent the first
season; summer twigs brown-tomentose; leaves
rather coarsely toothed; bracts nearly glabrous
on upper surface by flowering time; styles long,
style bases hairy
Tilia caroliniana, Carolina Linden   No. 12

Spring twigs light brown-tomentose the first season,
the tomentum on summer shoots very thick;
leaves less coarsely toothed; hairs rather
abundant on upper surface of bract at flowering
time; styles usually short and style bases smooth
or nearly so
Tilia georgiana, Georgia Linden   No. 13

1. Tilia neglecta Spach. Neglected Linden or Basswood.

THIS is a large tree that in our region seems to be found in
the native state only in the mountains and upper piedmont
of Virginia, North Carolina, Tennessee, and Georgia. How-

* Not native but common in cultivation.
** Position somewhat doubtful, needs further checking.

ever, like its near relative, *T. glabra*, it has been sent down from northern nurseries as a cultivated plant, and is sometimes found as a street tree or yard tree even in the coastal plain, as at Goldsboro, North Carolina.

Twigs glabrous, summer shoots at first sparsely pubescent but soon glabrous; leaves broadly ovate to cordate, mostly 3-6 (up to 7) inches long and 2½-4½ (up to 8) inches wide, apex long-pointed, base usually cordate, more rarely obliquely truncate or broadly cuneate, margin usually coarsely or some finely toothed, apiculate, deep green and soon glabrous above, lower surface paler, covered with gray or gray-brown short fascicled hairs and a few longer white

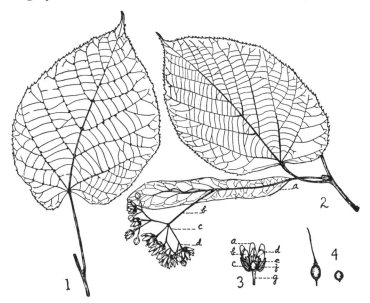

1, Twig, showing axillary tufts, x ⅓. 2, twig, showing bract with flower cluster, and leaf without axillary hairs. *a*, bract. *b*, peduncle. *c*, cyme branch. *d*, pedicel, x ⅓. 3, flower. *a*, petal. *b*, staminodium. *c*, sepal. *d*, anther. *e*, style base. *f*, ovary. *g*, pedicel, x ⅔. 4, fruits, x ⅓.

simple hairs, rather abundant on the thick sun leaves when young, scarce on the thin shade leaves, some persistent, axillary tufts usually present, petioles soon glabrous, stout, 1½-3 inches long; bract narrow, elliptic to oblanceolate, 3-6 inches long, ½-1 inch wide, apex rounded, base obliquely pointed, upper surface glabrous, a few fascicled hairs on the lower surface, stalk quite short or up to 1⅞ inches long; free part of peduncle 1¼-2 inches long, glabrous; pedicels nearly glabrous; flowers in broad clusters (generally 10-15), about ⅓ inch long, sepals about two-thirds as long as the petals, petals notched at the apex, staminodia nearly as long as the petals; style base woolly; fruits subglobose to ellipsoidal, apiculate, brown to tan-pubescent, about ⅓ inch in diameter, ripening in September. Flowering in early July.

The plant is closely related to *Tilia glabra*, and by Bush considered only a variety of that species (*Bull. Torr. Bot. Club* **54**: 238. 1927) ; but the persistent character of the fascicled hairs on the under surface of the leaf separates the plant rather satisfactorily from *T. glabra* and from *T. alabamensis;* more persistent hairs on the under surface of the leaf, lack of glaucousness, and the presence of axillary tufts separate it from *T. venulosa;* longer petioles, larger flowers, and larger fruits separate it from *T. heterophylla.* See *T. monticola* and *T. apposita* for comparisons with those species.

2. Tilia alabamensis Ashe. Alabama Linden or Basswood.

THIS large linden, much more common to the west of us, extends in the mountain region and piedmont of Georgia and North Carolina as far east as Polk County, North Carolina. A variety, *T. alabamensis* var. *oblongifolia* (Sarg.) Bush, has been described from northeastern and western Florida.

Twigs glabrous, even on summer shoots; leaves broadly ovate to long-ovate, 3-5 inches long, 2¾-4 inches wide, generally abruptly short-pointed, but on long leaves more gradually pointed, base obliquely truncate to cordate or even broadly cuneate, margin generally coarsely toothed, apiculate, the teeth more rounded and shallow on fast growing twigs and summer shoots, spring leaves practically glabrous at maturity, leaves on summer twigs light brown tomentose beneath; petioles rather stout, 1-2 inches long,

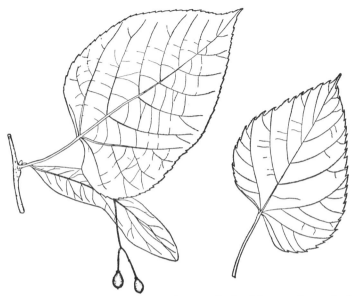

1, Twig with leaf, bract and fruits. 2, leaf with coarsely toothed margin. All x ⅖.

glabrous; stipules narrow, practically linear; bracts ligulate to oblanceolate, 3-5 inches long, ½-1 inch wide, usually pointed at the apex and gradually narrowed toward the base, stalk short, generally about ¼ (up to ¾) inch long, tomentose on both surfaces when young but completely glabrous by late summer; free part of peduncle 1-1½ inches long, soon glabrous; pedicels long and slender, nearly glabrous, forming loose broad clusters (we have no collections of this plant in flower); fruits globose to obovate, apiculate, about ¼ inch in diameter, light brown-tomentose when young, gray-brown-pubescent at maturity. Reported as flowering in early June.

There has been considerable confusion as to the position of this plant. Ashe (*Bull. Charleston Mus.* **14**: 31. 1918) described it as *T. alabamensis,* but later (*Charleston Mus. Quart.* **1**: 32. 1925) decided that as the flowers were so much like those of *T. floridana* it was only a long-leaved variety of that species. Bush (*Bull. Torr. Bot. Club* **54**: 247. 1927) claims that the flowers are not small but "large, much like those of *T. glabra,* the leaves are broad and short, not long and narrow, and the trees do not grow in swamps or low ground but along shaded creeks and river banks in rich soil.'' *Tilia alabamensis* differs from *T. glabra* in that the spring leaves are tomentose when unfolding, leaves on summer shoots have more tomentum beneath and usually lack the tufts of axillary hairs.

Bush has placed Sargent's *T. floridana* var. *oblongifolia* from Putnam, Leon, and Gadsden counties, Fla., as a variety of *T. alabamensis* with more elongated leaves, more prominent tufts of axillary hairs, and with slender, glabrous, reddish brown branchlets. We are not familiar with the variety.

3. Tilia venulosa Sarg.   Veiny Linden or Basswood.

This is a large tree that is found in the rich soil of rocky coves and wooded bluffs of streams in the Blue Ridge and western piedmont of Virginia, North Carolina, and South Carolina, as far east as Davidson County in North Carolina and as far south as Oconee County in South Carolina.

Bark of twigs purple, red-brown or yellow-brown, spring twigs soon glabrous, the summer shoots when young thickly covered with long brown hairs; leaves large, about the size and shape of *T. neglecta* but the under surface of the sun leaves usually more or less glaucous and all the leaves without axillary tufts and with fewer hairs that usually disappear entirely before the end of the summer; stipules ligulate, ½-1 inch long, ⅛-¼ inch wide; bracts oblong to spatulate, 2-5 inches long, ½-1 inch wide, the apex rounded, the base narrowed and rounded or pointed, nearly glabrous by flowering time, stalk $\frac{1}{16}$-¾ inch long; free part of peduncle 1-2 inches long, cyme branches and peduncle practically glabrous by flowering time, pedicels pubescent with appressed, tawny to white fascicled hairs, but practically glabrous by the time the fruit matures; flowers and fruits similar to *T. neglecta* or with the fruits slightly smaller, falling in August and September. Flowering in Davidson County, N. C., June 17, 1931, and in Buncombe County, N. C., July 5, 1917.

1, Twig with leaves and flowers, x ⅓. 2, twig with young leaves showing stipules, x ⅓. 3, flowers (one in section), x ⅔. 4, fruit nearly mature, x ⅓. 5, twig with buds, x ⅓.

This tree is closely related to *T. australis* described by Small from the mountains of Alabama, but the pedicels at the time of flowering are distinctly pubescent and the summer shoots are hairy. The presence of hairs on the young leaves and on summer shoots, the more or less glaucous character, and the absence of conspicuous tufts on the under surface of the leaf separate this tree from *T. glabra,* found to the north of us and as far south as Kentucky, but apparently not entering our region in the wild state though it is not at all uncommon as a cultivated tree. The hairiness of the summer shoots, more or less glaucous character of the leaves, and the sparseness or absence of hairs, even of axillary tufts on mature leaves, separate it from *T. neglecta*. The presence of hairs on the summer shoots and the absence of axillary tufts separate it from *T. alabamensis*.

Sargent has described a variety, *T. venulosa* var. *multinervis*, with 12 or 13 pairs of main veins to the leaf (8-10 in the typical species), with the base obliquely truncate rather than cordate, and with ellipsoidal fruit.

We are of the opinion that Ashe's *T. eburnea* is an extreme and rare variety of this species. It differs from the typical *T. venulosa* in that the leaf is more pubescent, usually remaining pubescent below, in abundant simple hairs among the fascicled hairs on the under side of the bract, and in smaller flowers. Except for these differences Ashe's original description of *T. eburnea* (*Bot. Gaz.* **33:** 231. 1902) resembles *T. venulosa* closely and in 1916 plants of *T. venulosa* were distributed as *T. eburnea*. The plants occur together in Oconee County, S. C., and both occur in Polk County, North Carolina. Sargent (*Bot. Gaz.* **66:** 429. 1918) considered *T. eburnea* as *T. heterophylla* var. *Michauxii*. However, the young fruits of *T. eburnea* are covered with the loosely packed, brown tomentum of *T. venulosa* rather than with the short, gray pubescence of *T. heterophylla*. It would be a taxonomic pity if the rules of nomenclature should require that this extreme and rare variety be declared the type and the abundant and well known *T. venulosa* be placed in the position of a variety.

4. **Tilia monticola** Sarg. **Mountain Linden** or **Basswood.**

THIS is a tree of moderate size of the mountains from Carroll County, Virginia, to near the Georgia line in Macon County, North Carolina, and westward into Tennessee.

Twigs red to brown, glabrous, even summer shoots practically glabrous; leaves about the size and shape of *T. neglecta* but the leaves thinner, the margin usually finely toothed, and the under surface of sun leaves made silvery white or white lightly tinged with brown by a close tomentum of white fascicled hairs with a few simple hairs scattered along the midrib and veins, tomentum sparse on shade leaves, axillary tufts usually absent but sometimes

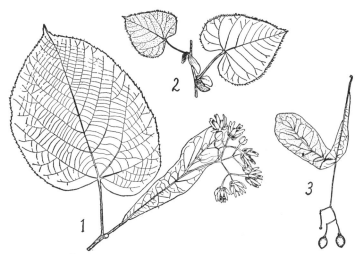

1, Spring twig with leaf, bract and cluster of flowers. 2, summer shoot with young leaves and stipules. 3, bract and fruits. All x ⅓.

present; stipules lanceolate to oblanceolate ⅓-⅔ inch long; bract nearly as in *T. neglecta,* but in our collections the base more gradually narrowed, stalk quite short or up to ¾ inch long, upper surface nearly glabrous or with a few fascicled hairs along the midrib and veins, fascicled hairs abundant on under surface; free part of peduncle ¾-1¾ inches long, glabrous, cyme branches glabrous, pedicels pubescent; flowers few in a broad cluster, large, about ½ inch long, sepals about two-thirds as long as the petals, staminodia nearly as long as the petals, base of style woolly, ovary gray-pubescent; fruit subglobose to short ellipsoidal, about ⅓ inch in diameter, apiculate, gray-brown, pubescent, ripening in September. Flowering in late June and early July.

This tree resembles *T. heterophylla* that grows through the same region as well as farther east, but the leaves will average larger and the under surface whiter, the petioles longer, the flowers larger and in smaller clusters, and the stipules are broadest near the middle rather than at the base. The thinner sun leaves that are much whiter beneath, the fine toothed margin, the larger flowers and the usual lack of axillary tufts separate it from *T. neglecta.* (Axillary tufts are sometimes absent in *T. neglecta.*) Sargent (*Bot. Gaz.* **66:** 510. 1918) says: "*T. monticola* with its larger leaves, snowy white on the lower surface and drooping gracefully on their long petioles, and its large flowers, is the showiest of the American lindens." Ashe (*Bull. Torr. Bot. Club* **53:** 28. 1926) thought that this is the plant Nuttall described as *T. Michauxii.*

5. **Tilia heterophylla** Vent. **White Linden** or **Basswood.**

The typical species is a large tree found through the mountains and upper piedmont of Virginia, North Carolina, South Carolina, Georgia, western Florida and westward. Several related trees considered by some authors as species, by others only as varieties, are also found in our region. See below for brief descriptions of these plants.

Twigs red to yellow-brown, glabrous; leaves similar in shape to *T. neglecta,* mostly 3-5 inches long, 2-4 inches wide, margin finely or coarsely toothed, under surface of the lower leaves nearly white, of upper leaves dingy or brownish white due to the close tomentum of fascicled hairs, some slightly glaucous and with or without axillary tufts below, petiole 1-2½ inches long, but rarely over 1½ inches long, soon glabrous; stipules lanceolate with a broadened or even

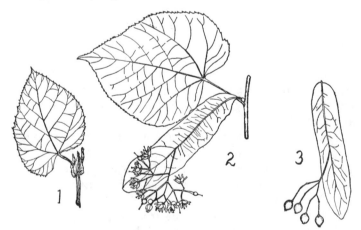

1, Summer shoot with young leaf and stipules. 2, twig with leaf, bract, and flower cluster. 3, bract with fruits. All x ⅖.

auriculate base, about ½ inch long; bract oblanceolate, 2-5 inches long, apex rounded or bluntly pointed, base gradually obliquely pointed or rounded, stalk very short or up to ¾ inch long, upper surface soon glabrous, lower surface covered with a short tomentum of fascicled hairs with a few longer, simple hairs; free part of peduncle mostly ¾-1 inch long, glabrous, cyme branches glabrous or nearly so, pedicels pubescent; flowers small, about ¼ inch long, in clusters of 10-25, sepals about two-thirds as long as the petals, staminodia nearly as long as the petals, base of style usually woolly; fruit subglobose to short ellipsoid, about ¼ inch in diameter, covered with a close, very short gray pubescence to near maturity then turning brown, ripening in September. Flowering in June.

See *T. monticola* and *T. neglecta* for comparisons with those species.

The variety *T. heterophylla* var. *Michauxii* (Nutt.) Sarg. is practically intermediate between *T. heterophylla* and *T. monticola*. It has an even wider range than the typical species, reaching as far north as New York, as far west as Missouri and Arkansas, but not reported from Florida.

In our opinion most of the plants referred to *T. heterophylla* from the piedmont and coastal plain from North Carolina to Alabama belong to *T. heterophylla* var. *tenera* Ashe. From North Carolina we have collections from many places, from the southeastern edge of Rowan County to the coast, and from Georgia, one from Dougherty County. In this variety the flowers are slightly larger (about ⅓ inch long) than in the typical *T. heterophylla*, the clusters are usually smaller, and the leaves are thinner and more triangular ovate, but there are intergrading forms.

Tilia heterophylla var. *amphiloba* Sarg., described from River Junction, Gadsden County, Florida, has fascicled hairs on the upper surface of the young leaves and the twigs are pubescent on summer shoots.

Tilia heterophylla var. *nivea* Sarg., also described from River Junction, Florida, has the flat closely interwoven, nearly white tomentum on the under surface of the leaf like

the typical *T. heterophylla,* but the ovary is woolly as in
T. caroliniana and the bract is velvety beneath. The relationship of this plant with *T. heterophylla* is quite doubtful.

6. **Tilia apposita** Ashe. **Linden, Basswood.**

THIS is a small tree reported only from the mountains of
northern Georgia.

Twigs reddish brown, glabrous by mid-June; leaves
cordate to broadly ovate, blade 3½-8 inches long, 3½-6½
inches wide, margin coarsely toothed, some teeth so coarse
as to approach lobes, under surface light gray with a rather
flat coat of fascicled hairs and a few simple hairs along the
midrib and larger veins, axillary tufts of brownish hairs
though present small and inconspicuous, slightly or strongly
glaucous; petiole up to 3 inches long; bract narrow, oblong to oblanceolate, 3½-5½ inches long and about 1 inch

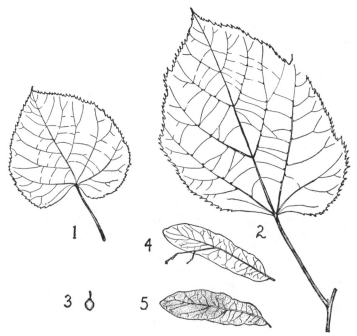

1, 2, Leaves. 3, fruit. 4, bract, upper surface. 5, bract, lower
surface. All x ⅓.

wide, apex rounded or bluntly pointed, base obliquely rounded or pointed, thick, stalk quite short or up to ⅓ inch long, lower surface covered with short fascicled hairs, in some so thickly covered as to appear velvety even in October; free part of peduncle ⅔-2¼ inches long, sparsely tomentose to nearly glabrous, cyme branches and pedicels tomentose; flowers not seen; fruit globose, ¼-⅓ inch in diameter, apiculate, covered with a gray-brown tomentum.

The under surface of the leaf of this plant resembles *T. heterophylla* but the blade is of a broader type, larger, and more coarsely toothed, and the petiole is longer. The leaves resemble those of *T. neglecta* still more, but they tend to be even more coarsely toothed, often nearly lobed, and are more or less glaucous beneath, the tomentum is more persistent and the axillary tufts are less conspicuous.

7. Tilia crenoserrata Sarg.   **Crenate-toothed Linden** or **Basswood.**

THIS is a small to medium sized tree that is found from southern Georgia (Dougherty County) to northeastern and central Florida.

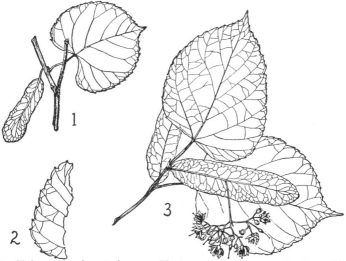

1, Glabrous spring twig on old tomentose summer shoot, x ⅓. 2, margin of leaf, x ⅔. 3, twig with leaves, bracts and flower cluster, x ⅓.

Spring twigs nearly glabrous by flowering time, but summer twigs tawny to dark brown-tomentose, the tomentum persistent even a year later and making a striking contrast in the alternating smooth and velvety patches of spring and summer growth; leaves mostly suborbicular, some cordate, usually 2½-4 (up to 5½) inches long, 2-3½ (up to 5) inches wide, abruptly pointed or almost rounded at the tip, base uneven, truncate to cordate, margin crenate-serrate, apiculate, or the whole tooth scarcely more than the apiculus, surface of mature spring leaves glabrous on both sides except for minute tufts on the veins beneath, lower surface sometimes slightly glaucous, both sides velvety on young leaves of summer shoots; petioles ¾-1¾ inches long, on spring growth soon glabrous, on summer shoots velvety; stipules lanceolate with a broad base; bracts mostly oblong, about 3-3½ inches long and about ¾ inch broad, irregular, mostly sessile; free part of peduncle about 1½ (1-2) inches long, pubescent; flowers numerous, 15-30, about ¼ inch long, sepals and staminodia two-thirds as long as the petals, style bases with or without tawny wool, ovaries woolly; fruit ellipsoidal, ¼-⅓ inch in diameter, conspicuously apiculate, rusty-tomentose, ripening from the middle to the end of August. Our collections do not show mature fruits and we have drawn the descriptions of the fruits from Sargent's *Manual of Trees* (2nd edition, p. 737). In Sargent's first edition this plant was described as *T. floridana* Small by mistake and figure 548 under that name is really *T. crenoserrata*. In the second edition he omits this figure under the latter name, giving no figure. It would seem that *T. crenoserrata* has not been illustrated under this name except in our figure.

Ashe has described a variety from Gainesville, Florida, with a longer, more acuminate point under the name of *T. crenoserrata* var. *acuminata*.

Tilia crenoserrata is closely related to *T. littoralis* but the leaves in the former are more orbicular, less acuminate pointed, except in the variety *acuminata* and even there the margin is more crenate than in *T. littoralis*, the tomentum on summer shoots more persistent, and the petiole generally longer. The shape of the leaf, blunt teeth, and the broad base of the bract separate it from *T. floridana*.

8. Tilia littoralis Sarg. Shore Linden or Basswood.

THIS is a small linden that has been reported only from Colonel's Island, Liberty County, Georgia, where it is found on the banks of creeks only a few feet above high tide.

Spring twigs soon glabrous, summer shoots gray-brown tomentose; leaves broadly ovate to suborbicular, abruptly short-pointed, mostly 3-4 inches long, 2-3½ inches wide, larger on summer shoots, base usually unsymmetrical, mar-

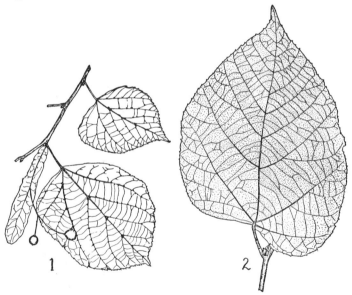

1, Glabrous spring twig with leaves, bract and fruits. 2, tomentose summer shoot with leaf and stipule. All x ⅓.

gin with shallow teeth or on fast growing shoots crenate, spring leaves soon glabrous except for axillary tufts and abundant marginal hairs, on summer leaves hairs abundant above, especially along the midrib and veins, and velvety below; petioles mostly ¾-1 inch long, on spring twigs slender and soon glabrous, on summer shoots thicker and tomentose; stipules lanceolate with a broadened base, ⅓-⅝ inch long; bract oblanceolate, mostly 2-4 inches long and ⅓-¾ inch (rarely 1½ inches) wide, tapering toward the base but with the base usually rounded and practically sessile, soon glabrous except for the ciliated margin and a few hairs along the midrib above; free part of peduncle ½-1½ inches long, sparsely tomentose; pedicels tomentose; flowers 9-30 in a cluster, about ¼-⅓ inch long, the sepals two-thirds as long as the petals, staminodia three-fourths as long as the petals, style bases woolly or glabrous, ovaries tawny-tomentose; fruits spherical to short-obovoid, apiculate, about ⅓ inch in diameter, pubescent. Flowering in June.

Bush (*Bull. Torr. Bot. Club* **54**: 241. 1927) considered the twigs of the summer shoots glabrous, but they are quite tomentose. The summer shoots of *T. littoralis* var. *discolor* Sarg., in which the leaves are nearly white (glaucous) on the under surface, are also tomentose.

This plant is closely related to *T. crenoserrata*. See that species for a comparison of the two.

9. Tilia lasioclada Sarg.   Woolly Linden or Basswood.

THIS is a medium sized tree found on rich wooded slopes and rocky bluffs from Oconee County, South Carolina, southeastward along both sides of the Savannah River in South Carolina, and Georgia to well below Augusta, and along the Chattahoochee River in western Florida.

Young twigs clothed with long straight, simple hairs, disappearing on some branches by early June, persisting on some for two or three years; leaves suborbicular, broadovate to cordate, mostly 4-6 inches long, 3-4½ inches wide, apex abruptly short-pointed, base obliquely truncate to deep cordate, margin coarsely to finely toothed, bright green and smooth above, lower surface lighter, some glaucous, permanently covered with a light tan to brown tomentum of long fascicled hairs and with a few simple hairs along the midrib and veins, the tomentum thickest on sun leaves, axillary tufts present or absent; petiole stout, mostly 1-1½ (up to 3) inches long, clothed when young

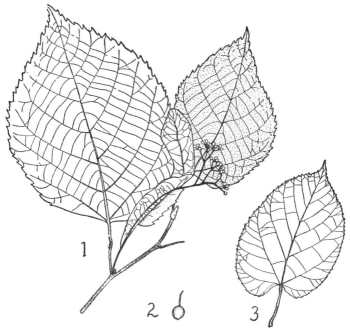

1, Twig showing leaves with truncate base, stipule, bract and cluster of flower buds. 2, fruit. 3, leaf with cordate base. All x ⅖.

with both fascicled and simple hairs but the simple hairs more persistent; stipules lanceolate, up to ½ inch long; bracts oblanceolate, 3-5 inches long, ¾-1 inch wide, apex rounded or bluntly pointed, base narrowed usually into an oblique point, sometimes rounded, practically sessile or with stalk up to ½ inch long, soon nearly glabrous except for a few fascicled and simple hairs, especially along the midrib, on both surfaces, the simple hairs more persistent; free part of peduncle ¼-1½ inches long, peduncle and cyme branches woolly with low fascicled hairs and longer simple hairs, pedicels pubescent; flowers 10-25 in a cluster, about ¼ inch long, sepals and staminodia described as about one-third as long as the petals; fruits subspherical, apiculate, about ⅓ inch in diameter, brown, pubescent.

The long, straight, simple hairs usually present on the twigs is the best means of identification for this tree. Ashe

(*Bull. Torr. Bot. Club* **53**: 31. 1926), from the presence of simple, long hairs on the under surface of the bract in this plant and in *T. eburnea,* has considered *T. lasioclada* only a variety of *T. eburnea.* However, there has been considerable confusion as to *T. eburnea,* which we are placing with *T. venulosa,* and since the usually long, simple hairs along the twigs make *T. lasioclada* so easy to identify we prefer to follow Sargent and to treat it as a species.

10. Tilia floridana Small. Florida Linden or Basswood.

THIS is a small tree up to 30 feet high which was described from rich woods in Jackson County, Florida. Bush (*Bull. Torr. Bot. Club* **54**: 246. 1927) says that it is a lowland or coastal species with a greater range than any other species except *T. glabra,* ranging from eastern North Carolina to Georgia, Florida, and westward, apparently confined to the Long-leaf Pine region. In our region we have no collections from uncultivated plants north of Florida.

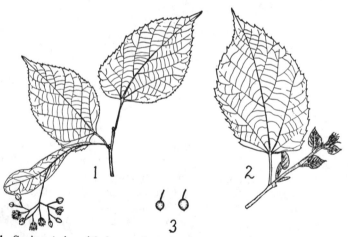

1, Spring twig with leaves, bract and cluster of flowers. 2, spring twig with leaf and summer shoot with young leaves and stipules. 3, fruits. All x ⅓.

Spring twigs soon glabrous, summer twigs thickly covered with a tawny tomentum; leaves ovate, usually 3-4 (2½-5) inches long, 1½-3 inches wide, acuminate-pointed, base uneven, usually truncate, but some slightly cordate and rarely a few pointed, margin coarsely toothed, spring leaves with short, stiff, simple hairs above and fascicled hairs on both surfaces until past flowering time, lower surface glaucous, leaves on summer shoots covered with a thick tawny tomentum when young; petioles mostly about 1 (½-2) inch long, a few fascicled hairs present until after flowering, on summer shoots densely tawny-tomentose; stipules nearly lanceolate, mostly ¼-½ inch long, slender, pointed; bracts small, mostly 2½-3½ (1¾-4½) inches long, about ½ (⅓-¾) inch wide, long obovate or oblanceolate, the apex rounded, usually the lower two-thirds of the blade narrowing gradually into a point and with a short stalk up to ¾ inch long, nearly glabrous by the time of flowering; free part of peduncle mostly 1-1½ inches long, sparingly pubescent at time of flowering, glabrous by the time the fruits mature; cyme branches and pedicels long and pubescent; flowers few in a widely spreading cluster, flowers about ¼ inch long, sepals and staminodia about three-fourths as long as the petals; style base and ovary tomentose; fruits nearly spherical but slightly longer than broad, about ¼ inch in diameter, apiculate, tomentose, ripening in September. Flowering about June 1.

This plant has been confused with *T. crenoserrata, T. Ashei,* and *T. alabamensis.* See under the first two mentioned for comparison with those species. *Tilia alabamensis* is found farther from the coast in the hill country; the twigs of its summer shoots are glabrous; and the flowers are reported (Bush) as about twice as large as in *T. floridana.* In the literature *T. floridana* is often credited as occurring as far north as Polk County, N. C., but we have the Ashe collection No. 102 of 1895 from Polk County, which we take is the authority for the citations and we are of the opinion that this collection is of *T. alabamensis.*

10a. **Tilia floridana** var. **porracea** n. comb. (**T. porracea** Ashe, Charleston Mus. Quart. **1**: 31. 1925). **Scurfy Linden** or **Basswood**.

Except for more abundant and more persistent hairs, the

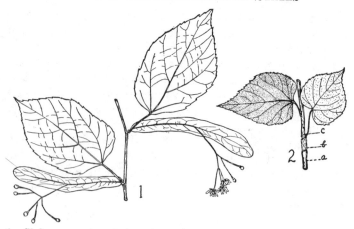

1, Glabrous spring twig with leaves, bracts and flower clusters. 2, twig showing a, glabrous spring growth of 1923; b, tomentose summer shoot of 1923; c, glabrous spring twig of 1924 with leaves. All x ⅓.

leaves generally remaining tomentose through the summer, and for narrower, nearly linear bracts, the description of this plant would be practically identical with that of *T. floridana*. We have several collections from Hickory Head and Turkey Head, Okaloosa County, Florida (Ashe), where we also have the typical *T. floridana*. We have a collection (Harbison) from near Mariana, Jackson County, Florida, the type locality for *T. floridana*, which seems intermediate.

11. Tilia Ashei Bush. Ashe's Linden or Basswood.

THIS is a small tree named for W. W. Ashe. It has been found only on slopes along streams and stream heads in western Florida.

Twigs soon glabrous, except on summer shoots where they are covered with a tawny-gray tomentum; spring leaves of about the size and shape of *T. floridana* but purple-bronze when unfolding and practically glabrous except for short, stiff, simple hairs on the upper surface and margin, the marginal hairs persistent, slightly glaucous beneath, leaves on summer shoots of a more orbicular type than the spring ones and with margins crenate or even

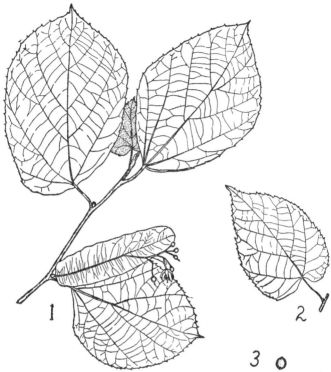

1, Fast growing spring twig with leaves, bract, flower cluster showing flower and young fruits, and young summer shoot. 2, leaf on
slow growing spring twig. 3, fruit. All x ⅖.

nearly plain except for the slender points and marginal
hairs, hairs abundant on both surfaces; petioles short, about
⅓-1 inch long; stipules nearly lanceolate, about ⅓ inch
long; bracts narrow-oblong, 2-4 inches long, ⅔-1 inch wide,
nearly sessile, practically glabrous; free part of peduncle
½-1 inch long, sparingly pubescent; cyme branches and
pedicels short and pubescent; flowers few in a rather compact cluster, flowers about ¼ inch long, sepals, petals, and
staminodia about the same length, style base woolly, ovary
tomentose; fruit nearly spheroidal, about ¼ inch in diameter, covered with tawny-gray tomentum, ripening in September. Flowering June 13.

Tilia Ashei is related to *T. floridana* but the spring

leaves when unfolding are practically glabrous except for marginal hairs that persist through the summer; the leaves on summer shoots are more orbicular than the spring leaves and have crenulate margins; the petioles are short, ⅓-1 inch long; the bracts are usually nearly sessile and with a broad base; and the flowers are in small, rather compact clusters. In *T. floridana* the spring leaves are more or less hairy until flowering time; the marginal hairs do not persist through the summer; the leaves on the summer shoots are not more orbicular than the spring leaves and are coarsely toothed; the petioles are somewhat longer, ½-2 inches long; the bracts are usually distinctly stalked and have a narrow base; and the flowers, in more open clusters, appear one or two weeks earlier than those of *T. Ashei*.

12. **Tilia caroliniana** Mill. (**T. pubescens** Ait.). **Carolina Linden** or **Basswood.**

Twig with leaves and flowers, x ⅓.

THIS is a medium sized tree found in our region in a rather narrow strip along the coast from New Hanover County, North Carolina, to Liberty County, Georgia, and in central and western Florida.

Twigs gray to red-brown, pubescent with fascicled hairs when young but glabrous except on summer shoots by midsummer; buds practically glabrous, leaves broadly ovate, nearly orbicular, mostly 2⅓-4 inches long, 1¾-3½ inches wide (much larger on strong shoots), apex abruptly long pointed, base cordate to obliquely truncate, margin coarsely toothed, the teeth often blunt except for the apiculus, tending toward crenate, teeth on strong shoots very distant and very large, upper surface covered with a loose coat of rather stiff brownish fascicled and simple hairs when unfolding, soon glabrous, lower surface sparsely tomentose with distant fascicled light brown hairs, coarser and stiffer than those in the *T. heterophylla* group, consequently their ends are rather distant from the surface and give the lower surface a brownish mealy appearance; petioles slender, mostly ¾-1 (up to 1½) inch long, stouter on strong shoots, pubescent, later nearly glabrous; stipules linear to lanceolate, about ⅓ inch long; bract oblanceolate, mostly 2¾-4 inches long, ½-¾ inch wide, apex usually rounded, more rarely bluntly pointed, base pointed or rounded, nearly sessile or stalk up to ⅓ inch long, by flowering time nearly glabrous or with a considerable number of fascicled hairs along the midrib above and over the lower surface; free part of peduncle slender, about ¾-1½ inches long, sparsely pubescent, cyme branches slightly more pubescent, pedicels very pubescent; flowers in clusters mostly of 10-15, about ⅓ inch long, sepals about as long as the staminodia and about three-fourths as long as the petals, style long, in our collections the base of the style and ovary quite woolly; fruits globose to short ellipsoidal, about ¼ inch in diameter, apiculate, the tomentum worn down to a pubescence by maturity, brown. Flowering on James Island, S. C., on June 7.

This plant can be distinguished from *T. heterophylla* var. *tenera*, that extends into its range, by the pubescence on the young twigs, the coarser hairs that are not pressed so closely to the under surface of the leaf and by the young fruits that are covered with longer hairs. The above leaf difference will also distinguish it from *T. heterophylla* var.

nivea found in western Florida but the young ovaries and young fruits of these two are similar. It is closely related to *T. georgiana* found through most of its range but that plant is more hairy, especially on the twigs and winter buds, the leaves are usually less coarsely toothed, the flowers usually smaller with short styles that are glabrous at the base, and the fruit is slightly larger. However, we have a collection from near Ocala, Florida (Ashe No. 138) that appears to be intermediate. It may be a hybrid or further collections may show *T. georgiana* to be only a variety of *T. caroliniana*.

13. Tilia georgiana Sarg. Georgia Linden or Basswood.

THIS is a medium sized tree found in our region near the coast from near Charleston, South Carolina, to Brunswick, Georgia, and in central and western Florida.

Young twigs thickly coated with a light brown tomentum that persists as a dark coat through the second year though considerably worn down, tomentum on summer

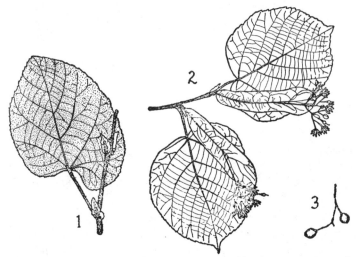

1, Summer shoot with stipules and young leaf velvety beneath.
2, spring twig with stipules, leaves, bracts and clusters of flowers.
3 fruits. All x ⅓.

shoots thicker and darker than on spring twigs; young buds tomentose, later pubescent or nearly smooth; leaves about like those of *T. caroliniana* with the margin somewhat less coarsely toothed and more crenate and the fascicled brown hairs on the lower surface of the leaf more abundant, so abundant on fast growing shoots as to remain velvety throughout the summer; stipules ligulate to lanceolate with a broadened base, some auricled, ⅓-⅔ inch long; bracts oblong to long obovate, mostly 2½-3½ (up to 4½) inches long, ½-1 inch wide, apex rounded, base rounded or bluntly pointed, some obtuse, practically sessile, upper surface sparsely covered with fascicled hairs, thickly so along the midrib and with an occasional simple hair, fascicled hairs more abundant on the lower surface; free part of peduncle mostly 1-1½ inches long, pubescent, cyme branches and pedicels pubescent; flowers in clusters of 10-15, about as in *T. caroliniana* except that the flowers are usually smaller, about ¼ inch long, with the style usually shorter and the style base glabrous or nearly so; fruit globose, ½-⅓ inch in diameter, apiculate, when young covered with a fairly close gray tomentum, turning brown at maturity, ripening early in September. Flowering at Brunswick, Georgia, on June 19.

This plant is closely related to *T. caroliniana* found through most of the same territory and may be only a very hairy variety of it. See that plant for a comparison of the two. At Colonel's Island, Georgia, *T. georgiana* and *T. littoralis* grow together and the leaves on the summer shoots of these two plants are quite similar, the greatest difference being a slightly longer petiole in *T. georgiana*. The rather small summer leaf of the sketch of *T. georgiana* shows how unsymmetrical the base may be on that plant. The spring leaves of *T. littoralis*, soon glabrous except for axillary tufts and marginal hairs, are quite different from the hairy leaves of *T. georgiana*.

To the most hairy form Sargent has given the name *T georgiana* var. *crinita* but fast growing branches are very hairy and could easily mislead one.

STERCULIACEAE (CHOCOLATE FAMILY)

STERCULIA L.

1. Sterculia platanifolia L. f. [Firmiana platanifolia (L.) Br.] Japanese Varnish Tree, Chinese Parasol Tree.

THE Japanese Varnish Tree, a native of China and Japan, is sparingly escaped in the lower coastal part of South Carolina, in Georgia and Florida and westward. It is a peculiar tree with very large simple leaves and green bark even on branches or trunks ten years old or more. The fruit is also peculiar in that the pods are not closed even when young so the seeds can be seen clearly from the outside.

TERNSTROEMIACEAE (TEA FAMILY)

STEWARTIA L.

Fruit a pointed 5-angled pod; stamens yellow (purple in the variety *grandiflora*
    Stewartia pentagyna, Mountain Stewartia   No. 1
Fruit a globular pod without conspicuous ridges; stamens purple
    Stewartia Malachodendron, Stewartia   No. 2

1. Stewartia pentagyna L'Hér. Mountain Stewartia.

THIS shrub or small tree is essentially a mountain plant occurring not infrequently in the mountains of Kentucky, Tennessee, Virginia, and North Carolina southward to Georgia. Harbison has found it common in the Cumberland Mountain and Sand Mountain regions of Tennessee and Alabama. Harbison said it was more plentiful at the head of Tallulah River in Georgia than in any other place he had ever seen. At that station it is mostly if not all of the yellow-stamened form. We have collections of it as far east as Montgomery County, North Carolina. Curtis says that it grows in Wake County, N. C., and Grimes (*Rhodora* 24: 150. 1922) reports it from Williamsburg, Virginia, but is this not rather *Stewartia Malachodendron?* See that species.

Stewartia pentagyna. 1, Twig with mature fruit, x ½. *Stewartia Malachodendron.* 2, branch with open flower and bud, x ½. 3, twig with mature fruit, x ½. 4, seed, x 1.

Leaves oblong-elliptic, acuminate, about 2-5 inches long, margins ciliate and with minute teeth, lower surface with scattered hairs; petioles up to ½ inch long, pubescent; flowers up to 4 inches broad, creamy white, petals crimped toward the eroded margins; stamens very numerous, with whitish filaments and yellow anthers; pistil with five separate styles; fruit a pointed pod with five sharp angles. A tree near Satolah, Rabun County, Georgia, is 24 feet high and 3⅓ inches in diameter.

There is a variety of *S. pentagyna* with bright purple stamens making the flowers almost identical in appearance with those of *S. Malachodendron,* which has been given the name *grandiflora* by Bean. In North Carolina this form seems to be less common than the one with pale stamens. We have it from 5 miles south of Highlands, N. C., near the Georgia line and from Transylvania County near Little Toxaway Falls. It seems to be more common farther west. Harbison has found it in a number of places in the mountains of Georgia and in the Cumberland Mountains of Tennessee.

The Stewartias are exacting in cultivation, even more so apparently than the heaths. This is indicated by the fact that although of such striking beauty they are rarely found in gardens. The *grandiflora* form of *pentagyna* is the one usually cultivated.

2. **Stewartia Malachodendron** L. (**S. virginica** Cav.). **Stewartia.**

This is a shrub or small tree up to about 20 feet high, which grows in fertile, well drained deciduous woods, usually near streams and frequently associated with Beech. It is essentially a coastal plain plant. The highest elevation we know of its being found is at Cullman, Alabama, at an elevation of 2,000 feet. It is much more common in Mississippi than in the southeastern states. It occurs also in Tennessee and Virginia. We have specimens from Darlington and Williamsburg counties, South Carolina, and from Stanly, Jones, and Edgecombe counties, North Carolina. It has been found by T. G. Harbison in Onslow, Bertie and Craven counties, North Carolina, at Dover, Georgia, and at Round Lake, Florida, and H. A. Rankin reports it from Cumberland and Bladen counties, North Carolina. Fernald (*Rhodora* 38: 428. 1936) reports *Stewartia Malachodendron* from Accomac and Norfolk counties, Virginia.

Bark smooth, dark brown; leaves elliptic, apiculate or mucronate, about 2¾-3 inches long, the lower surface with scattered hairs and the veins pubescent with whitish hairs, margins ciliate and with minute sharp teeth; petioles, twigs and buds pubescent; flowers of great beauty, up to 4 inches broad, the five large petals creamy white and crimped toward the eroded margin; stamens very numerous, purple, making a highly decorative center; pistil with five united styles; fruit a globular capsule without conspicuous ridges. There is a fine specimen of *S. Malachodendron,* which is 5 inches in diameter at the base and 14 feet high, in the garden of D. R. Coker at Hartsville, South Carolina. It was brought in from the neighboring woods. This is more tender than *S. pentagyna* and we have not found it offered for sale by nurseries.

GORDONIA Ellis.

1. Gordonia Lasianthus Ellis. Loblolly Bay.

THIS medium sized evergreen tree with a narrow compact head is found in bays and on the edges of swamps in the coastal plain from Virginia to Florida and westward. It is quite plentiful on the coastal half of the plain and extends inward to the sandhills (Hartsville, S. C., and Cumberland County, N. C.). In northern Florida it is rare west of the Suwannee River (Harper).

Bark marked with narrow flat ridges separated by shallow, or in old trees very deep, anastomosing furrows; wood soft and light; leaves thick and leathery, narrowly elliptic, 2-6 inches long, shallowly toothed along the edges; flowers white, fragrant, about 2½ inches across, both sepals and petals silky; stamens numerous, yellow, united into a cup below; fruit a dry woody ovoid pod about ⅔ inch

1, Twig with leaves, open flower, and buds.   2, flower bud.   3, open fruit. All x ⅖.

long and silky on the surface; seeds small, with wings. This is one of the most beautiful and unique trees of the southern states.   Being a member of the tea family, it is closely related to the well known cultivated shrub *Camellia japonica* and to our native *Stewartia*.   It is a beautiful tree at all seasons but particularly so in July when the flowers open. Rankin says that veneer blocks 27 inches thick cut from this species come into Fayetteville, and larger trees are reported. Unfortunately it does not do well in cultivation unless its habitat is closely duplicated.   It was in full bloom in the coastal region of North and South Carolina on July 11, 1932.

There is in America one other species of *Gordonia, G. alatamaha,* which has had a very interesting history. It was discovered in one small area on the Altamaha River in Georgia by John and William Bartram, supposedly in 1765. In 1773 William Bartram returned and gathered seeds. In two subsequent visits William collected plants and seeds and introduced the plant into cultivation in Philadelphia and England. The first plants to reach England may not have been sent by Bartram (see Jenkins, The Historical Background of Franklin's Tree, *Penn. Mag. Hist. and Biog.,* July, 1933). Dr. Moses Marshall found this plant again in the same place in 1790. Since that time it has never been seen in the wild state but it is still in cultivation in America and in Europe. The flowers are much like those of the common *Gordonia* but the leaves are deciduous, the stamens separate below, and the seeds are without wings. Reports in recent years that this tree has been rediscovered in its original location have been proved to be unfounded. For further notes on the history of this tree, together with biographical data, see Jenkins as above cited. The tree was first named *Franklinia* after Benjamin Franklin, hence the title of the article. For good colored illustration of *G. alatamaha,* see *Addisonia* 18: pl. 583. See later article by Harper and Leeds in *Bartonia,* No. 19, 1938.

TAMARICACEAE (TAMARISK FAMILY)

TAMARIX L.

1. Tamarix gallica L. Tamarisk, Salt Cedar.

THE Tamarisk, a native of the Mediterranean region, has escaped in South Carolina in considerable quantity, at least on Pawley's Island and in the neighborhood of Beaufort and southward. Soon after the Revolution it began to be used to hold the banks of the causeways through the salt marshes. Some old specimens of early planting are still living. Dr. Hal M. Stuart writes of one in the town of Beaufort, which is at least ninety years old and about 30 feet high with a gnarled and twisted trunk larger than his body. It is easily recognized by the slender branches covered with minute scale-like leaves similar to those of cedar, and by its delicate plumes of very small, pinkish flowers. Plants cultivated at Chapel Hill were in full bloom the week of April 11-18, 1936, and lasted a long time.

Tamarix gallica. 1, Flower, x 20. 2, twig with leaves and flowers, x ⅔. 3, twig with leaves, x 16.

ARALIACEAE (GINSENG FAMILY)

ARALIA (Tourn.) L.

1. **Aralia spinosa** L. **Hercules Club, Angelica Tree, Prickly Ash.**

THIS small prickly tree or shrub with few or no branches occurs in rich woods or along streams from the coast to the mountains as far south as northern Florida. However, it is local in its distribution and entirely absent over large areas. In some localities it is rather abundant, as along Swift Creek in Wake County, North Carolina. Near Highlands, N. C., we have found it at an elevation of about 3,700 feet.

Leaves very large, twice or thrice compound, 2-4 feet long, all borne in an umbrella-like group at the top, leaflets broadly ovate and toothed; flowers greenish white, small but very numerous, forming large panicles in the top of the tree; fruit a very small, juicy, black berry. The largest plant of this species that we have measured grows near the South Carolina coast between Little River and Myrtle Beach. This plant is 20 feet high and 2½ inches in diameter. However, Harper reports specimens in Early County, Ga., 6 inches in diameter and 25 feet tall. This is rather handsome in cultivation but not so much so as the more robust Chinese Aralia. Both increase by suckers. Flowering near Myrtle Beach, S. C., July 15, 1932.

CORNACEAE (DOGWOOD FAMILY)

NYSSA L.

1. Leaves usually less than 6 inches long, entire (rarely with a few teeth) 2
   Leaves often over 6 inches long, entire or with large distant teeth; fruits purple, about 1 inch long, borne on long stalks (as in all the species, a fleshy drupe)
   Nyssa aquatica, Tupelo Gum   No. 1
2. Fruit red, about one inch or more long, very acid, a tree of the southern coastal swamps
   Nyssa ogeche, Ogeechee Lime   No. 2
   Not as above 3
3. Fruits often three on a common stem; stone indistinctly ribbed
   Nyssa sylvatica, Black Gum   No. 3
   Fruits often two on a common stem; stone distinctly ribbed
   Nyssa biflora, Water Gum   No. 4

1. **Nyssa aquatica** L. (**Nyssa uniflora** Wang.) **Tupelo Gum.**
THIS is a large tree of the deeper swamps near the coast from southeastern Virginia to northern Florida and westward, and extending up the Mississippi valley.

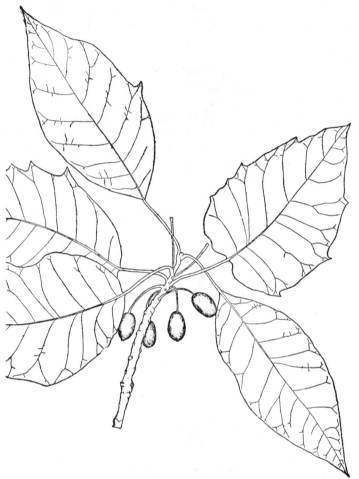

Branches with leaves and mature fruits, x ⅓.

Leaves large, 4-12 inches long, ovate, long-pointed, edges entire or with a few prominent teeth, smooth or nearly so and dark green above, pale and hairy beneath; male flowers borne in a many-flowered cluster at the tip of a long peduncle, female flowers solitary; fruits large, dark purple, about 1 inch long, one to the stem, stones with sharp, prominent ridges. The tree may reach a diameter of 4 feet above the base, which is often much enlarged so that it may be up to 15 feet in diameter. A section of the Tupelo Gum in the museum in Raleigh from Craven County, N. C., has a diameter of 2 feet 9 inches. This section is peculiar in showing bark only ¼ inch thick on one side and up to 2⅞ inches on the other. Dr. F. P. Porcher says (*Resources of Southern Fields and Forests*, 2nd ed., p. 386): "The roots are white, spongy and light, and are sometimes used in the Southern States as a substitute for cork; I am informed by a friend, who has had bottle corks cut from them that they answer perfectly, and the floats for the nets of fishermen are generally made of the tupelo." Dr. Porcher also states that the wood of the roots is suitable for making shoes, and that he has had shoes made of this for negroes on a plantation in South Carolina.

2. **Nyssa ogeche** Marshall (**N. capitata** Walter). **Ogeechee Lime, Sour Tupelo**.

THIS is a rare and local small tree, often shrubby in habit with several stems, that is confined to swamps or swamp borders in the southwestern corner of South Carolina and neighboring areas in Georgia and Florida. It grows along the lower Apalachicola and west to the mouth of the Choctawhatchee River (Harper). The westernmost limit known in Georgia seems to be a colony on the Ochlochnee River a few miles west of Thomasville, discovered by Miss Rebecca Bridgers and visited by us in 1941. There were a number of large trees characterized by much swollen bases. The largest one was 16½ feet in circumference two and a half feet from the ground, at which point it was smaller than higher up where the branching began.

Leaves oblong, sometimes more rounded, up to about 6 inches long and 2 inches broad, more or less undulate but scarcely toothed with a rounded tip and a little mucro, pale beneath and pubescent along the midrib and veins; male flowers in heads, female flowers solitary on short stalks, some of the trees bearing male and female flowers, others bearing perfect flowers; fruit large, dull or bright red at maturity, oblong, up to 1 inch long and ⅝ of an inch thick;

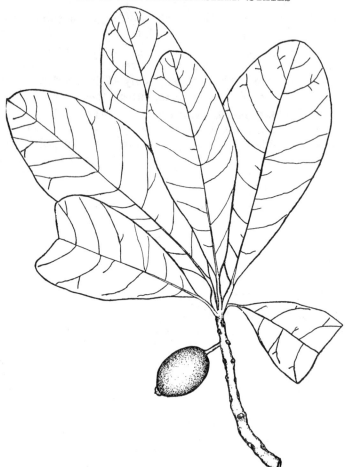

Nyssa ogeche. Twig with leaves and mature fruit, x ⅔.

the pulp very acid and well known in its limited area as making a good preserve. The name of this tree is derived from the Ogeechee River in Georgia and from the use of its acid juice as a substitute for limes.

3. **Nyssa sylvatica** Marsh. **Black Gum, Sour Gum.**

THIS is a tree which is common throughout our area, growing both in swamps and uplands and to moderate elevations in the mountains.

Twig with leaves and fruits, x ½.

Bark thick, up to 2⅞ inches, deeply furrowed; leaves ovate or obovate, 2-6 inches long, smooth and shining when mature except for brownish hairs along the midrib, margins even or rarely with a few teeth or lobes, turning bright red in late summer or early fall; fruits 1-3 on a common stem, very often 3, dark blue, about ½ inch long, sour and bitter; the stone more or less ribbed. The robins are very fond of the fruits. The Black Gum is usually a narrow, cylindrical tree of medium size with short, somewhat drooping branches. Its pleasing shape, glossy foliage, and freedom from attacks of insects and disease make this tree a very desirable one for streets or lawns. A conspicuous characteristic of the Black Gum is the way in which the tree begins to "grow shorter" upon reaching old age. For many years the old Black Gum holds a bald stump aloft above its green branches as death, followed by decay at a respectful distance, creeps down from the top. In cut-over woods the old Black Gum with its stumpy top usually towers above the second growth trees, as the wood is so tough that woodmen usually do not attempt to cut and handle it. Rarely sprouts are sent up from runner-like roots for several yards around the tree. A section of Black Gum in the museum in Raleigh from Craven County, N. C., has a diameter of 2 feet 10 inches. Flowering April 19 to May 4.

4. **Nyssa biflora** Walt.   **Water Gum, Sour Gum, Black Gum.**

Twig with leaves and mature fruits, x ⅝.

THIS is a small or medium sized tree found on the edges of ponds and streams in most of the coastal plain from Montgomery County, Maryland, to northern Florida, and in Tennessee. The base of the tree is usually swollen and when growing in water erect roots rise above the surface.

Leaves ovate or obovate, blade 1½-4 inches long and ¾-1½ inches broad, pale below; petioles ¼-½ inch long, hairy; male flowers borne in a cluster at the tip of a long peduncle; female flowers borne in pairs on long peduncles; fruits often in pairs, dark blue, about ⅓-½ inch long. This tree is very similar to *N. sylvatica* and Fernald (*Rhodora* 37: 435. 1935) treats it as a variety. The stones are supposed to be more prominently ridged but this difference is often obscure. As in Tupelo Gum, the wood is very light. Flowering at Mitchell's Mill, Wake County, North Carolina, May 29, 1932.

CORNUS (Tourn.) L.

Leaves opposite; flowers surrounded by 4 large white
   or pink bracts; fruits red
                        Cornus florida, Dogwood   No. 1
Leaves alternate; fruits blue-black on red stems
                Cornus alternifolia, Blue Dogwood   No. 2

1. Cornus florida L. Flowering Dogwood.

THIS is a low tree, very conspicuous in flower, that is scattered plentifully through all fertile, well drained woods from the coast nearly to the tops of the high mountains in all our area.

The dogwood is the best known and possibly the most popular small tree in our area. Virginia has adopted it as the state flower, and "Dogwood Festivals" have been held at Chapel Hill and Southern Pines, N. C., when it is in flower.

Bark brownish gray, checkered; twigs smooth, green or reddish, often with swollen places containing insect larvae; leaves ovate, opposite, blade bright green above, pale below, about 3-5 inches long and 1½-2 inches broad, the veins curving upward; flowers small, yellowish, borne in many-flowered clusters surrounded by four large white or sometimes decidedly pinkish bracts; fruit a bright red drupe. The largest Flowering Dogwood that we have measured is near the Harbison Spring on the south side of Mt. Satulah in Macon County, N. C. This handsome tree is 40 feet

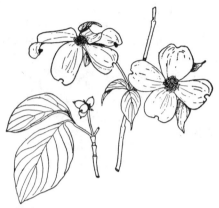

Twig with mature leaves and fruit;
twig with flowers and young leaves.
All x ¼.

high, has a spread of 53 feet and is 1 foot 7 inches in diameter at the base and 11½ inches in diameter three feet from the ground. R. W. Graeber has reported a tree on the farm of H. B. Jones in the "Rocky Hock" section of Chowan County, N. C., as 2 feet 2⅕ inches in diameter two feet from the ground and one on the farm of W. T. Perry in the same county as 1 foot 10⅕ inches in diameter at breast height. The Flowering Dogwood is highly decorative in cultivation and should be more used on lawns. It is very variable in the size and other characters of the floral bracts. There is a tree in Chapel Hill with enormous flower heads which are up to 5½ inches across. Beside it is another tree with delicate flesh pink flowers of the usual size. There is another tree in Chapel Hill in which the bracts are very persistent, continuing the display for a week or ten days longer than the others. These superior forms should be propagated. Though this dogwood never makes a large tree, its wood has considerable use in the making of tools, where toughness is needed, such as handles, mauls, and wedges and as the lever for tightening the chain about a load of lumber. In the mountains of North Carolina it is used for flooring. Porcher *(Resources of South-*

ern Fields and Forests, p. 59, 1863) says: "This well known plant possesses tonic and anti-intermittent properties, very nearly allied to those of cinchona; in periodic fevers, one of the most valuable of our indigenous plants. 'Dr. Gregg states that, after employing it for twenty-three years in the treatment of intermittent fevers, he was satisfied that it was not inferior to Peruvian bark.' . . . It also possesses antiseptic powers." Flowering March 24 to April 21.

A double form (*C. florida* f. *pluribracteata* Rehder) and one with yellow fruits (*C. florida* f. *xanthocarpa* Rehder) are found in North Carolina, the latter at Saluda and High Rock, the former near Hillsboro. The double form was propagated and distributed by the late J. Van Lindley.

2. Cornus alternifolia L. Blue Dogwood.

THIS is a low tree or shrub that is much more common in the north than the south. In Virginia, the Carolinas, and

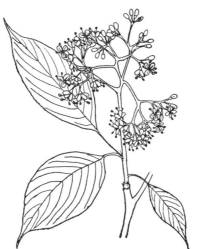

Twig with leaves and flowers, x ½.

northern Georgia it is found mostly in rich woods near streams in the mountains (up to 6,000 feet) but, strange to say, it also occurs near Williamsburg, Virginia, in Wake County, North Carolina, in southwestern Georgia, and at River Junction, Florida.

Bark, except on old trees, smooth and greenish; leaves alternate, often clustered at the tips of the branches, ovate, with acuminate tips, smooth, light green below, entire or rarely with a few obscure teeth, blade about 2-3 inches long and 1-2 inches broad; petioles smooth, slender, ½-1½ inches long; flowers small, cream-colored, borne in a loose, flat cluster; fruit dark blue on bright red pedicels. This tree differs from the more common dogwood in the green bark, alternate leaves, blue berries, and the absence of the conspicuous white floral bracts.

In addition to the Blue Dogwood and the Flowering Dogwood, there are seven other dogwoods in our area. All are essentially shrubby, but three at times may become small trees. Like the Blue Dogwood, they all lack the floral bracts of the common Flowering Dogwood.

ERICACEAE (HEATH FAMILY)

ELLIOTTIA Muhl.

1. Elliottia racemosa Muhl. Laurel.

THIS small tree, more often a shrub, is included here among the trees because it is one of the most unique plants of our section, not only for its rarity and local distribution but also because it is the only species of the genus known and commemorates in its name one of the greatest American botanists, Stephen Elliott of South Carolina. It was first discovered, probably by Elliott himself, at Waynesboro in Burke County, Georgia, early in the nineteenth century and first named by Muhlenberg, but without description, in his *Catalogue of North American Plants* in 1813. The description first appeared in Elliott's *Sketch of the Botany of South Carolina and Georgia* in 1821. In Georgia it occurs in Burke, Telfair, Coffee, Columbia, Candler, and Bulloch counties and also near the Oconee River (county not given). It has also been found along the Savannah River near Augusta, Georgia, and in South Carolina at Hamburg, immediately opposite Augusta, by

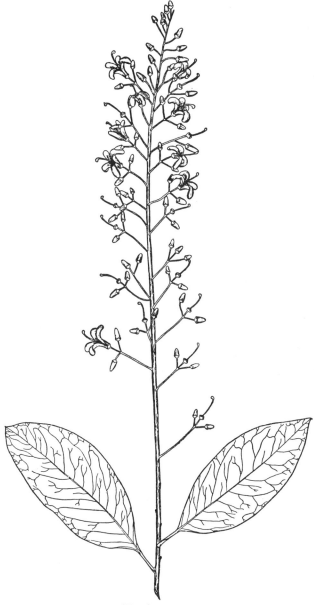

Elliottia racemosa
Twig with raceme of flowers at different ages, x ½.

Olney in 1853. Both of these latter stations have now disappeared. It has been thought that the flowers were self-sterile and that plants increased by runners, but recent observations by Mr. W. A. Knight, Mr. Frank M. Crayton, and Dr. E. T. Wherry, who have discovered new stations, seem to have proved the contrary. A number of plants are now being grown in Mr. Knight's garden at Biltmore, N. C., and in Washington, D. C. Dr. C. C. Harrold of Macon, Ga., has purchased several of the most populous colonies of *Elliottia* and is protecting them. He deserves our thanks.

Leaves alternate, long-elliptic, 2½-6 inches long, pointed, margins even, smooth above and pubescent below; flowers very showy, about ½ inch long, white, borne in terminal spikes up to 10 inches long, sepals 4 or rarely 3 or 5, valves of the ripe pod 4 or varying to 2 to 5; fruit a small dry pod. This little tree has the appearance of *Clethra*. It seems to prefer rather rich, moist soil in the neighborhood of bays, but it is also found on sandy ridges. Near Metter, Ga., where the plants occur by thousands, Dr. Wherry measured one plant 35 feet high and about 3 inches in diameter. Flowering in cultivation at Biltmore on Aug. 13, 1936. For articles concerning this interesting plant, see Sargent, *Garden and Forest* 7: 206, 1894; Harper, *Plant World* 5: 87, 1902; and Trudell, *Bartonia* No. 9: 11, 1925-1926, and No. 10: 24, 1927-1928.

RHODODENDRON L.

Leaf blades about 3½ times as long as broad; calyx
   lobes broad and blunt
          Rhododendron maximum, Great Laurel   No. 1
Leaf blades about twice as long as broad; calyx lobes
   very short and pointed
          Rhododendron catawbiense, Rose Bay   No. 2

1. Rhododendron maximum L. Great Laurel, White Rhododendron.

THIS is a shrub or small tree, sometimes 25 feet high with a trunk 10 inches in diameter, that is one of the most abundant, conspicuous, and well known plants of the mountains from Pennsylvania to Georgia. In North Carolina it descends rather abundantly as far down as Hickory, and is rare and local as far east as Davidson County, where it is

Branch with flowers, x ⅓.

known to occur on a bluff about 2 miles northeast of Yadkin College and at Piedmont Springs in Stokes County. In South Carolina it descends to Paris Mountain, Greenville County.

Leaves evergreen, thick and leathery, oblong, pointed, about 3½ times longer than broad, paler beneath and in most cases glabrous; petioles stout and woolly when quite young, becoming glabrous; flowers in large terminal clusters, white to pink, pedicels and flower axis viscid, calyx lobes broad and blunt, about 3/16 inch long; fruit a long sticky capsule, containing many seeds. A tree near "Hoot Owl Glen," Highlands, N. C., measured in 1932, was 23 feet high and 9 inches in diameter two feet from the ground. Flowering in Davidson and Davie counties near Yadkin College, N. C., June 17, 1931.

2. Rhododendron catawbiense Michx. Rose Bay, Purple Rhododendron.

THIS is more of a shrub than *R. maximum*, but occasionally it becomes a small tree with a diameter of 4 or 5 inches. The Rose Bay has a very remarkable distribution.

Branch with flowers, x ⅓.

In Virginia and Georgia, so far as we know, it is found only in the mountains. In North Carolina it ascends to the highest mountains, often forming dense stands on their "bald" tops (Roan, Craggy), but descends also down the eastern slopes (not western) in a scattered and limited way to much lower altitudes as at Asheville, Black Mountain, Bat Cave, and Lenoir. It skips then to the tops of a few isolated mountains as Table Rock, King's, Crowder's, and

Pilot and on mountain sides about Piedmont Springs, near Danbury, Stokes County, where it grows abundantly along with *R. maximum*. Then, which is most surprising of all, it skips again to bluffs along streams in Alamance, Orange, Durham, Wake, Nash, and Johnson counties down to about a hundred feet above the sea (Selma). In South Carolina *R. catawbiense* is scarce. We have plants from Peattie collected from Rocky Spur, Greenville County, South Carolina, by Edward Holmes. The farthest extension westward is in the four most northeastern counties of Alabama.

Leaves oblong to oval, about 3-5 inches long and 1½-2½ inches broad, about twice as long as broad, evergreen, smooth, dark green above and light green or whitish below; petioles ¾-1¼ inches long; flowers lilac-purple (magenta), calyx lobes pointed and very short, under ⅛ inch long; fruit a long sticky capsule, containing many seeds. The form of lower altitudes in North Carolina, from Alamance to Johnson counties, has larger, broader leaves and longer flowers than the typical. It has been given the form name *insularis* by Coker (*Journ. Eli. Mitch. Sci. Soc.* **35**: 81. 1919). Flowering near Chapel Hill, April 11 to May 15.

In addition to the above there are two shrubby species of Rhododendron native in the Carolinas, *R. carolinianum* Rehd. and *R. minus* Michaux, the latter also in Georgia. For a map showing the distribution of the four species of Rhododendron in North Carolina see the *Mitchell Journal* as cited above. Since the publication of this map *R. catawbiense* has been found in Alamance and southwest Nash counties and both *R. catawbiense* and *R. maximum* in Stokes County.

KALMIA L.

1. Kalmia latifolia L. Mountain Laurel, Ivy.

THIS shrub or small tree is extremely abundant in the mountains and extends along the bluffs of rivers all the way to the coast (Wilmington, N. C., and Georgetown, S. C.) and to western Florida, and westward it is found as far as middle Tennessee.

Leaves elliptic-lanceolate, blade about 2-4 inches long and ¾-1¼ inches broad, smaller and narrower than those

Twig with mature fruits; branch
with leaves and flowers. All x ¼.

of Rhododendron, evergreen, thick and leathery; flowers
saucer-shaped, white or pink, provided with curious pockets
for the anthers; fruit a viscid, globose, 5-lobed capsule.
The leaves are poisonous when eaten and will kill cattle.
The Indians are said sometimes to have committed suicide
with them (*Bull. Torr. Bot. Club* **12**: 53. 1885). A tree near
Highlands, N. C., measured in 1932 was 1 foot 1 inch in
diameter two feet above the ground, not including any
swelling. Another one near it was 30 feet high and 10⅔
inches in diameter. Quite recently Mr. Jim Shelton has discovered in the Great Smoky Mountain Park a giant laurel
that measures 6 feet 10 inches in diameter through the base.
One limb of this plant measures 2 feet 7 inches in diameter
(see *National Geog. Mag.* for August, 1936, and *Science
News Letter*, August 1, 1936, for photographs). In cultivation this is fine and should be more used along shaded banks.
Harper makes the interesting observation that *Kalmia* usually grows in places where there are no earthworms in the
soil, *Economic Botany of Alabama*, p. 289. When insects
walk about the flowers the stamens which are under tension
snap out of the corolla pockets and throw pollen dust on the

insects. This helps to bring about cross pollination. (For flower structure see p. 4). Flowering May 10 to May 16.

Our three other species of *Kalmia*, *K. angustifolia* L., *K. cuneata* Michx., and *K. carolina* Small, are small shrubs.

OXYDENDRUM DC.

1. Oxydendrum arboreum (L.) DC.   Sour Wood.

This small tree is scattered rather plentifully in good, well drained soil through most of our woods from the mountains (under 4,000 feet) through the piedmont and then retires to bluffs of streams and descends to the coast from Virginia to western Florida.

1, Twig with leaves and flowers. 2, fruits. All x ½.

Twigs smooth with reddish bark; trunk bark gray, deeply furrowed, up to 1 inch thick; leaves elliptic, shiny, pointed, serrate, with a decidedly sour taste, turning a bright red in the fall; flowers small, white, fragrant, borne on slender, finger-like racemes which are grouped at the ends of the branches in summer; fruit a small, dry, 5-angled, 5-valved capsule. The flowers remind one of the Lily of the Valley and make a very pretty centerpiece with ferns. The bees seek them and from them make the esteemed sour-wood honey. In the mountains this tree may reach a height of 60 feet and a diameter of about 15 inches. A tree in Amelia County, Va., is 27 inches in diameter four feet from the ground (Lewis, *Garden Gossip,* May, 1939). This tree like most of the heath family is fond of humus and is hard to get started in cultivation. It is so attractive, however, that it should be much more used, particularly in front of evergreen. Flowering in June and July.

VACCINIUM L.

1. **Vaccinium arboreum** Marsh.   **Sparkleberry.**

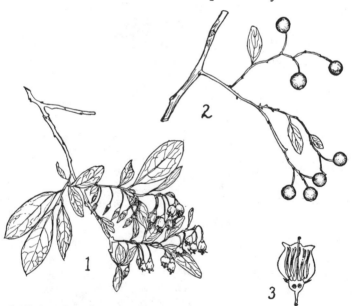

1, Twig with leaves and flowers, x ½.   2, mature fruits, x ½.
3, section of flower, x 1½.

This small tree is found in good, well drained (usually sandy) soil from the lower mountains to the coast from Virginia to Florida and westward. It is most plentiful in the coastal plain and is partial to the neighborhood of streams and ponds.

Bark gray; leaves obovate to oblong, 1-1¾ inches long, margins with minute teeth; flowers small, white, bell-shaped, borne on slender pedicels; fruit a small, dry, sweetish, scarcely edible black berry that ripens late in the fall and hangs on for much of the winter. Often the Sparkle-berry is only a shrub, but it may reach a height of about 30 feet in favorable situations. Near Dovesville, Darlington County, S. C., there is a tree which is 13 inches in diameter. Flowering about May 23.

SAPOTACEAE (SAPODILLA FAMILY)

BUMELIA Sw.

1. Leaves glabrous
   Bumelia lycioides, Buckthorn .... No. 1
   Leaves not glabrous 2
2. Leaves with a silky, shining, golden buff tomentum on the lower surface, flower stalks ¼-⅚₆ inch long
   Bumelia tenax, Buckthorn .... No. 2
   Leaves with a dark red-brown, dull, woolly tomentum on the lower surface, flower stalks ½-⅝ inch long
   Bumelia lanuginosa, Gum Elastic .... No. 3

1. Bumelia lycioides Gaertn. f.   Buckthorn, Ironwood.

This is a small, openly spreading tree confined mostly to the borders of streams and sandy low grounds in the coastal plain from Virginia to northern Florida and extending into the piedmont, also southeastern and middle Tennessee. It is rather local in its occurrence and is rarely seen. In North Carolina it is known from the coastal region (Brunswick County) and from Lincoln, Stanly, and Rowan counties in the piedmont. At Myrtle Beach, South Carolina, it is rather scattered in the dense growth among the dunes, and in the sandy flats back of the dunes south of town it forms con-

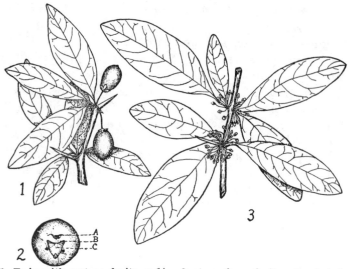

1, Twig with mature fruits, x ½.   2, stone from fruit, x 2.   3, twig
with flowers, x ½.

spicuous clumps.   It is said by Dr. Dudley Jones to be
found near Summerton in Clarendon County, South Carolina.   This tree occurs around Athens (Julian Miller),
and in Dooly and Early counties, Georgia.   It is found on
calcareous bluffs of the Apalachicola River in Gadsden
County, Florida (Harper).

Bark of trunk smooth, reddish gray; twigs often with
sharply pointed thorns up to ¾ inch long, leaves thickly
borne on short spurs, except in strong sprouts, mostly 2-4
inches long and up to about $1\frac{3}{16}$ inches broad, the base
tapering and often with a little mucro, both surfaces glabrous, bright green, the lower conspicuously netted-veined;
flowers small, inconspicuous, in ample clusters on the same
spurs with the leaves, sometimes at the bases of thorns;
fruit an oblong black drupe about ⅔ inch long, with a thin,
pulpy, bitter-sweet flesh (considered edible); stone large,
smooth, shining, with a greasy feel, oval, the distal end with
an abrupt little point, the proximal end of very peculiar
form with two holes of unequal sizes (fig. 2A, C) separated
by a little elevated handle (fig. 2B).   A large specimen of
this buckthorn was seen in Dooly County, Georgia, which

is about 25 feet high and 8 inches in diameter. Harper says
that in Early County, Georgia, it reaches a height of 50
feet and a diameter of one foot. On the Carolina coast it
is more shrubby than arborescent in form and is rarely
found over 12 or 15 feet high.

Fernald (*Rhodora* **38:** 439, 1936; **41:** 478, 1939) describes a new variety *virginiana* of *B. lycioides,* occurring
in several counties in southeastern Virginia and even as
"a solid thicket" at Upper Brandon on the James.

2. Bumelia tenax Willd. Buckthorn, Ironwood.

THIS small tree is found in very sandy soil along the coast
from North Carolina to Florida, and is also reported from
southwestern Georgia. It seems not uncommon on the
South Carolina sea islands. We have specimens from Sul-
livan's Island, South Carolina, and from McIntosh County,
from Colonel's Island, Liberty County, and from Brunswick, Georgia.

Branches tough; bark on twigs deep reddish brown;
leaves borne on short spurs, small, densely clustered, blade

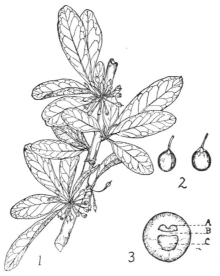

1, Twig with leaves and flowers, x ½. 2, mature fruits, x ½.
3, stone from fruit, x 2.

about ¾-1¾ inches long (up to 2½ inches on vigorous shoots), oblanceolate, tapering evenly to the very short petiole, tips rounded or notched, upper surface glabrous and shining, lower lustrous with a dense, golden-buff, closely appressed tomentum; flowers in dense clusters on the same spurs with the leaves, very small, the greenish corolla only slightly exserted beyond the tomentose calyx, pedicels about ⅓ inch long, tomentose; fruit a globose to oblong black drupe about ⅓-½ inch long; stone as in *B. lycioides* but less pointed and the holes in the proximal end of different shape. A tree on Colonel's Island is 35 feet high. This species is easily distinguished from *B. lycioides* by smaller leaves which are silky-tomentose below, in the somewhat smaller berries, and in being more closely confined to the coast.

3. Bumelia lanuginosa Pers. Gum Elastic, Woolly Buckthorn.

THIS is a small tree which occurs sparsely in the coastal region of southern Georgia and northwestern Florida and westward. The New York Botanical Garden has a collection by Rev. M. A. Curtis of *B. lanuginosa* from North Carolina, exact location not given, which has the reddish brown tomentum typical for the species.

Leaves borne on short spurs, elliptic, blades on strong shoots up to 4 inches long and 1¼ inches wide, much smaller on the average, entire, covered below with a dark reddish brown, woolly, dull tomentum as are the petioles, flower stalks, calyx lobes, and young twigs; flowers in dense clusters on the same spurs with the leaves, small, borne on peduncles ½ inch long or longer; fruit a black drupe as in the other species.

The form with a pure white tomentum has been described as the variety *albicans* by Sargent (*Journ. Arn. Arb.* 2: 168. 1921). It is an eastern Texas form and is confined to that section in Sargent's second edition of *Trees*. He at first referred a plant from Wilmington, North Carolina, to this variety, but evidently changed his mind about it later.

EBENACEAE (EBONY FAMILY)

DIOSPYROS L.

1. Diospyros virginiana L. Persimmon.

THIS common and well known tree in our states extends throughout all our territory except the higher mountains. It is most plentiful in the upper coastal plain and lower piedmont. Harper thinks that the persimmon is probably not native in northern Florida.

Twig with fruit and leaves; twig
with female flowers. All x ⅖.

Bark dark gray, strongly checkered; leaves ovate-oblong to elliptic, blade about 2-5½ (rarely 7) inches long and 1-2 (rarely 3½) inches broad, entire, dark green above, light green below, at maturity smooth on both surfaces; flowers of two sorts, male and female, borne on different trees, female flowers larger (about ½ inch broad) than the male flowers (about ³⁄₁₆ inch broad), greenish yellow, corolla bell-shaped with spreading, recurved lobes, very thick and succulent, falling to the ground unwithered very soon after opening, odor fragrant (for details of flower structure see figs. 3 and 4 on page 4); fruit a globose (rarely oval) berry, dull orange to reddish or purplish brown, sometimes with nearly black areas even before ripening, about ¾-1¼ inches, rarely more than 1⅝ inches in diameter; seeds large, flat, dark brown, and very hard. The female trees bear the well known fruits, which are quite variable in nearly all characters. Contrary to popular belief, some trees ripen their fruit well before frost, and in some the fruit is nearly or quite seedless. There is a tree in the town of Chapel Hill on which many of the fruits are seedless and in Yazoo City, Mississippi, in a pasture grow two persimmon trees on which all the fruits are seedless (Harbison). Also Mr. Kelly W. Huss, of Cherryville, N. C., and Dr. G. D. Green, of Waynesville, N. C., have seedless persimmons on their places. In an area about 1½-3 miles east of Chapel Hill there occurs a very remarkable form of the persimmon in which the fruits are almost entirely without astringency while they are still firm and some time before they would be considered ripe. They are also of a very superior quality. A number of named varieties of our persimmon are now offered by nurseries. Flowering May 12 to May 17.

A truly alarming disease of persimmon is reported as having crossed eastward over the Mississippi River. It is due to an imperfect fungus, *Cephalosporium*. No control has been found. It kills the trees in a few weeks and apparently takes all as they come (*Science,* Suppl., p. 10, Sept. 1, 1939).

STYRACACEAE (STORAX FAMILY)

SYMPLOCOS Jacq.

1. **Symplocos tinctoria** (L.) L'Hér. **Sweet Leaf, Horse Sugar.**

THIS small tree or shrub is abundant around bays and flats in the coastal plain and in northern Florida, west of the Suwannee River, rare and mostly along bluffs in the piedmont, and less rare, but not common in the lower mountains. A tree in the Kalmia Gardens, Hartsville, S. C., is six inches in diameter and about twenty-three feet high.

Twigs hairy or becoming smooth; leaves thick, long-ovate, pointed, edges slightly toothed or obscurely crenulate to almost even, taste sweet, lower surface of leaves

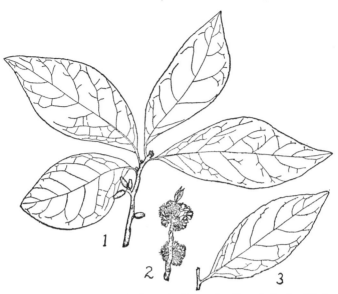

1, Twig with leaves and fruits.   2, flower heads.   3, leaf with less
even margin.   All x ⅓.

and the petioles hairy when young and remaining so or
becoming smooth; flowers small, light yellow, fragrant,
borne in bunches along the twigs; fruit a small, dry, cylin-
dric, hairy or glabrous drupe, containing one seed.   The
leaves are greedily eaten by cattle and horses, and are
noticeably sweet and partly evergreen.   The leaves and
bark are the source of a fine yellow dye, and from this the
plant is often called Yellow-wood.   Near Chapel Hill it is
found only on the bluffs of New Hope Creek and Price's
Creek.   The coastal plain form is predominantly glabrous
soon after the leaves are grown, while the mountain form
is habitually hairy so far as our specimens show.   This
mountain plant has been recently described as a new variety
by Harbison, *S. tinctoria Ashei* (*Journ. Eli. Mitch. Sci.
Soc.* 46: 218. 1931).   The coastal form is the typical.   It
was first described and figured by Mark Catesby in 1731
from coastal South Carolina.   Linnaeus gave the plant its
specific name, using Catesby's work for his description.   A
well formed specimen of Horse Sugar in bloom is distinctly

an ornamental plant and the delicate, aromatic fragrance is a great addition to its value. Dr. Raynal reports a *Symplocos* tree "in a narrow deep valley just off the road at Blowing Rock," which is 8 inches in diameter and 30 feet high. Flowering in Wilson County, N. C., on April 8, 1932, and at Tarboro, N. C., on April 19, 1931.

HALESIA Ellis.

1. Flowers not over ½ inch long
       Halesia parviflora, Little Silverbell　　No. 1
   Flowers over ½ inch long 2
2. Flowers with the corolla not deeply cut; fruit with four broad wings
       Halesia carolina, Silverbell　　No. 2
   Flowers with the corolla deeply cut; fruit with two broad wings
       Halesia diptera, Two-wing Silverbell　　No. 3

1. Halesia parviflora Michx. Little Silverbell.

This is a shrub or a small tree up to 30 feet high, occurring in our territory only on dry sandy soil in northwest Florida and southern Georgia. Its range is mostly farther west. We have Florida specimens from Old Town by the Suwannee River, La Fayette County (Harbison), and from Rocky Run, Okaloosa County (Ashe).

Leaves ovate-elliptic, long acuminate, the small ones

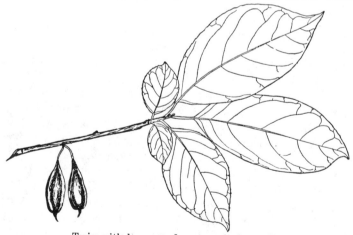

Twig with leaves and mature fruits, x ½.

more rounded, about 2-4 inches long, veins pubescent beneath as are the petioles, twigs and buds; flowers bell-shaped, white, not over ½ inch long; fruits clavate, up to 1⅜ inches long, with a sharp beak and 4 rather narrow wings with one or more ridges between them. As an ornamental this tree is inferior to the other species.

2. **Halesia carolina** L. (**H. tetraptera** Ellis and **Mohrodendron carolinum** Britton). **Snowdrop Tree, Silverbell.**

THIS tree is found along streams in the mountains and in the piedmont, mostly the upper part, rarely in the coastal plain, from Virginia to Georgia and Tennessee, and in northern Florida. We have one record (F. G. Tarbox, Jr.) of its occurrence within two miles of the coast near Brookgreen Gardens, S. C. Except for this, the farthest

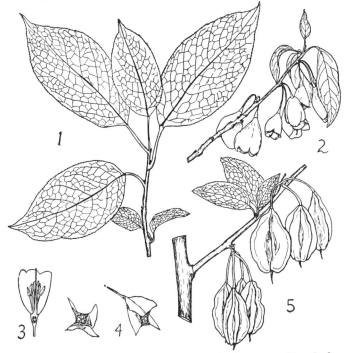

1, Twig with leaves, x ⅖. 2, twig with flowers, x ⅖. 3, longitudinal section of flower, x ⅗. 4, mature fruits in section, showing seeds, x ⅖. 5, twig with fruits, x ⅖.

eastern record we have is on the Cape Fear River about twenty-eight miles below Fayetteville, N. C. (Dr. C. G. Vardell). We have specimens from the Cape Fear six miles below Fayetteville (H. A. Rankin). Mr. J. S. Holmes has found it in the southeastern corner of Anson County, N. C., and Gibbes's Catalogue reports it from Columbia, South Carolina.

Leaves oblong or ovate, about 3-5 inches long, usually with a long point, tomentose beneath, margins very finely toothed; flowers opening while quite small with the petals green, but growing much larger and petals becoming white, pinkish toward the base, corolla bell-shaped, ⅓-1 inch long, shallowly lobed (except in the variety *dialypetala* Schneider, in which the corolla is cut nearly to the base), drooping, very pretty; young fruit 4-celled with 4 ovules in each compartment, two pendulous and two upright, mature fruit a dry pod 1¼-1¾ inches long, usually with 4 compartments but often with one aborted, and with 4 broad wings. In the piedmont section it is a small tree, but in the Smoky Mountains it may reach a diameter of over 3 feet and a height of 100 feet. At Highlands, N. C., there is a tree which has a diameter of 2 feet 4⅓ inches four feet from the ground and a height of about 80 feet (*Garden Magazine*, Feb. 1917). Dr. Stanley Cain of the University of Tennessee reports two trees of *Halesia monticola* in the Great Smoky Mountains that are 3 feet 9 inches thick at breast height. This tree is a fine object when in bloom and does well in cultivation. It is difficult to eradicate from pastures as the cut stumps sprout indefinitely. Flowering in Davidson County, N. C., on April 23, 1916, and on April 29, 1932. The flowers open in infancy.

The large tree in the mountains has been given the specific name *H. monticola* Sargent, but we think it best to include this tree under *H. carolina* as the differences given between these species are not constant. *Halesia monticola*, according to Sargent, is found in the mountains at an altitude of 3,000 feet or more and has flowers and fruits larger than in *H. carolina*. However, trees bearing fruits up to 1¾ inches long grow in the piedmont region of North Carolina and trees with large flowers (petals up to 1 inch long) may bear small fruits. The name *H. monticola* var. *vestita* Sargent has been given to a plant with more tomentose leaves collected at Marion, North Carolina, by Harbison. Both Britton and Small state that the filaments of *H. carolina* are glabrous, but all the specimens which we have examined have villous filaments at least toward the base. The flowers sometimes vary to pink adding much to the beauty of the tree. Near Franklin, N. C., there is a fine example of this pink form. It has been given the form named *rosea* by Sargent. It is being propagated and probably will soon be offered in the trade.

3. Halesia diptera Ellis. Two-wing Silverbell.

This is a smaller plant than *H. carolina*, often only a shrub, and it has a more southern distribution. In our states it is

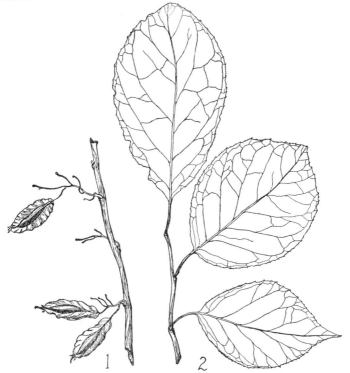

1, Twig with mature fruits.   2, twig with leaves.   All x ⅓.

reported only from damp woods and swampy places in the lower coastal region of South Carolina, Georgia and northern Florida. It is evidently a rare plant in South Carolina and we do not have any authentic record from that state. Harbison wrote us (letter of Feb. 19, 1932) that he thought he had seen it at Andrews, South Carolina. In Georgia it occurs in the coastal plain and is reported by Harper from along the Flint River in Meriwether County. We have collected it from the Bluffs of the Apalachicola River at River Junction, Florida.

Leaves ovate to obovate, rounded or pointed at the tip, about 3-6 inches long and 2½-4 inches broad, margins with distant teeth; flowers white, drooping, with the corolla lobes deeply divided; fruit with two broad wings and one or more narrow wings or ridges between them. This species and *H. carolina* are very ornamental and their cultivation should be encouraged. A tree at River Junction, growing among *Tumion*, is 8 inches in diameter and 35 feet high, as measured by us in 1933.

OLEACEAE (OLIVE FAMILY)

FRAXINUS (Tourn.) L.

1. Leaflets quite sessile

                                    Fraxinus nigra   No. 5
   Leaflets petiolate................................ 2
2. Twigs with 4 angles or wings

                          Fraxinus quadrangulata   No. 6
   Twigs without such angles...................... 3
3. Wing of fruit not extending down the short plump seed portion; an upland tree

                          Fraxinus americana, White Ash   No. 1
   Wing of fruit extending partly or all the way down the seed portion.............................. 4
4. Trees of coastal swamps; the wings extending to the base of the seed............................ 5
   Trees not of the coastal swamps; seed and wing very narrow

                          Fraxinus pennsylvanica, Red Ash   No. 7
5. Seed portion very flat, extending well beyond the middle of the fruit........................ 6
   Seed portion plump, not extending to the middle of the fruit

                          Fraxinus profunda, Pumpkin Ash   No. 2
                                    and
                          F. profunda var. *Ashei*   No. 2a

6. Leaflets usually 5, thick and leathery
>>> *Fraxinus pauciflora*, Water Ash   No. 3
Leaflets usually 7, not thick and leathery
>>> *Fraxinus caroliniana*, Water Ash   No. 4

1. Fraxinus americana L. White Ash.

THIS is the largest, most useful, and most widely distributed ash in our region, reaching a diameter of 4 feet 10 inches at breast height in the Great Smoky Mountains (Cain). It occurs abundantly in the mountains and piedmont in rich moist soil and extends down the valleys into the coastal plain south to northern Florida.

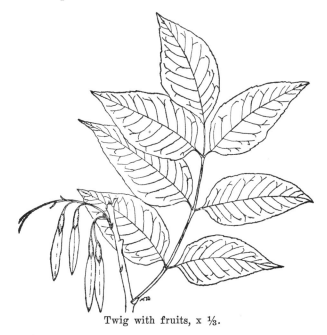

Twig with fruits, x ⅓.

Twigs smooth; leaflets 5-9 (usually 7), decidedly whitish (silvery) below, typically smooth on both sides, margins even or finely toothed; petioles smooth; flowers in panicles appearing before the leaves, the male and female flowers on separate trees; entire fruit ⅜-1½ inches long, seed short and plump, the wing long, varying from lanceolate and pointed to broader, oblong and notched at the end, about ⅛-¼ inch broad, not extending down the sides of the seed part.

A number of other species have been described, which are so similar to the White Ash and have so many intergrading forms that we find it impossible to distinguish them with any certainty. Plants otherwise as in *F. americana* but with twigs, petioles and the under side of the leaves (at least the veins) pubescent have been called *F. biltmoreana* Beadle. Very close to this, if not the same, is *F. catawbiensis* Ashe. *Fraxinus Smallii* Britton has the fruit of the White Ash and the green under side of the leaf as in the Green Ash. It is suggested by Sargent that it is a hybrid between *F. americana* and *F. pennsylvanica* var. *lanceolata*.

2. Fraxinus profunda Bush. Pumpkin Ash.

UNTIL 1932 this species included the variety *Ashei* described below. Palmer separates the variety almost entirely it seems on the glabrous twigs and glabrous or almost glabrous lower surface of the leaves. He confines the species *F. profunda* to those with densely pubescent leaves and twigs. This typical form is more western and northern but is reported along the Apalachicola River in Florida, apparently the only record from our territory. The variety is the common form in all our states. We describe it in full. Except for the glabrous twigs and glabrous or nearly glabrous leaves that description may be applied to *F. profunda*. (See Palmer in *Journ. Arn. Arb.* **13:** 417. 1932.)

2a. Fraxinus profunda var. Ashei Palmer. Pumpkin Ash.

This is a medium sized, slender tree, which is found in swamps in the coastal plain from eastern Maryland to the Apalachicola River in western Florida. We have specimens in our herbarium collected in Maryland from the Eastern Shore (Besley), in Virginia from the Potomac River swamp south of Washington and from Alexander Island (Ashe), in North Carolina from Wake, New Hanover and Pender counties (Ashe), in Florida from Hil-

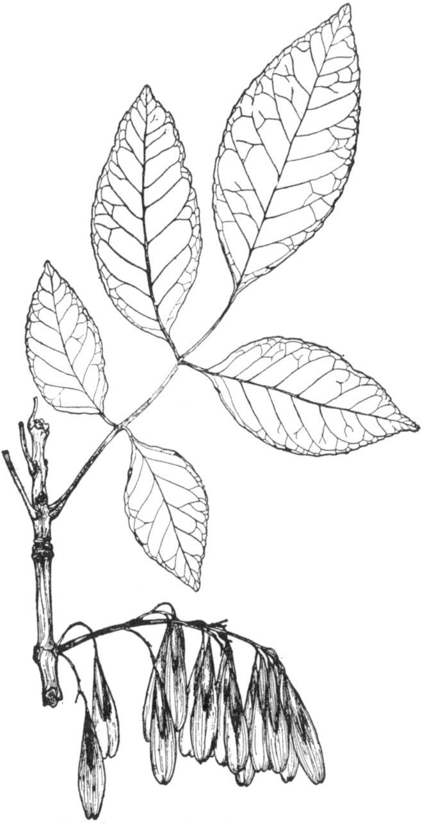

Fraxinus profunda var. *Ashei.*
Twig with leaf and fruits, x ⅓.

dreth, Suwannee County (type, Ashe), and from Columbia, Alachua, Marion and Gadsden counties (Ashe).

Twigs and leaf stalks glabrous; leaflets 5-9, ovate, pointed or long acuminate, blade 2-5½ inches long and 1½-2½ inches broad, typically glabrous beneath, varying to tomentose along the veins, margins slightly toothed to nearly entire; fruits usually about 1¾-2 (2½) inches long and 5/16-⅜ inch broad, the wing extending obviously at least to the middle of the plump seed part. The leaflets of the Florida specimens in our collections are all typically glabrous, while the North Carolina, Virginia, and Maryland specimens are pubescent on the midrib.

3. Fraxinus pauciflora Nutt.   Water Ash.

THIS is a small tree resembling *F. caroliniana* but confined to the swamps of southern Georgia (along the Flint and St. Mary's rivers and at Homerville) and Florida (near Jacksonville, in Lee County and vicinity, and in the valley of the Apalachicola River).   We have a specimen from near Homerville, Georgia, collected and determined by W. W. Ashe.

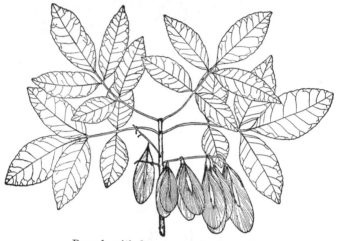

Branch with leaves and fruits, x ⅓.

Leaves small for an ash, leaflets usually 5, elliptic to ovate-lanceolate, the blade about 1¾-2½ inches long and ⅝-1⅜ inches wide, lateral ones on short stalks, texture thick and leathery in appearance, quite glabrous on both sides as are the petioles, margin shallowly toothed or undulate; fruits as in *F. caroliniana* but their stalks often shorter.

4. Fraxinus caroliniana Mill.   Water Ash.

THIS rather small tree in our states inhabits as a rule only the deeper swamps of the lower half of the coastal plain from the Potomac River near Washington, D. C., according to Sargent, south to Florida.   Except for *F. profunda* and its variety and *F. pauciflora* it is the only species of the genus with such a habitat.   In North Carolina we have

1, Leaf. 2, leaflet with more serrate margin. 3, mature fruits. All x ⅓.

collected it as far inland as Wake (Mitchell's Mill on Little River) and Robeson counties (Ashpole Swamp) and Boynton reports it from a rocky creek at Wadesboro, Anson County, and in a mill pond at Rockingham, Richmond County.

Leaves large, leaflets 5-9 (usually 7), oval to lanceolate, blade 1½-3½ inches long and 1-1¼ inches wide, with or without sharp points, rather remotely toothed or with numerous sharp teeth, pale beneath, sometimes pubescent on the midrib, upper leaflets little if any longer than the lower, the stalks very short or up to ½ inch long; petioles and twigs glabrous; flowers in crowded panicles, distinctly yellow; fruits variable, about 1½-1¾ inches long, typically with a rounded point and not notched at the end, strongly characterized by the very broad wing, $3/8$-$^{15}/_{16}$ inch broad, that extends practically to the base of the fruit, sometimes with three wings. The wood of the Water Ash is very light, even lighter than White Pine, and is inferior to most other ashes. Flowering at Mitchell's Mill on April 9, 1932.

We have a collection from Mitchell's Mill with distinctly tomentose leaves and much narrower fruits that is evidently Sargent's variety *Rehderiana*. Plants of the typical species are more abundant in the same locality. We suggest that this variety may be a hybrid between *F. caroliniana* and *F. pennsylvanica*.

5. Fraxinus nigra Marsh. Black Ash.

ALTHOUGH this tree is extended as far south as Virginia in most of the manuals, we have located only one specimen from that state (U. S. Nat'l Herb., J. Ball, 1890; information from Mr. H. A. Allard). It is listed in *Flora of the District of Columbia* (Hitchcock and Standley, 1919). It should be looked for and if found it can easily be recognized by the sessile leaflets and wings which extend to the base of the seed.

6. Fraxinus quadrangulata Michx. Blue Ash.

THIS is a fine tall tree with narrow outline that occurs in our area only in Tennessee. It is usually found in fertile upland woods and seems to prefer limestone soil. Dr. Gattinger, is his *Flora of Tennessee*, gives it as extensively distributed in that state, but it seems not to be common there or anywhere else. In the University of Tennessee herbarium there is a collection by Dr. Gattinger from the vicinity of Nashville.

Leaves $7\frac{1}{2}$-11 (12) inches long; leaflets 5-9 (11), ovate-lanceolate or lanceolate, acuminate, strongly or shallowly toothed, thick, glabrous on both surfaces or pubescent along the midrib below, short-stalked or sessile. Twigs yellowish brown, glabrous with four obvious angles or wings. Flower buds short and plump; flowers perfect. Fruits about $1\frac{1}{8}$-$1\frac{1}{2}$ inches long, the broad wing surrounding the flattened seed, apex rounded, emarginate or sometimes pointed.

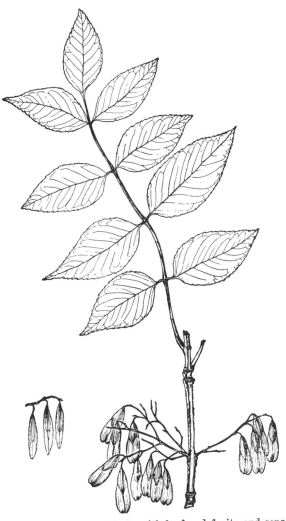

Fraxinus quadrangulata. Twig with leaf and fruits and separate fruits showing variation in shape, x ⅓.

7. Fraxinus pennsylvanica Marsh. Red Ash.

THIS is a common tree along rivers and low grounds in the piedmont and lower mountains of our area south to northern Florida. Sargent extends it to central Georgia and

some others into Florida. Fernald reports it from Norfolk, Va.

Young twigs velvety; leaves pinnately compound, leaf-

Fraxinus pennsylvanica 1, branch with compound leaf and cluster of
fruits. *Fraxinus Darlingtonii* 2, fruits. All x ⅓.

lets 7-9, entire or obscurely toothed, green above and light green and pubescent below; petioles pubescent; fruits with a very narrow seed and a long spatulate wing pointed below, 1/4-5/16 inch broad (rarely with three wings), which suddenly narrows at the seed and extends at least half way down its sides. This species may be separated from the other ashes by the long and very narrow seed and wing.

The form with perfectly smooth leaves and twigs has been separated by some as a variety or even as a distinct species (*F. pennsylvanica* var. *lanceolata* Sarg. or *F. lanceolata* Borkh.). This form has the common name of Green Ash. In Chapel Hill we have both extremes and also intermediates, all growing in low grounds and otherwise indistinguishable, so that we are inclined to consider them as variations of one species, as does Dr. Britton. Another form, pubescent like the type and with a very narrow wing only about 1/8-3/16 inch wide, has been called *F. Darlingtonii* Britton. This occurs in Orange, Davie, and Davidson counties, North Carolina, and in Darlington County, South Carolina.

FORESTIERA Poir.

1. Forestiera acuminata (Michx.) Poiret (**Adelia acuminata** Michx.) **Swamp Privet.**

THIS is a spreading, deciduous shrub or small tree said to reach a height of 30 feet, which is essentially of more western range but occurs rarely and locally as far north as Richmond County, Georgia (Harbison), and on the banks of the Suwannee and Apalachicola rivers in northern Florida, and in Tennessee. Small extends it to South Carolina.

Leaves opposite, oblong-ovate, pointed at both ends, obscurely serrate above the middle, about 2-4 inches long; flowers small, inconspicuous, without petals, in small axillary clusters, appearing before the leaves, some male, some female, and some perfect on different trees; fruit a small, elongated, purple, berry-like drupe. A close relative from

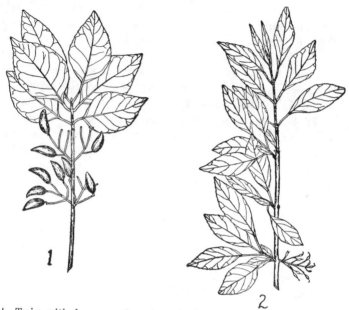

1, Twig with leaves and mature fruits.   2, twig with leaves and very young fruits.   All x ½.

the Orient, and seen more often in cultivation, is *Fontanesia fortunei*, a small tree of vigorous growth and shiny leaves.

CHIONANTHUS L.

1. **Chionanthus virginica** L.   **Fringe-tree, Flowering Ash, Old Man's Beard.**

THIS is a small tree or shrub scattered through rich woods in all of our area, especially in moist soil along the streams, most abundant in the piedmont section, but extending sparingly along streams in parts of the coastal plain and into the mountains to an altitude of 4,900 feet (Whiteside and Satulah Mountains, N. C.), south to the Everglades in Florida.

Leaves oval to obovate, pointed or rounded at the end, thin and pubescent beneath and along the margins when young, but at maturity thick, dark green above, lighter and nearly smooth below, 3-8 inches long; flowers in large

1, Branch with flowers. 2, twig with mature fruits. All x ⅓.

drooping clusters, fragrant, petals linear, about 1 inch long, white, usually with tiny purple spots at the base inside; fruit resembling a small olive, to which family the tree belongs, ½-¾ inch long, dark blue or nearly black, often with a glaucous bloom, flesh thin; stone large. This tree is very showy in the spring and is often cultivated for ornament. Thomas Meehan (*Proc. Acad. Nat. Sci. Phil.*, June 21, 1887) notes that in reality there are male and female plants of this tree, although the distinction has not gone so far as to suppress either the stamens or pistils. There are said to have been purple-flowering specimens of the Fringe-tree in Clayton's garden in Virginia (*Phil. Med. and Phys. Journ.* 2: pt. 1, 141. 1805). Flowering from April 11 to May 11.

OSMANTHUS Lour.

1. **Osmanthus americanus** (L.) B. & H. **Devilwood, Wild Olive.**

THIS small evergreen tree or shrub is found from Princess Anne County, Va. (U. N. C. Herb., George C. Mason, coll., 1936; reported also by Fernald, *Rhodora* **42**: 374. 1940), to Florida and westward among the sand dunes and on hammocks near the coast and in sandy flat woods for some

1, Branch with mature fruits, x ½. 2, section of female flower, x 6. 3, twig with flowers, x ½.

distance inland. In Georgia it extends inland to the Pine Mountains in Meriwether County.

Leaves oblong, usually 3½-4¾ inches long including the long petioles, smooth and shining; flowers small, cream-colored, borne in compound, axillary clusters, very fragrant; fruits resembling a small olive, bluish purple when ripe, about ½ inch long, or somewhat longer. We have never seen them one inch long, the length given by Sargent. The appearance of the tree is something like the Dahoon Holly, but the leaves are opposite. The wood is "devilishly" hard to split, hence the common name. This tree is very attractive in cultivation and is hardy in Chapel Hill. The manuals say that the fruit ripens early in the fall, but this seems to be an error. Fruited sprays collected on Ocracoke Island, North Carolina, on September 3, 1931, have fruits not more than two-thirds grown and of a greenish color. On Smith's Island, North Carolina, fully mature fruits were still abundant on trees on April 6, 1918, and the flowers were in bloom at the same time. Trees cultivated at Chapel Hill, N. C., were in bloom April 16, 1936.

BIGNONIACEAE (BIGNONIA FAMILY)

CATALPA L.

1. **Catalpa Catalpa** (L.) Karst. **(Catalpa bignonioides Walt.) Catalpa.**

THIS fast growing tree is native in our states only in southwestern Georgia and western Florida but it is thoroughly naturalized (though not common) along streams and gullies throughout the southeastern states.

Leaves large, heart-shaped, 4-12 inches long, hairy beneath; flowers about 1½ inches long, white with purple dots and two rows of yellow dots within, fragrant, borne in large terminal panicles; fruit a slender, cylindrical pod, 10-12 inches long, with vast numbers of small winged seeds. The durable wood is excellent for fence posts. The big black caterpillars that eat up the leaves are a nuisance on

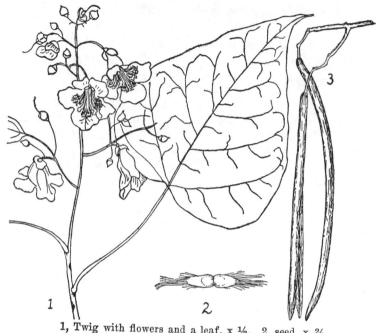

1, Twig with flowers and a leaf, x ⅓. 2, seed, x ⅔.
3, fruits, x ⅙.

cultivated trees. The fishermen see this from a different angle and plant Catalpas to get the caterpillars for bait. Flowering from May 15 to June 5.

2. Catalpa speciosa Warder.

THIS is a much larger tree than *C. Catalpa*, occurring native in our area only in the low grounds of western Tennessee, but has escaped in other parts of that state. In addition to its larger size, it is distinguished from *C. Catalpa* by the larger flowers which are fewer in the inflorescence and by the thicker pods.

SCROPHULARIACEAE (FIGWORT FAMILY)

PAULOWNIA Sieb. & Zucc.

1. Paulownia tomentosa (Thun.) Steud. **Paulownia, Princess Tree, Cotton Tree.**

THE Princess Tree, introduced from China or Japan, is a fast growing, coarse tree with large, heart-shaped leaves, 6-12 inches long, or on young shoots much larger, very hairy beneath; flowers fragrant, about 2 inches long, purplish, in large clusters often over a foot long. In winter the tree is loaded with smooth, pointed, ovate pods, 1-1½ inches long, and has conspicuous clusters of velvety buds. Though inferior to many of our native trees, it has been extensively planted in yards and has now sparingly escaped in waste places. Walker counted the seed in a Paulownia pod and found "almost exactly 2,000." He estimated the number borne on the trees as over 21 million. If each of these developed into a plant, which produced the

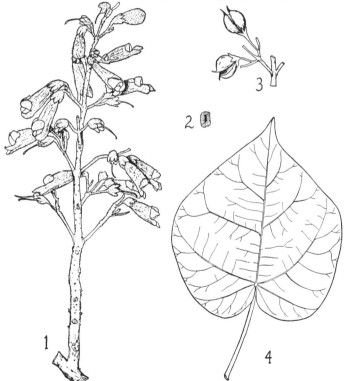

Paulownia tomentosa. 1, Flower cluster, x ⅙. 2, seed, x 1⅓.
3, open fruits, x ⅙. 4, leaf, x ⅙.

same number of seeds the next generation, in the third generation there would be plants enough to cover 20,442 worlds the size of ours (*Amer. Forestry* **25**: 1486. 1919). The wood is very light and is used by the Japanese for making their wooden shoes. Flowering April 12 to April 23.

RUBIACEAE (MADDER FAMILY)

PINCKNEYA Michx.

1. **Pinckneya pubens** Michx.   **Georgia Bark, Fever Bark, Maiden's Blushes.**

THIS is one of the most remarkable and interesting plants in our states.   Georgia Bark is a subtropical tree which occurs only in the southwestern corner of South Carolina and thence southward into Georgia (Altamaha Grit region)

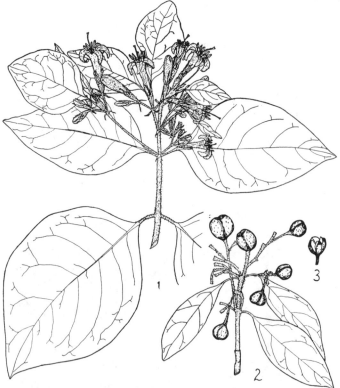

1, Branch with flowers.   2, mature fruits.   3, open fruit.   All x ⅓.

and Florida. The New York Botanical Garden has specimens from the following three places in South Carolina: "Bluffton," "Beaufort District," and "Seaboard." Dr. Mellichamp of Bluffton, S. C. (*Garden and Forest* 2: 15. 1889) says the following about the *Pinckneya* that he found near Rose Dhue, S. C. (8 miles from Hardeeville in the extreme southern part of the state): "Here is the usual swamp growth of *Nyssa,* Maple, one or two small cypresses, and a single high-climbing vine of *Decumaria;* but the tree which will most attract our attention will be the (to us) rare *Pinckneya pubens.* We see the greenish and pale yellow capsules in thick clusters among the mellowing leaves, but they will soon be ruddy-tinged when the later frosts come. This spot is, so far as I know, its farthest northern limit, and I have seen it in only one other place not far off, and a single small shrub near the Savannah River." Mrs. Wilder of Beaufort, S. C., says there are one large plant and several small ones on the farm of Mr. Johnson near Bluffton, S. C. We have specimens in our herbarium from 10 miles east of Tallahassee, Leon County, Florida, from near Sopchoppy, Wakulla County, and Monticello, Jefferson County, Florida, and from Screven, Evans, Wayne, Decatur, and Randolph counties in Georgia, and it is also found in a number of places around Thomasville. Mr. William L. Hunt has brought us a specimen of a white form from near Bainbridge which he says is a purer white than the dogwood. All intermediate shades between this and the rose-colored forms occur. For an exact Florida location near Bristol, Liberty County, see R. M. Harper in *Torreya* 26: 81, 1926. Harper also reports this plant from swamps near the Apalachicola River, in the middle part of northern Florida, and in the west Florida Pine Hill section (*Rept. Fla. Geol. Survey* 6: 163. 1914). Murrill reports it from Green Cove Springs, Florida. Thanks to Professor Herman Kurz, of Tallahassee, we received fine flowering specimens on May 22, 1933. Bartram found *Pinckneya* associated with *Franklinia alatamaha* at the original station for the latter species (Fort Barrington). For other early references to *Pinckneya,* see Harper and Leeds, *Bartonia* No. 19: 1, 1937.

Twigs densely tawny-pubescent when young, usually

becoming glabrous the second year; leaves opposite, more or less ovate, the blade about 6-7 inches long, at maturity slightly pubescent above and densely pubescent below especially along the veins; petioles also pubescent; triangular stipules between the petioles falling early; floral habit unique for this country; flowers borne in more or less clustered panicles, the corolla tubular, petals greenish yellow with bright red spots on the inside, greenish yellow on the outside, but the inflorescence made quite conspicuous by the remarkable enlargement of some of the calyx lobes into leaf-like extensions which are bright rose pink with greenish veins; many of the flowers without such enlargements but enough present to make the inflorescence very showy; usually only one of the five calyx lobes is enlarged, often two, in which case they are usually of unequal size; large calyx lobes may reach a width of 1¾ inches and a length of 3 inches; fruit a dark brown somewhat flattened capsule, up to ⅝ inch broad, with two cells containing many small winged seeds. *Pinckneya* reaches the size of a small tree, occasionally with a diameter of 6 inches, but it has more the habit of a shrub with several shoots from the base. In connection with the flowers one would think of the Flowering Dogwood, but it will be noticed that there is no morphological similarity in the conspicuous elements in the two cases, as the showy part in the dogwood is made of floral bracts and is not a part of the flower. At least one other plant in this family, *Mussaenda erythrophylla,* has the calyx the conspicuous part. In this species only one lobe becomes enlarged and colored. *Pinckneya* is a close relative of the Cinchona tree of South America that furnishes the quinine of commerce and has been thought, especially by the older writers (Michaux, Porcher, *et al.*), to contain quinine and to have the same properties for curing malaria. However, modern tests fail to show any trace of quinine or related alkaloids (W. T. Sumerford, *Journ. Amer. Pharm. Assoc.,* Sci. Sect., 32: 101. 1943). Porcher (p. 443, 1869) quotes Dr. Fauntleroi of Virginia who, while he does not claim it to be a substitute for quinine, concludes that it has other medicinal value.

For colored plates of this species see Michaux, *North*

American Sylva, pl. 49; Barton, *A Flora of North America*, pl. 7; *Flore des Serres et des Jardins de l'Europe*, pl. 1937; and Audubon, *Birds of North America* III, pl. 176 (as *P. pubescens*). The color of the calyx lobes in Michaux's plate is too green. Barton's plate is the best, but none of these plates show the true lively pink of the calyx lobes. For photographs see *American Botanist* 36: 1, 1930.

CAPRIFOLIACEAE (HONEYSUCKLE FAMILY)

VIBURNUM L.

1. Leaves small, usually less than 2 inches long, entire
   or obscurely toothed
   　　　Viburnum obovatum, Small Viburnum　　　No. 1
   Leaves larger, serrate 2
2. Upper surface of leaves shining; petioles and veins
   on lower side of leaves red pubescent; buds short
   and broad, red
   　　　Viburnum rufidulum, Blue Haw　　　No. 2
   Upper surface of leaves dull..................... 3
3. Petioles and veins on lower side of leaves reddish
   scurfy; buds very long and slender, red; leaves
   mostly long-pointed
   　　　Viburnum lentago, Nannyberry　　　No. 3
   Petioles and leaves glabrous; buds long and slender,
   usually gray scurfy; leaves mostly short-pointed
   　　　Viburnum prunifolium, Black Haw　　　No. 4

1. **Viburnum obovatum** Walter.   **Small-leaved Viburnum.**
THIS is a small tree with stiff, straight branches growing in coastal swamps from Virginia to Florida. It seems to be local in its distribution. In the sandy flood plain of the Black River just at the south side of the bridge at Kingstree, South Carolina, we find this tree very plentiful in company with *Sebastiania ligustrina, Ilex decidua, Crataegus* sp., etc. We also have specimens from the Ogeechee Swamp in Georgia and from Perry and Oneco, Florida. These last specimens have fruits much shorter in proportion than the ones from South Carolina and the leaves average smaller. Other differences are negligible.

Bark of trunk dark and checkered; twigs spurred much like an apple, gray-brown, red, punctate, pliable; buds narrow, reddish brown, pubescent; leaves thick, deep green, shining and glabrous above, light green and punctate below with minute, reddish hairs, small, ⅝-2 inches long, great majority ¾-1½ inches long, oblong-elliptic to somewhat spatulate, margins revolute, even, or with several undulations or teeth in the distal half, blunt; petioles very short or none, punctate; cymes sessile, up to 2⅝ inches broad, few to many-flowered; fruit about ⅜ inch long including the little beak, flattened, 3⁄16 inch broad, through bright red to black and shining when fully ripe, flesh almost none, nearly tasteless, stone shaped like the fruit,

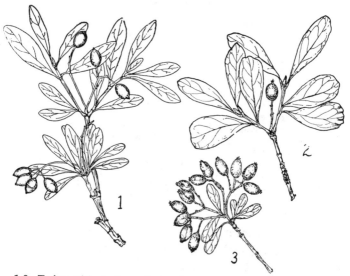

1-3, Twigs with fruits and showing variation in leaves, x ½.

about 5⁄16 inch long and 3⁄16 inch broad, flat, slightly marked, with shallow grooves on both sides. There are usually several trunks from the base, the larger reaching a diameter of 4 inches and a height of 15 feet. Small has described from swamps in western Florida as *V. Nashii* plants with long fruits and stones as in our South Carolina specimens. It seems to us that it is better to call these forms of *obovatum*. We have a good fruiting specimen determined as *V. Nashii* from a swamp at Perry, Taylor County, Florida.

2. Viburnum rufidulum Raf.   Blue Haw, Rusty Black Haw, Southern Black Haw.

This is a small tree of either damp or dry woods from the coast to the lower mountains from southern Virginia to Hernando County, Florida, and reported from central Tennessee. At Chapel Hill it is much more common than *V. prunifolium*.

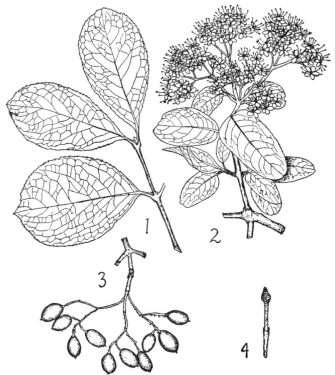

1, Twig with leaves. 2, branch with flowers. 3, mature fruits.
4, twig with bud. All x ½.

Bark rough, with much the appearance of *V. prunifolium;* buds short, broad below, pointed above, scurfy, with red, fascicled, scale-like hairs (hairs usually about 0.2 mm. long) on single-celled colorless stalks; leaves oval to obovate, about 2-4 inches long and 1-2½ inches broad, thick, margins finely toothed, green and shining above and when young covered below with a red tomentum of scale-like hairs, which wears off during the season but is always to be detected on the veins and petioles of the smaller basal leaves; flowers small, white, borne in clusters 3-6 inches across; fruits deep blue, about ⅓-½ inch long with more flesh than in *V. prunifolium*, the stone elliptic and flat. Trees in Chapel Hill reach a diameter of 5 inches and a height of 17 feet. In Chapel Hill, where both *V. rufidulum* and *V. prunifolium* are common, the former can be distinguished easily by the larger (usually), shining leaves with the reddish tomentum, by the larger flower clusters, which bloom about ten days later, by the larger, bluer fruits and by the larger, shorter buds, covered with much longer fascicled, scale-like hairs not mixed with crystals, therefore red. While usually larger, the leaves of *V. rufidulum* may in some specimens be much smaller than the size given above, as for example, 1-1⅗ inches long and ⅝-1 inch broad. The older botanists (Elliott, Curtis, Chapman) did not distinguish this species from *prunifolium*, but the two are quite different. The cymes of *V. rufidulum* are very large, up to 6 inches across, usually 3-4 inches. Only two other American species occasionally reach this size, but these average smaller and are not so impressively strong and heavy. A good specimen of this small tree is one of the finest of our native ornamentals. Flowering begins about May 2 to May 12.

3. Viburnum lentago L. Nannyberry, Sweet Viburnum, Sheepberry.

THIS is a small spreading tree, more often a shrub, of rich woods near streams, essentially of northern distribution. It is rare and local in the southeastern states and its occurrence at all in North Carolina has not been a certainty (although recorded by Curtis) until we found the plant in Wilkes County and on Craggy Mountain in Buncombe County. We have also collected it in Giles County, Virginia. Sargent extends its range south only to West Virginia, Small and Britton to Georgia. Gattinger does not include it for Tennessee.

1, Fruit (diagrammatic), x 2⅔. 2, twig with leaves and mature fruits, x ⅓. 3, twig with leaves, x ⅓.

Young twigs green then reddish, sparingly pubescent or scurfy; buds long-pointed, reddish, minutely scurfy; bark of trunk reddish, checked into small plates, both bark and wood with a disagreeable odor. Leaf blade oval or elliptic with a long or short apiculus, base rounded or slightly cuneate, about 2½-4 inches long and 1¼-2½ inches broad, reddish scurfy on the midvein below, less so above; margin with fine, closely set teeth with incurved tips; petioles about ½-¾ inch long, more or less wing-margined, scurfy. Inflorescence sessile or short-stalked; flowers creamy white and somewhat fragrant. Fruit blue-black with a bloom, oval, ⅓-½ inch long, sweet and edible.

This plant is often confused with the Withe-rod (*Viburnum cassinoides*), a very variable, large shrub quite abundant in wet soil throughout our mountains. The buds of the Withe-rod are very much like those of the Nannyberry and often the leaf is also long-pointed, but it is never so finely toothed and the flower or fruit cluster is always borne upon a long common stalk, or peduncle.

4. **Viburnum prunifolium** L. Black Haw.

THIS low tree is common in damp woods and along streams throughout the middle and western sections of Virginia, the

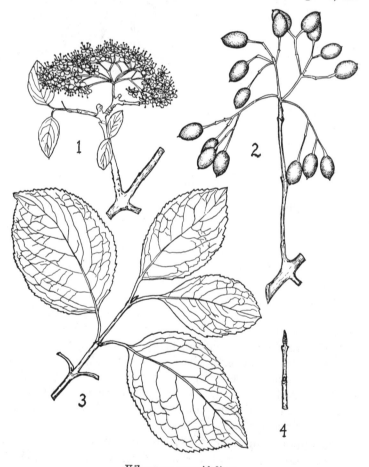

Viburnum prunifolium
1, Twig with flowers. 2, mature fruits. 3, leaves. 4, twig with bud.
All x ½.

Carolinas, Tennessee, and the mountainous parts of South Carolina and Georgia. In Virginia it is reported in the swamps of Chisel's Run, on the peninsula, and in Prince George and Norfolk counties, and in North Carolina it occurs at least as far east as Greene County.

Bark very rough, resembling the bark of the Dogwood; buds long, slender, covered with very small, fascicled, red, scale-like hairs (usually less than 0.1 mm. long), which are mixed with whitish crystals usually in such quantity as to give a gray appearance to the bud; leaves ovate to obovate, small, 1-3 inches long, ½-2 inches broad, margins finely toothed, smooth, a dark, but rather dull green; flowers small, white, borne at the ends of the branches in clusters 2-4 inches across; fruits bluish black, with a faint glaucous bloom, not so blue as in *V. rufidulum*, ¼-⅓ inch long, flesh thin, sweetish, stone flat. In some parts of the state most of the plants have been dug up for the bark of the roots, which is used in medicine. See the Blue Haw for contrast. A tree near Cheraw, S. C., is 24 feet high and 5 inches in diameter two feet above the ground. Flowering April 1 to April 22.

Several other species of *Viburnum* occur in our area but they are essentially shrubs. Two of these, however, *V. cassinoides* L. (Withe-rod or Shonny Haw) and *V. nudum* L. (Smooth Withe-rod) appear rarely as slender little trees.

BIBLIOGRAPHY*

Ashe, W. W.
    1894 The Forests, Forest Lands, and Forest Products of Eastern North
           Carolina. N. C. Geol. Surv. Bulletin 5.

Ayers, H. B., and Ashe, W. W.
    1905 The Southern Appalachian Forests. U. S. Geol. Surv. Professional
           Paper No. 37.

Bartram, William
    1791 Travels through North and South Carolina, Georgia, East and West
           Florida etc. (1928 printing). Macy-Masius, 551 Fifth Ave.,
           New York.

Britton, N. L., and Shafer, J. A.
    1908 North American Trees. Henry Holt and Co., New York.

Britton, N. L., and Brown, Addison
    1913 Illustrated Flora of the Northern United States, Canada, and the
           British Possessions. Charles Scribner's Sons, New York.

Catesby, Mark
    1731 and 1748 Natural History of Carolina, Florida, and the Bahama
           Islands. Vols. I and II. London.

Chapman, A. W.
    1897 Flora of the Southern United States. Third edition. Cambridge
           Botanical Supply Co., Cambridge, Mass.

Coker, W. C.
    1905 Observations on the Flora of the Isle of Palms, Charleston, S. C.
           Torreya 5: 135.
    1912 The Plant Life of Hartsville, S. C. For sale by the Botany Depart-
           ment of the University of North Carolina, Chapel Hill, N. C.

Coker, W. C., and Totten, H. R.
    1916 The Trees of North Carolina. Chapel Hill, N. C.

Croom, H. B., and Loomis, H.
    1833 Catalogue of Plants Observed in the Neighborhood of New Bern,
           N. C. Spectator Office, New Bern, N. C.

Croom, H. B.
    1837 A Catalogue of Plants Native or Naturalized in the Vicinity of New
           Bern, North Carolina. G. P. Scott and Co., Printers. New
           York.

Curtis, M. A.
    1834 Plants Growing Spontaneously around Wilmington, North Carolina.
           Boston Journ. Nat. Hist. 1: No. 2.
    1860 The Woody Plants of North Carolina. Geol. and Natural Hist.
           Surv. of N. C. Part III.
    1867 A Catalogue of the Indigenous and Naturalized Plants of North
           Carolina. Geol. and Nat. Hist. Surv. of N. C. Part III.

Davis, John H.
    1930 Vegetation of the Black Mountains of North Carolina: An Ecological
           Study. Journ. Eli. Mitch. Sci. Soc. 45: 291.

Elliott, Stephen
    1821 and 1824 A Sketch of the Botany of South Carolina and Georgia.
           Vols. I and II. J. R. Schenck, Charleston, S. C.

Elliott, Charles N.
    1931 Key to Georgia Trees. Georgia Forest Service Bull. 13.

Gattinger, A.
    1887 The Flora of Nashville. Published by the author, Nashville, Tenn.
    1901 The Flora of Tennessee. Gospel Advocate Publishing Company, Nash-
           ville, Tenn.

Gibbes, Lewis R.
    1835 A Catalogue of the Phaenogamous Plants of Columbia, S. C., and its
           Vicinity. Columbia, S. C.

Gray, Asa
    1908 New Manual of Botany. Seventh edition. American Book Company,
           New York.

    * Only the more important books and comprehensive local catalogues are
included here. Many other references are in the text. See the introduction.

Harbison, T. G.
   1931   A Preliminary Check List of the Ligneous Flora of the Highlands Region, North Carolina. The Highlands Museum and Biological Laboratory. Publication No. 3.

Harper, Roland M.
   1914   Geography and Vegetation of Northern Florida. Fla. Geol. Surv. Sixth Ann. Rept., p. 165.

Harshberger, John W.
   1903   An Ecological Study of the Flora of Mountainous North Carolina. Bot. Gaz. **36:** 241 and 368.

House, Homer D.
   1913   Woody Plants of Western North Carolina. Darmstadt, Germany.

Ivey, G. F.
   1934   The Physical Properties of Lumber. The Southern Publishing Co., Hickory, N. C.

Kearney, T. H.
   1901   Report on a Botanical Survey of the Dismal Swamp Region. Contr. U. S. National Herbarium **5:** 321.

Massey, A. B., and C. R. Ball
   1944   The Willows of Virginia. Bull. V. P. I. **37,** No. 9.

Peattie, Donald C.
   1928-1931   Flora of the Tryon Region. Journ. Eli. Mitch. Sci. Soc. **44:** 95, 141, and 180; **45:** 59 and 245; **46:** 129.

Pinchot, Gifford, and Ashe, W. W.
   1897   Timber Trees and Forests of North Carolina. N. C. Geol. Surv. Bull. **6.**

Rehder, Alfred
   1927   Manual of Cultivated Trees and Shrubs. The Macmillan Company, New York.

   1940   Second edition (revised) of above.

Sargent, C. S.
   1891-1902   Silva of North America. Vols. I-XIV. Houghton, Mifflin and Co., Boston, Mass.

   1905 and 1913   Trees and Shrubs. Vols. I and II. Houghton, Mifflin and Co., Boston, Mass.

   1922   Manual of the Trees of North America. Second edition. Houghton, Mifflin and Co., Boston, Mass.

Small, J. K.
   1913   Flora of the Southeastern United States. Published by the Author. New York Botanical Garden, New York.

   1913   Florida Trees. Published by the Author. New York Botanical Garden, New York.

   1934   Manual of the Southeastern Flora. Science Printing Co., Lancaster, Pa.

Sudworth, George B.
   1927   Check List of the Forest Trees of the United States, Their Names and Ranges. U. S. Dept. Agric. Misc. Circ. **92.**

Tarbox, F. G., Jr.
   1944   Some Native Hollies Rare and Common. Brookgreen, S. C.

Trelease, William
   1924   The American Oaks. Mem. Nat. Acad. of Sci. Vol. XX.

Walter, Thomas
   1788   Flora Caroliniana. J. Wenman, London.

Wells, B. W.
   1932   The Natural Gardens of North Carolina. University of North Carolina Press, Chapel Hill, N. C.

Wood, Thomas F., and McCarthy, Gerald
   1885-1886   Wilmington Flora; A List of Plants Growing about Wilmington, N. C., with Date of Flowering, with a Map of New Hanover County. Journ. Eli. Mitch. Sci. Soc. **3:** 77.

ABBREVIATIONS

Abbreviations for periodicals referred to in the text are given below.

Amer. Journ. Sci. and Arts. American Journal of Science and Arts. Also called Silliman's Journal.

Bot. Gaz.   Botanical Gazette.

Bull. Charleston Mus.   Bulletin Charleston Museum.

Bull. Mo. Bot. Gard.   Bulletin Missouri Botanical Garden.

Bull. N. Y. Bot. Gard.   Bulletin New York Botanical Garden.

Bull. Torr. Bot. Club.   Bulletin Torrey Botanical Club.

Charleston Mus. Quart.   Charleston Museum Quarterly.

Geol. Surv. Ala. Mon.   Geological Survey of Alabama Monograph.

Journ. Arn. Arb.   Journal of the Arnold Arboretum.

Journ. Eli. Mitch. Sci. Soc.   Journal of the Elisha Mitchell Scientific Society.

Journ. Hered.   Journal of Heredity.

Mem. Torr. Bot. Club.   Memoirs of the Torrey Botanical Club.

N. C. Geol. and Econ. Surv.   North Carolina Geologic and Economic Survey.

Penn. Mag. Hist. and Biog.   Pennsylvania Magazine of History and Biography.

Phil. Med. and Phys. Journ.   Philadelphia Medical and Physical Journal.

Proc. Acad. Nat. Sci. Phil.   Proceedings of the Academy of Natural Science of Philadelphia.

Tech. Bull.   Technical Bulletin (United States Department of Agriculture).

GLOSSARY

Achene. A small dry hard one-celled and one-seeded indehiscent fruit.

Acuminate. Tapering at the end.

Acute. Terminating with a sharp or well defined angle.

Adnate. United.

Alternate. Not opposite to each other on the axis.

Anther. The polleniferous part of a stamen.

Appressed. Lying close and flat against.

Attenuate. Slenderly tapering.

Auricle. An ear-shaped appendage.

Auriculate. Furnished with auricles.

Axil. The upper angle formed by a leaf with the stem or veins with other veins.

Axillary. Situated in an axil.

Berry. A fruit in which the ovary becomes a fleshy or pulpy mass enclosing one or more seeds.

Blade. The expanded portion of a leaf.

Bract. A more or less modified leaf subtending a flower or belonging to a cluster of flowers.

Bud. The rudimentary state of a stem or branch; an unexpanded flower.

Calyx. The outer perianth of the flower.

Campanulate. Bell-shaped.

Canescent. Hoary with a gray pubescence.

Capsule. A dry dehiscent fruit composed of more than one carpel.

Carpel. A simple pistil, or one member of a compound pistil.

Catkin. A delicate, usually pendulous spike or thread of flowers as in oaks, hickories, willows, and poplars.

Ciliate. Marginally fringed with hairs.

Clavate. Club-shaped.

Compound leaf. One divided into separate leaflets.

Compressed. Flattened, especially laterally.

Coniferous. Cone-bearing.

Cordate. Heart-shaped.

Coriaceous. Leathery in texture.

Corolla. The inner perianth of a flower.

Corymb. A flat-topped or convex open flower cluster, with its marginal flowers opening first.

Crenate. Dentate with the teeth much rounded.

Cuneate. Wedge-shaped.

Cuspidate. Tipped with a cusp or sharp and rigid point.

Cyme. A usually broad and flattish inflorescence with its central or terminal flowers blooming earliest.

Deciduous. Not persistent; not evergreen.

Decurrent (leaf). Extending as a line down the stem below the insertion; extending down the petiole as a wing.

Dehiscent. Opening regularly by valves, slits, etc., as a capsule or anther.

Dentate. Toothed.

Dioecious. Unisexual, with the two kinds of flowers on separate plants.

Dorsal. Upon or relating to the back or outer surface of an organ.

Drupe. A fleshy or pulpy fruit with the inner portion hard and stony inclosing the seed, e.g., peach (one-celled and one-seeded or sometimes several-celled or with more than one seed). In some cases the outer part is scarcely fleshy as in the Sumachs.

Entire. Without toothing or division.

Epidermis. The superficial layer of cells.

Exserted. Projecting beyond an envelope, as stamens from a corolla.

Fascicle. A close bundle or cluster.

Filament. The part of a stamen which supports the anther.

Filiform. Thread-shaped.

Fimbriate. Fringed.

Floccose. Clothed with flocks of soft hair or wool.

Glabrate. Somewhat glabrous, or becoming glabrous.

Glabrous. Smooth; not rough, pubescent or hairy.

Gland. A secreting protuberance or appendage.

Glandular. Bearing glands or of the nature of a gland.

Glaucous. Covered or whitened with a gray or blue powdery or waxy surface layer (or "bloom") as in the fruit of blueberry, some plums, etc.

Hirsute. Covered with rather coarse or stiff hairs.

Hispid. Beset with rigid or bristly hairs or with bristles.

Incised. Cut sharply and irregularly, more or less deeply.

Indehiscent. Not opening by valves, etc.; remaining persistently closed.

Inflorescence. The flowering part of a plant.

Involucral. Belonging to an involucre.

Involucre. A circle or collection of bracts surrounding a flower cluster or a single flower.

Lanceolate. Shaped like a lance-head.

Leaflet. A single division of a compound leaf.

Ligulate. Tongue-shaped.

Linear. Long and narrow.

Lobe. Any segment or division of an organ, especially if rounded.

Membranaceous or *membranous.* Thin, rather soft, and more or less translucent.

Midrib. The central or main rib of a leaf.

Monoecious. With stamens and pistils in separate flowers on the same plant.

Mucro. A short and small abrupt tip.

Mucronate. Tipped with a mucro.

Multiple fruit. One that results from the aggregation of several flowers into one mass.

Nut. A hard indehiscent one-celled and one-seeded fruit, though usually resulting from a compound ovary.

Obcordate. Inverted heart-shaped.

Oblanceolate. Lanceolate with the broadest part toward the apex.

Oblong. Longer than broad and with nearly parallel sides.

Obovate. Inverted ovate.

Orbicular. Circular.

Ovary. The part of the pistil that contains the seeds.

Ovate. Egg-shaped, with broader end down.

Ovule. The body which after fertilization becomes the seed.

Palmate (leaf). Radiately lobed or divided (like a hand) as in the buckeyes.

Panicle. A loose irregularly compound inflorescence with pedicellate flowers.

Pedicel. The support of a single flower in a cluster.

Peduncle. A primary flower stalk, supporting either a cluster or a solitary flower.

Pendulous. More or less hanging.

Perfect (flower). Having both pistil and stamens.

Perianth. The floral envelope, consisting of the calyx and corolla (when present), whatever their form.

Pericarp. The matured ovary.

Petiole. The stalk of a leaf.

Pilose. Hairy, especially with long soft hairs.

Pistil. The seed-bearing organ of the flower, consisting of ovary, stigma, and style (when present).

Pistillate. Provided with pistils, but lacking functional stamens.

Plumose. Having fine hairs on each side like the plume of a feather.

Pod. Any dry and dehiscent fruit.

Pome. A kind of fleshy fruit of which the apple is the type.

Pubescent. Covered with hairs, especially if short, soft, and down-like.

Pulverulent. Powdered; appearing as if covered by minute grains of dust.

Punctate. Dotted with depressions or with translucent internal glands or colored dots.

Pyriform. Pear-shaped.

Raceme. A simple inflorescence of pediceled flowers upon a common more or less elongated axis.

Recurved. Curved downward or backward.

Reflexed. Abruptly bent or turned downward.

Reniform. Kidney-shaped.

Revolute (leaf margin or apex). Rolled or turned downward or toward the under surface.

Rugose. Wrinkled.

Samara. An indehiscent winged fruit as in the maples and elms.

Scabrous. Rough.

Serrate. Having sharp teeth pointing forward.

Sessile. Without stalk of any kind.

Silky. Covered with close-pressed soft and straight hairs.

Sinus. The cleft or recess between two lobes.

Spatulate. Gradually narrowed downward from a rounded summit.

Spike. A form of inflorescence with the flowers sessile or nearly so upon a more or less elongated upright common axis.

Stamen. One of the pollen-bearing organs of the flower.

Staminodium. Modified stamen; in Linden petal-like.

Staminate (flowers). Bearing stamens but without pistils.

Stipulate. Having stipules.

Stipule. An appendage at the base of a petiole or on each side of its insertion.

Stoma (pl. stomata). An orifice in the epidermis of a leaf.

Strigose. Beset with appressed sharp, straight, and stiff hairs.

Subulate. Awl-shaped.

Succulent. Juicy; fleshy.

Sulcate. Grooved or furrowed.

Suture. A line of dehiscence.

Tomentose. Densely hairy with matted wool.

Toothed. Having teeth; serrate.

Trifoliate. Having three leaflets.

Truncate. Ending abruptly, as if cut off transversely.

Turbinate. Top-shaped.

Umbel. An inflorescence in which the peduncles or pedicels of a cluster spring from the same point, as in carrot.

Undulate. With a wavy surface or margin.

Unisexual. Of one sex, either staminate or pistillate only.

Valve. One of the pieces into which a capsule splits.

Ventral. Belonging to the anterior or inner face of an organ; the opposite of dorsal.

Verticillate. Disposed in a whorl.

Villous. Bearing long soft hairs.

Viscid. Glutinous; sticky.

Whorl. An arrangement of leaves, etc., in a circle around the stem.

Wing. Any membranous or thin expansion bordering or surrounding an organ.

Woolly. Clothed with long and tortuous or matted hairs.

INDEX